Italian Dumplings and Chinese Pizzas

Critical Studies in Italian Migrations

Nancy C. Carnevale and Laura E. Ruberto, *series editors*

This series publishes scholarship on Italian migrations, mobilities, and other related transnational concerns. Authors include both emerging and established scholars with differing theoretical and methodological approaches, all rooted in humanities and social science disciplines. Books in the series seek to engage and extend questions of identity and community pertinent to the fields of ethnic studies, gender studies, and migration studies, among others.

Italian Dumplings and Chinese Pizzas

Transcultural Food Mobilities

Gaoheng Zhang

FORDHAM UNIVERSITY PRESS
NEW YORK 2026

Copyright © 2026 Fordham University Press

All rights reserved. No part of this publication may be reproduced, stored in a retrieval system, or transmitted in any form or by any means—electronic, mechanical, photocopy, recording, or any other—except for brief quotations in printed reviews, without the prior permission of the publisher.

Fordham University Press has no responsibility for the persistence or accuracy of URLs for external or third-party Internet websites referred to in this publication and does not guarantee that any content on such websites is, or will remain, accurate or appropriate.

Fordham University Press also publishes its books in a variety of electronic formats. Some content that appears in print may not be available in electronic books.

Visit us online at www.fordhampress.com.

For EU safety/GPSR concerns: Mare Nostrum Group B.V., Mauritskade 21D, 1091 GC Amsterdam, The Netherlands, gpsr@mare-nostrum.co.uk

Library of Congress Cataloging-in-Publication Data available online at https://catalog.loc.gov.

Printed in the United States of America

28 27 26   5 4 3 2 1

First edition

CONTENTS

	Introduction: Transcultural China-Italy Food Mobilities	1
1.	Chinese Migrants' Food Entrepreneurship and Italians' Culinary Tourism, 1962–2020	25
2.	Romantic Waitresses vs. "Kung Food" Workers: Gendering the Chinese Restaurant	53
3.	The Chinese Who Eat Dogmeat: Racialization of Chinese Food Consumption	83
4.	Fighting "Yellow Mozzarella": Italians Safeguard Food's Authenticity	105
5.	Pizza Hut, Fine Dining, and Trattorie: Italian Gastronomy Tourism in China	127
6.	Slow and Fast, Sweet and Sour: Chinese Foodie Travelers in Italy	161
	Conclusion	191
	Acknowledgments	197
	Notes	201
	Bibliography	239
	Index	255

Italian Dumplings and Chinese Pizzas

INTRODUCTION

Transcultural China-Italy Food Mobilities

In March 2020, Italy made worldwide news as it officially became the first country outside of China hardest hit by the SARS-CoV-2 virus. However, while the COVID-19 epidemic was already raging in China in January and early February, there were still no officially confirmed cases in Italy. The Italian media's coverage of the infectious disease focused on the situations in China and those involving the country's Chinese migrants. Labeling the phenomenon "corona-psychosis," the Italian press covered a surge of anti-Chinese racist incidents in the country. Among the highlighted issues were racial slurs, inappropriate jokes, dirty looks, and physical attacks on Chinese migrants, other Asians, and people who appeared to be Asian.[1]

In reaction to these incidents, many people fought the discrimination and misinformation that linked Chinese people to the spread of the coronavirus. These stakeholders came from a spectrum of social classes and professions and utilized different modes of communication. Chinese migrants, such as entrepreneurs, students, and highly skilled workers, wrote firsthand accounts under lockdown that were published online and in print.[2] The Chinese ambassador and general consuls in Italy issued public communications on their websites, attempting to steer the direction of public opinion in Italy about the evolving epidemic in China and its impact on Italy.[3] Mainland Chinese news outlets, particularly starting in March, published and circulated articles in the country's vibrant digital domain to battle what they perceived to be Italian racism.[4] Italian bureaucrats (including the Italian president Sergio Mattarella) and health experts also contributed their time and energy to educating the public about the looming epidemic, aided as they were by Italian journalists working for newspapers and television networks.[5]

A paradigmatic case illustrating these sociopolitical and media confrontations concerns one of the first ethnic Chinese-owned businesses impacted by the epidemic in Italy and worldwide: Chinese restaurants. In Italy, food-related initiatives were among the first activities through which government entities and community organizations advocated for ethnic Chinese. On February 8, the mayor of Milan, Giuseppe Sala, and the mayor of Rome, Virginia Raggi, both ate in Chinese restaurants in their respective cities as a gesture of support for two of the country's largest Chinese communities.[6] On February 20, the food-focused Italian-Chinese migrant collaboration "La notte delle bacchette" (The Night of Chopsticks) took place in Milan.[7] The initiative sought to address the plight facing Chinese and Italian restaurants in the city's Via Sarpi neighborhood, a key center of Chinese social and community life in Italy, where foot traffic had abruptly diminished. According to the official regulation of the initiative, these eateries would each offer a "solidarity dish." Half of the revenue from these sales would be donated to an Italian organization providing Chinese orphanages with resources to fight the COVID-19 epidemic.

As another significant event that emerged from civil society and engaged both Italians and Chinese migrants, the Italian street artist Laika created an artistic poster and displayed it on February 4 at the entrance to the covered public markets at Piazza Vittorio in Rome.[8] Being the commercial center of the capital city's Chinese community, Piazza Vittorio hosted many Chinese restaurants, including Hang Zhou.[9] Its owner, Sonia Zhou, or Zhou Fenxia, was the focus of Laika's poster. In it, Zhou is depicted as wearing a protective medical suit and carrying a bowl of rice. In a speech balloon typical of comic books and graphic novels, we read: "There is an epidemic of ignorance around . . . We have to protect ourselves from it!!!"[10] The slogan characterized some Italians' hesitation to consume Chinese food and the recent string of racist incidents as manifesting "an epidemic of ignorance." In so doing, the poster's catchphrase questioned the legitimacy of the prevailing connotation of "epidemic" that focused on the spread of the coronavirus.

In raising public consciousness about the plight of Italy's Chinese restaurant and catering sector during the health crisis, Laika's poster capitalized on Zhou's media fame. At the dawn of the COVID-19 pandemic, Zhou was undoubtedly the most celebrated Chinese migrant food entrepreneur in mainstream Italian media.[11] Previously, she had received extensive coverage in the country's premier food and wine magazine, *Gambero Rosso*, two of its main dailies, *Corriere della Sera* and *La Repubblica*, and one of its leading newsweeklies, *L'Espresso*, as well as in Italian national television shows and major English-language news outlets, such as the Canadian-American lifestyle magazine *Vice*. Through Laika's artwork and the media's coverage of it, including the British newspaper *The Guardian*, Zhou became an influential critic of anti-Chinese racism.[12] While the poster articulated an antiracist perspective more broadly, and although other activists and politicians also worked to combat anti-Asian racism, Zhou's connection to food made her pleas for customers to return to Chinese restaurants particularly visceral. Indeed, Raggi's abovementioned restaurant visit on February 8 occurred at Hang Zhou, where the two women posed for photographs to help debunk the association of Chinese food with the COVID-19 virus, thereby reassuring the public about the safety of Chinese food.

As a media-savvy food entrepreneur even before the pandemic, Zhou fashioned for the media an identity that deployed both ethnocultural essentialization of her Chinese heritage and transcultural Italianization. Such an identity performance enhanced the experiences of Italian culinary tourists in her restaurant, who also appreciated that her outfits evoked China and her lifestyle referenced Italy. *L'Espresso* praised her as "a Chinese person who is very Italian," and she called herself "an Italian by adoption" in *Gambero*

Rosso.¹³ Moreover, *L'Espresso* described her lifestyle as reminiscent of the Roman myth of *la dolce vita* (the good life), in a fond reference to Federico Fellini's 1960 film of the same title.¹⁴ These remarks exhibited Italians' positive reception of her personal style, which *Vice* quoted her as being acutely aware of: "I understand what Italians want."¹⁵ Thus, Zhou's identity performance for media exposure was self-consciously expressive of Italian-Chinese friendship and conviviality. The outcome of her mediated self-fashioning was the status of being the Italianized entrepreneur in Chinese food par excellence. This image helped Laika's artwork endorse the Italian-Chinese migrant cooperation in February 2020 when fighting public panic about a possible epidemic in Italy.

Zhou's story encapsulates several core connections that my book addresses: the connections between China and Italy, labor migration and culinary tourism, and food and its transnational and transcultural mobilities. Moreover, Zhou's case study highlights the links between food as material objects and commercial products, and the sociocultural issues and identities that they communicate in the media and cultural domains, including anti-Asian racism and migrant entrepreneurial identity-making in Italy. As my book demonstrates, it was not coincidental that food narratives such as Zhou's and Laika's played such a critical role in culturally mediating Italian-Chinese sociocultural relations during the initial period of the COVID-19 pandemic. Rather, as I show throughout the book, food mobilities articulated in popular culture have been essential in negotiating complicated socioeconomic and geopolitical dynamics between the two countries for decades.

By food mobilities articulated in popular culture, I mean mobilities relayed in narratives about social events and phenomena concerning food which popular culture produces and circulates. Drawing from both Tim Cresswell's definition of mobility and Stephen Greenblatt's insights into cultural mobilities, I view food-related cultural mobilities as the combined effect of physical movement of people and objects, sociocultural meaning-making, and power negotiation among competing discourses or stakeholders.¹⁶ A cultural analysis of food mobilities, particularly in the China-Italy case, which began in the 1980s, also draws from pertinent historical scholarship. As the editors of *Food Mobilities: Making World Cuisines* maintain, the emergence of modern cuisines has been intertwined with the "historical mobility of peoples, plants and animals, food goods, and commodities."[17] In the volume, a focus is placed on the historical lens on such mobilities in revealing their relevance to cuisine. I, too, demonstrate that China-Italy food-facilitated cultural mobilities have been in constant flux in line with historical contingencies.

The main aim of my research is to demonstrate how China-Italy food mobilities relayed in popular culture helped forge Chinese and Italians' socioeconomic identities in recent decades by fundamentally shaping contemporary Chinese and Italian consumer cultures. Analyzing China-Italy food mobilities this way also involves parsing a broad spectrum of historical processes and social mechanisms that food-assisted popular culture articulates. Such an interpretation of food-assisted, intersecting physical and cultural mobilities helps strengthen a nuanced scholarly view of tolerance, hospitality, and empathy during transcultural events and processes.

I follow the view of transculturation, or transculturality, embraced by the editors of *Engaging Transculturality*, which was nurtured at Heidelberg University while studying Asia and Europe in a global context. Transculturality is a fundamental social process that privileges an understanding of interactions among cultural entities in multilayered, nonlinear, and transgressive ways.[18] The transcultural China-Italy food mobilities I analyze can be partially viewed as contributing to the intellectual project championed by *Transcultural Italies*, which examines Italian migrant communities in some parts of the world and their transculturality.[19] Through the optics of transcultural mobilities, my analysis sheds light on how culinary dynamics address alterity and build understanding in a world of increasing political and cultural polarization.

The title of my book, *Italian Dumplings and Chinese Pizzas*, is meant to reinforce the transcultural agenda of my intellectual project. In the common understanding of national cuisines, pizza is an iconic Italian food and dumplings are commonplace in the Chinese diet. Hence, pairing nationalities with their foods in this title would elicit some surprise. However, as those who are familiar with Chinese and Italian foods know, in some regions of the two countries, Italians eat dumplings (e.g., *ravioli*) and Chinese make baked, steamed, or fried flatbread with toppings or fillings (e.g., *laobing*) frequently. Furthermore, the title prompts the reader to ponder the ethnic identity of dumplings made in Italy by Chinese migrants or Chinese Italians and pizzas made in China by Italian migrants, Chinese Italians, or Chinese without apparent ties with Italy. How feasible is it to assign national or ethnic identities to these culinary products? Is it useful to label these culinary dynamics with distinctive national or even transnational (such as Chinese-Italian) titles? Why do some of us tend to view pizzas made by the Chinese in Italy in restaurants or Chinese dumplings (say, *jiaozi*) made at an Italian household as exceptional occurrences? What are the deeper reasons for which we—including scholars—ought to care for such labeling dilemmas?

When unraveling these questions about pizzas, dumplings, and many more China-Italy food dynamics, we need to know how important food and food narratives are for migration and tourism between China and Italy. Next, I propose a critical framework through which to approach the socioeconomic and historical complexity of these highly mobile transcultural culinary phenomena. Finally, to appreciate culture in action, I explain the technicality of analyzing food narratives at the textual and discursive level in interaction with the empirical world. The rest of this Introduction provides such a route for covering the main lineaments of studying transcultural China-Italy food mobilities and the implications of such a study for transcultural food mobilities more generally.

The Centrality of Food in Contemporary China-Italy Cultural Mobilities

The history of China-Italy cultural mobilities is the longest East-West contact in written record. There have been unbroken cultural interactions based on human mobilities since the circulation of Marco Polo's travel account written in the final years of the thirteenth century. Another well-known story from this history in the pre-modern period concerns the dissemination of largely accurate information about China and Chinese people in Europe for the first time. Beginning in the sixteenth century, the Italian Jesuit missionary Matteo Ricci and his followers from various European states produced a significant body of literature about all things Chinese that catalyzed the study of China in Europe. Despite the influence of Polo and Ricci's work, movements and exchanges of people, ideas, objects, and trade between the Chinese empire and various political entities in the Italian peninsula did not exponentially increase until the mid-nineteenth century. At this time, intensified industrialization and technological advances made transoceanic trips more available to travelers with the means and resources to do so. With the establishment of the Kingdom of Italy in 1861, the newly formed nation-state's needs to establish diplomatic ties with China and to participate in the European scrambles in Africa and Asia also emerged.

As Valentina Pedone and I have suggested in *Cultural Mobilities Between China and Italy*, three time periods since the early twentieth century can be identified in which China-Italy mobilities have been particularly fruitful and impactful in both directions.[20] The first constellation of mobilities occurred in the 1920s–1930s when Italy's only Asian colonial possession—a concession in Tianjin—became firmly established and when the presence of elite Chinese tourists and students in Italy became notable for the first time in history. The second key period refers to the 1950s–1970s, in which select Italian delegates—typically authors, journalists, and artists—visited Maoist China, who then spread its ideals among their colleagues in the Euro-American intellectual circle.

The final stage in contemporary China-Italy mobilities is meaningful for my book as it concerns the 2000s and 2010s migrations between the two countries. Labor migration is the most significant type, and it intersects with leisure tourism, business travel, and international student mobility. Indeed, since the 1980s, dramatic socioeconomic transformations have occurred in both countries, which have impacted their mobility patterns and narratives. Never before in history have there been so many Chinese working and traveling in Italy, and vice versa. In the 1980s, labor migration and leisure tourism across the two countries became the most consequential forms of human mobility influenced by globalization. These mobilities have engendered sociocultural, political, and economic negotiations in both Italy and China which migrant-managed food entrepreneurship and middle-class consumers' culinary tourism vitally contributed to.

During the 1980s, Chinese cuisine became the first non-European food widely available in Italy, thanks to the widespread presence of Chinese eateries. Only American fast food, which established itself in Italy around the same time, enjoyed comparable popularity as a destination for Italians' culinary tourism. In the late 2010s, local populations viewed Milan's vibrant Chinese foodscape[21]—serving Italian culinary tourists and everyday consumers, as well as Chinese international students, visitors, and migrants—as enhancing the fashion capital's cosmopolitanism. The larger context of this phenomenon is mass immigration to Italy, which began in the 1980s when Italy rapidly changed from an immigrant-sending country to an immigrant-receiving country. Since then, the Chinese have remained the fourth largest migrant group in numbers. The Chinese migration is distinguished by its members' strong entrepreneurialism. No other immigrant group from a single country has formed such a strong ethnic labor market in Italy (e.g., in the restaurant, garment, and retail sectors) capable of competing and sometimes outcompeting their Italian counterparts.

Meanwhile, in the early 1990s, together with American hamburgers and fried chicken, the American food chain Pizza Hut's pizzas and spaghetti were the first non-Asian foods that post-Mao Chinese customers recognized as "Western." Since the 2000s, Italian cuisine has firmly established its reputation as fine dining among middle-class Chinese, which only French gastronomy can rival, thanks to the efforts of Italian food entrepreneurs and workers. Italian migrants often work in the "Made in Italy" sectors, which sell food, fashion, design products, furniture, and machinery to China's rising middle class. Since the 2010s, increasing numbers of Chinese culinary tourists have been traveling to Italy to sample local food, thereby negotiating their existing Italian culinary repertoires acquired in China. The impetus for these consumer and social changes can be traced to China's Open Door Policy, which was institutionalized in 1978. "Chinese-style modernization" attracted overseas investment, promoting the consumption of Western commodities and adoption of Western lifestyles. Middle-class Chinese also began traveling abroad, initially as visiting government officials and for family reunions, and then increasingly as labor migrants, businesspeople, international students, and leisure tourists.

My book is divided into two parts to address these socioeconomic realities and their cultural dynamics. The study is not an empirical investigation but is about how China-Italy food mobilities enjoyed complicated, stimulating, and ambivalent cultural lives in mass media, cinema, and literature. Although the existing social scientific and historical studies on the subjects of my book are slim, they provide a wide array of empirical details from which I draw for my analysis. However, the real weakness of this literature lies in leaving out an interdisciplinary analysis of an extremely rich and heterogeneous body of publicly available cultural texts. Without such an analysis, however, we would not understand why some popular perceptions of China-Italy food dynamics seemed to contradict what was actually happening from the 1980s through the 2010s.

One example of this seeming contradiction concerns the anachronistic, and yet persistent, stereotype that Chinese people eat dogs (Chapter 2). A key reason for this and other apparent contradictions is a lack of critical attention to the agendas and actions of transnational Chinese and Italian stakeholders when constructing and debating meanings through food cultural mobilities. Instead, I interrogate how and why food discourses have provided cultural resources and created new cultural meanings for recent Chinese-Italian interactions. For example, according to the cultural logic that I analyze about the dogmeat stereotype, often it was not the case that stakeholders truly or simplistically believed in the tales told by these narratives. Instead, these narratives served to racially demarcate Italians from the Chinese. Some cultural workers also reiterated the stereotype in order to satirize it, thereby exposing the instability of its semantics.

In performing a cultural diagnosis on China-Italy food mobilities, my book pursues a notable avenue of research linking food studies with popular culture. Kathleen LeBesco and Peter Naccarato highlight how the media helps food extend its influence to popular culture more generally.[22] Likewise, Fabio Parasecoli maintains that the pervasive presence of food in contemporary Western popular culture influences self-perceptions and self-representations of oneself both as an individual and as a member of diverse social groups.[23] Meanwhile, LeBesco and Naccarato's observation on how food and popular culture share many contact zones points to multiple possibilities for research at the conjunction of popular culture and food studies.[24] For example, popular culture's focus on everyday life and practices resonates with critical studies of food and foodways. Indeed, although "popular culture" is difficult to define, its general distance from elitist forms of cultural production resonates with food studies.[25]

My research agenda is close to Parasecoli's elaboration on the potential for cross-pollination between food and cultural studies in that both disciplines critique popular culture and seek to catalyze change.[26] Parasecoli reviews the three paradigms—structuralist, culturalist, and Gramscian—which Bob Ashley, Joanne Hollows, Steve Jones, and Ben Taylor identified in one of the only scholarly volumes dedicated to food and cultural studies in the early 2010s.[27] The structuralist approach examines food as a cultural system and code that continuously produces signs. The culturalist approach considers the value of the lived experiences of people and their agency over existing structures. The Gramscian approach focuses on ongoing negotiations between hegemonic, allied, and subordinate cultural groups and social classes. Ashley et al. advocated for the Gramscian approach as it avoids the tendency to stress domination in the structuralist approach and the predilection for resistance or transgression in the culturalist approach.

Considering this scholarly tradition, my book sets out to analyze how cultural workers intend to stimulate progressive societal change. However, my study does not embrace a simplistic vision of the "power-resistance" model, which tends to flatten the complexity of sociocultural actions, as Eva Illouz warns.[28] For example, I highlight migrants' acts of irony expressed against the foil of a hegemonic Italian representation of Chinese food. Meanwhile, I pay attention to the fact that it was in combating the relative semantic stability of certain Chinese food stereotypes that migrants were enabled to articulate their agency.

Operationalizing these principles, in Chapters 1–4, I analyze how, for many Italians, representations of Chinese migrant food provided a culturally digestible and rhetorically powerful demarcation between "natives" and foreigners and between slow and fast foods. Such demarcation is highly gendered and racialized, and it frequently updates previous Chinese American stereotyping. Food-circulated discourses about various "Chinamen" and *cinesine* (petite Chinese women), or about the Chinese who eat dogmeat, are symptomatic of differentiating Italian "natives" starkly apart from Chinese migrants in the cultural domain which cannot always be effectuated in everyday economic and social life. The demarcation strengthens a set of essentialized Italian identities under duress in the context of globalization and immigration, as is the case involving ways to protect authentic Italian food under supposed Chinese threat. Pro-migrant Italian and migrant authors have challenged this view and proposed their own perspectives on food-related issues in the cultural field.

Chapters 5–6 address the other main subject of the book. In narrating Italian and Italianate gastronomy tourism, middle-class Chinese showed a thirst in self-identifying as cosmopolitans in China's post-socialist era. Food-assisted Chinese cosmopolitanism has had an ambivalent relationship with Slow Food. Sweet appreciation for a fulfilling and socially conscious lifestyle co-exists with skepticism soured by the movement's apparent resistance to speed, industrialization, and globalization—qualities that the Chinese cherished during their modernization. This ambivalence can be partially explained by referring to Pizza Hut China's emphasis on hybridized food, a culinary business model that has been deeply ingrained in the Chinese encounter with Italian cuisine. This culinary experience runs against Slow Food–influenced Italian gastronationalism, which, however, some Chinese cultural workers have enthusiastically adopted to enhance Chinese culinary nationalism. To consider another reason, while Italian cuisine allowed 2010s Chinese culinary tourists to gain sophistication in tastes, it also showed them the importance of fighting what they perceived to be Slow Food–influenced food parochialism.

Framing Chinese and Italian Cuisines on the Move

As the above section argues, transcultural China-Italy food mobilities are a complicated phenomenon requiring a careful critical cultural analysis. My book is the first critical attempt at creating a framework that analyzes the phenomenon by seriously assessing the confluence of diverse mobilities and its impact on food cultures. The framework foregrounds three interfaces in their cultural dimensions: two-way labor migrations between China and Italy, labor migration and culinary tourism, and contacts with American business and popular cultures. In this section, I draw from a diverse scholarship broader than the China-Italy context in order to explain the framework's connotations.

FOOD, MIGRATION, AND MOBILITIES

The major scholarly premise of this framework derives from the existing critical literature's highlight of the intimate association between food and migration, both in historical and cultural domains. As Donna Gabaccia argues, food and mobility have been interconnected throughout history, given their universal presence in human life.[29] Tiana B. Hayden and Dhan Zunino Singh propose "the lens of food (in)mobility as a way of contributing to transport history's understanding of the movement of non-human things."[30] Sarah Gibson works with notions of culture as traveling and dwelling to argue that food mobilities are equally significant to food's rootedness in soil or a national culture. Individuals such as migrants may perceive food as a site of home, belonging, and cultural identity that are more or less fixed. But often, food travels to dwell in people's lives in such diasporic contexts. As Gibson sums up, "Whether it is the food that moves or the food that moves us, the consumer who travels to eat or indeed eats to travel, or the consumer who eats to dwell or dwells to eat, eating is inextricably bound up with the geographies and spaces of mobilities."[31]

The intellectual project of this literature focused on food, mobility, and culture respond to key research agendas proposed by Kevin Hannam, Mimi Sheller, and John Urry. These critics emphasize the necessity to study the relation between migration, tourism, and travel; these physical mobilities' relationships with virtual and informational mobilities; and the dynamics between materialities and mobilities.[32] Indeed, as Daniel E. Bender and Simone Cinotto note, "food mobilities can be understood, necessarily as plural, as an amalgam of material, social, and imaginative mobility, what Urry calls 'interdependent mobilities.'"[33] However, as the authors of the volume *Food Mobilities* collectively argue, the historical dimension of mobilities or food has not been thoroughly examined in previous literature about food mobilities. It is critical to fine-tune this scholarship to demonstrate how mobilities move foods only through history. My focus on the cultural dynamics of food mobilities in this book closely resembles the agenda of this historical scholarship but sheds more light on narratives and discourses.

The close association between food, migration, and culture has not been adequately explored in critical literature for the China-Italy context. To be sure, there are abundant food studies about Italy and China individually. As two countries associated with rich culinary cultures, Italy and China have both attracted a notable amount of scholarship from interdisciplinary historical, anthropological, and cultural studies on their foodways and cuisines.[34] However, historical and social scientific understanding of Chinese migrant food in Italy, which is incorporated into Chapter 1, is rather slim. Scant scholarship exists on Italian food cultures in China; I address all of it in Chapter 5. The meager existing scholarship is not justified given the historical and cultural importance of Italian food in China since the 1990s, and vice versa, as I have relayed above. Previously, Jeffrey Pilcher adopts the culinary practices of Italian and Chinese migrants as two exemplary case studies to trace the development of transformed or creolized cuisines. Pilcher views these processes as emerging through migrant experiences and contributing to culinary globalization.[35] However, my book provides the first comprehensive analysis of the multilayered China-Italy food cultures via migrations.

LABOR MIGRATION

When discussing food and migration in the Chinese-Italian context, I privilege perspectives on labor migrations between the two countries, particularly those pertaining to the restaurant sector. Both Chinese and Italian restaurants in each other's countries have been a fundamental source of economic income and reputational support for migrants employed in the sector. Migrant-managed restaurants are also places of ethnic, national, or cultural belonging for many more migrants not employed in the restaurant sector. The largest body of migration and food research in the Chinese and Italian contexts is the existing historical scholarship on Chinese and Italian migrant foodways in the American context. Drawing from this literature, I examine two-way labor migrations between China and Italy for their cultural relevance to gendered and racialized identity-making for my own analytical framework to approach transcultural food mobilities.

For example, in presenting a history of Chinese American cuisine from early immigrant restaurants in the nineteenth century to contemporary restaurant chains, Haiming Liu contends that American societal perception of Chinese food was often influenced by racial rather than culinary standards.[36] For Simone Cinotto, Italian immigrant food was a central consumer choice that helped articulate class, race, gender, and power relations based on generational differences.[37] In her study of the migrant marketplace—where food was a central commodity—in both North and South America from the late nineteenth to mid-twentieth centuries, Elizabeth Zanoni also presents Italian migrants as "gendered and global consumers" who defined themselves through the commodity of food.[38]

In addition to the gendered and racialized aspects of food-related migrant identity-making, I highlight food's authenticity and misrepresentation in my analyses, which are central issues for understanding many migrant-host cultural dynamics. The springboard from which I launch my analysis is the relevant research on Chinese and Italian food and migration. Writing on the globalization of Asian food and its manifestations in the United States, Robert Ji-Song Ku challenges the idea of food's authenticity and suggests that it may be "an illusion and a trap."[39] Meanwhile, researching Italian food cultures, Emanuela Scarpellini argues that encounters between cultures are always "a kind of translation, which never completely reflects the original and is inevitably transformed by the cross-cultural contact."[40] Some historians claim that the adaptation of ethnic or migrant food is usually not a one-way process. For example, J.A.G. Roberts traces how, when, and why Western inhabitants incorporated Chinese food, which by now has become a more widespread cultural trend in North America.[41] As Zanoni demonstrates, since the nineteenth century, the debate regarding the authenticity of Italian-origin food items, including pasta and tomato sauces, has been vigorous in Italy's competition with countries such as the United States and Argentina, where Italian diasporas were significant.[42]

When discussing Chinese and Italian food's authenticity, I contextualize this issue's socioeconomic background and reveal its geopolitical and symbolic purposes for cultural workers. Somewhat surprising results can derive from these discussions. For example, Chapter 6 shows that China's cinematic competition with the United States can be effectuated via representations of Italian cuisine, which is made by both "native" Italians and Chinese migrants.

LABOR MIGRATION AND CULINARY TOURISM

In John Urry's theorization of mobilities, migration and tourism are two important mobility forms within the category of the physical or corporeal travel of people.⁴³ These are two extremely vibrant forms of mobility in today's world owing to globalization, both of which are deeply connected with culinary cultures.⁴⁴ But as Chiara Rabbiosi suggests, tourism is a type of mobility that has received considerably less attention than migration in its power to forge Italian food and Italianness.⁴⁵ Associating tourism with the myth-making of Italian food, Fabio Parasecoli argues that the expansion of the tourism industry shaped perceptions of Italy and its culinary culture.⁴⁶ For Roberta Sassatelli, food culture helps Italians signify their national identity, thereby consolidating Italianness in a global context, which importantly involves non-Italians' tourism in Italy and Italian food.⁴⁷

It is my contention that the China-Italy story is well-positioned to bring to the fore the intersection of (cultural forms of) labor migration and leisure tourism—and Chinese leisure tourism in Italy in particular—in spreading food cultures. I develop this argument by drawing from Lucy M. Long's concept of culinary tourism. For the critic, culinary tourism consists in "adventurous eating, eating out of curiosity, exploring other cultures through food, intentionally participating in the foodways of an 'other,' and developing food as tourist destination and attraction."⁴⁸ Migrant cuisines in Italian and Chinese cities provide occasions for such culinary tourism.

Tourism through food can also take the form of physical travel to the destination country. Roberts cites the development of Western tourism in China as a factor for increased acceptance of Chinese food available in the West.⁴⁹ Scarpellini lists increased opportunities for average Italians to travel abroad as one reason for growing interest in ethnic cuisines in Italy's migrant-managed eateries.⁵⁰ Meanwhile, analyzing Chinese tourists' interest in Italian wine and food, Michael Volgger and Harald Pechlaner analyze their consumer behavior to make practical suggestions for the Italian tourism sector.⁵¹

As my subsequent chapters show, the China-Italy situation is a rare case in which to acutely observe how both countries' culinary tourism is influential for each other's identity-making and how this tourism is complexly intertwined with labor migration.

AMERICAN BUSINESS AND POPULAR CULTURES

To return to the above-examined Zhou's case, how do we interpret the appearance of "Cantonese fried rice" and "chicken with almonds," two common American Chinese dishes, alongside dishes more commonly found in China, on its menu?[52] Although there is no conclusive research done on this topic, according to anecdotes relayed in Chapter 1, two factors were at play. Some chefs working in the first Chinese restaurants opened in Milan and Rome in the mid-twentieth century came from Western European countries, where these and other American Chinese specialties had already been widely adopted. Moreover, beginning in the 1980s, when Italian culinary tourists dined in Chinese eateries, they expected to see dishes they had first experienced in American and European cities with large Chinese diasporic communities, such as New York City and London, where these dishes were served.

As Zhou's and many other examples in this book demonstrate, American business and popular cultures often impacted matters associated with tourists and migrants between China and Italy. We cannot exclude a critical consideration of these American resonances when analyzing recent Chinese-Italian encounters. The United States influenced Italian-Chinese food exchanges from both business and cultural perspectives, and American business and popular cultures mediated cultural scripts and arguments about the Italian and the Chinese people more generally. I interrogate how and why ethnic Chinese and Italian narrators—frequently migrants and tourists themselves—deployed American cultural stereotypes, preoccupations, and comparisons when creating their stories about Italy-China cases during the period under consideration. Except for Chapter 4, this is a critical concern that informs all other chapters of my study. I have designed this component to show how transculturality in China-Italy food mobilities can break the confines of the two countries to reach a much broader cultural significance.

The most crucial benefit of the framework that I have explained in this section for a fruitful analysis of transcultural food mobilities is that it helps destabilize a tendency in mainstream migration studies to disregard other mobilities that are significantly intersected with a particular migration being analyzed. In the narratives concerning China-Italy mobile subjects, migration and tourism have often occurred on a continuum. A particularly powerful third country's culture has significantly impacted cultural representations of migration and tourism occurring between two other countries.

Consider the field of cultural representations of foreign migrations to Italy, including the Chinese one. An almost exclusive critical focus is placed on the Global South-to-North migrations largely set within postcolonial milieus.[53] While this more established analytical framework yields valuable insights about such movements and critiques Eurocentrism, it is not always applicable to circulations of people, objects, and ideas on the ground, and largely not to the Italian-Chinese case. Despite the greater scholarly attention paid to South-to-North migrations, the global North does not have a higher rate or a longer history of mobility than elsewhere. Additionally, migrants' interpersonal relationships are not limited to their relationship with members of the dominant groups within the host society.[54] A book-length analysis of the agency of both the migrants and the "natives" in forging food identities is rarely seen in scholarship about Italy's global mobilities.[55]

As will be clear in the pages to follow, food dynamics effectively exposes such a critical lapse. From the 1980s through the 2010s, narratives about China-Italy food dynamics were apt in culturally condensing variegated human mobile experiences, making them more digestible and visceral. Such food-related narratives also provided cultural resources to social actors when making sense of, and sometimes acting upon, aspects of migration and tourism that are not covertly about culinary preferences. China-Italy food cultures on the move showcase transculturality in a brilliantly relatable and expressive way.

Food as Communication in Popular Culture

In my book, food narratives are viewed as public communications that cultural workers create to inform and potentially change people's behavioral, conceptual, and cultural mappings. This critical position means, first and foremost, that I select primary texts from popular culture intended for consumption by a broad spectrum of audiences. To borrow Gitanjali G. Shahani's terminology when discussing methodologies in literary food studies, I am "omnivorous" in my selection of popular media, cinematic, and literary texts that I believe are key to an understanding of current Italian-Chinese food dynamics.[56] The most significant sources for my analysis include creative fiction, such as graphic and detective novels; personal documentary accounts, including memoirs and restaurant reviews; digital promotional materials, such as restaurants' self-introductions and product advertising; the news media; and comedy, crime, and arthouse films. Much of this body of sources refers to more popular and vernacular forms of writing, which is increasingly becoming the focus of existing scholarship.[57] My book also draws from a sizeable amount of critical literature that has investigated the intersection of literature,[58] media,[59] and cinema[60] with food.

To better probe the potential impact of these public narratives on people's approaches to food, my book is engaged in a contextualized textual and discourse analysis that is sensitive to meaning-making, knowledge creation, and power relations in transcultural settings. A primary outcome of my study is to gain a critical assessment of the hegemonic and alternative representations of culinary narratives, which are composed through competing frames and articulate discursive negotiation of power dynamics. Typical questions that I ask include: What persuasive, cultural, and sociopolitical agendas did the content creators intend these representations to accomplish? What meanings did these media and cultural representations convey about Chinese and Italian cuisines on the move, and to whose benefit? How did cultural stakeholders strategically deploy cultural resources available to them to achieve these meanings and agendas?

The importance of these research questions can be appreciated with reference to the current interdisciplinary field of food and communication. This scholarship is well-established and has recently adopted more expansive research agendas and approaches.[61] This book's primary research orientation aligns with Arthur Lizie's formulation of communication food scholarship. The main objective of my research is to analyze how culture acts upon specific food narratives related to migration and tourism through what Ann Swidler has called "strategy for action."[62] Through this critical lens, I ask questions such as: How does culture orient social actors in navigating the challenge of making sense of food preparation, distribution, consumption, and other related dimensions? What cultural resources are available for them to interpret food within larger sociopolitical milieus? Lizie articulates the main agenda of communication food scholarship from the perspective of meaning-making and the stakeholders and the mediums involved in this process:

> Communication food scholarship looks at how, what, and to what effect meaning is created as message producers (typically, but not exclusively, corporations) create messages about food (advertisements, commercials, films) that circulate in culture and are interpreted by audiences.[63]

Lizie's concept of food-related meaning-making can be further appreciated by referring to cultural sociologist Wendy Griswold's "cultural diamond." In this simple and elegant model, four entities form a diamond-shaped diagram of intersecting relationships, with "social world" and "cultural object" on the top-to-bottom axis and "creator" and "receiver" on the left-to-right axis.[64] My analytical compass is tilted toward the left side of the diamond, that is, the tensions among the "social world," "creator," and "cultural object." For most case studies, I explore the creation of meanings through cultural objects, which for Griswold means "shared significance embodied in form, i.e., an expression of social meanings that is tangible or can be put into words."[65] Food discourses, which have embodied forms in cultural formats and convey sociocultural meanings through words and other codes, are such cultural objects.

Griswold, Lizie, and Swidler's theorizing helps me analyze the dialogue between Karl Marx's interpretation of culture as holding up a mirror to society and Max Weber's tendency to favor culture's influence on society.[66] As Roger Dickinson points out, most food studies consider the media as a reflection of changing public attitudes and practices, while its role in the social processes that drive such changes is less frequently examined. However, as Dickinson contends, cultural studies research on food has the potential to shift food and its media representation toward the center of the analysis.[67] Indeed, more recent studies of popular media forms featuring food attempt to demonstrate their cultural significance and symbolic power. According to Dickinson, such cultural studies work on food treats "media representations as repositories of meaning that can be uncovered using techniques of discourse analysis."[68] I examine how food cultures both reflect and act upon social dynamics through activities such as migrants' activism, gendered racialization, and the branding and marketing of Italian and Chinese cuisines.[69] My multilingual and multisited study is the first book to incorporate these critical frames and tools into a single interpretive matrix through which to approach transcultural China-Italy food mobilities.

Chapter Outline

In Chapter 1, I examine how Chinese migrant-managed food entrepreneurship in Italy developed in close interaction with Italians' Chinese culinary tourism in the last six decades. The start date of my survey is 1962, when the opening of Milan's first formal Chinese restaurant gained significant media and social attention. The deepening crisis in Italy's Chinese restaurant sector in early 2020 caused by the COVID-19 pandemic provides a fitting end for my discussion. Operationalizing Long's insights into culinary tourism, in the first part of the chapter, I examine the 2003 SARS outbreak and the COVID-19 pandemic as two watershed moments. I provide a concise historical account of the most consequential empirical conditions of Italy's Chinese restaurant sector, which sought to meet Italian culinary tourists' needs. While empirical research on Chinese food in Italy only began in the 1990s, Italian media chronicled the phenomenon for a longer period. More intriguingly, as I show in the second part of this chapter, as covered by Italy's largest-circulating newspaper, *Corriere della Sera*, from the 1960s to the present day, Italians' Chinese culinary tourism in Milan interacted with Chinese American food culture in various stimulating ways. Chapter 1 offers a first taste of the complexity of studying China-Italy mobilities and food cultures, in which migration, tourism, and media circulation intersect across countries and cultures.

Italy's Chinese foodscape, as described in Chapter 1, diverges significantly from its cultural dynamics. This difference is manifest when analyzing relevant representations in influential Italian popular films and graphic novels since the 1980s, which is the focus of Chapter 2. The springboard from which I launch my analysis is a sociocultural place: the Chinese restaurant, the most recognizable and widespread symbol of Chinese migrant communities and identities for the average contemporary Italian. My analytical focus on food-related Chinese identity-making is on gender stereotyping in Italian popular culture. Following a section on 1980s–1990s comedy films that promote a migration-restaurant-crime frame, I ask the following questions for more recent and layered depictions: How did formulaic depictions of diasporic Chinese women in several 2000s popular films promote specific cultural scripts about Chinese restaurants? In fighting such negative stereotyping, how did 2010s pro-migrant graphic novels—authored by both white Italians and Chinese migrants or their descendants—create positive stereotyping of Chinese restaurants through molding positive Chinese masculinities? When probing the reasons for Italian variants of "Chinamen" and *cinesine* (petite Chinese women), I highlight the role played by previous American popular culture about Chinese migrants. A significant part of Italian popular cultural understanding of Chinese restaurants since the 1980s has been highly gendered in a cliché way. These discourses are symptomatic of differentiating Italian "natives" starkly apart from Chinese migrants in a cultural way that cannot always be effectuated in everyday economic and social life.

Chapter 3 addresses the most enduring negative stereotype concerning Chinese food in Italy, which accuses migrants of eating unhealthy dogmeat dishes and offering them in restaurants, habits said to be characteristic of the Chinese overall. In Italy, this hackneyed stereotype enjoyed influential cinematic treatments during the 1960s and 1970s. This food taboo resonated with content creators in the 2000s and 2010s, as evidenced by an important example of migration literature and TikTok posts by Chinese Italians. The food cliché acutely racializes Chinese migrants and then resolutely demarcates them from Italians within sociocultural spaces. Chinese migrant foodways and cuisines are not the only foil against which Italian narratives perform the Italian-alien differentiation. However, Chinese food has so far provided a compelling example that exhibits a broad range of food issues and approaches for Italian content creators to elaborate on. Thus, in Chapter 3, an analysis of narratives of this alimentary stereotype provides an especially sharp view of the communicative frames and representational agendas of food-circulated discourses about populations with migratory backgrounds in Italy. I also probe the origins of this stereotype in Italy, tracing them to specific inspirations drawn from American mass media and popular culture.

Mozzarella is a signature Italian food product. In a recent Italian fiction film, *mozzarella gialla* (yellow mozzarella) is the nickname Italian entrepreneurs use to refer to a mozzarella supposedly made by Chinese migrants. This and other cultural texts from the 2000s and 2010s reflected an urban myth about authentic Italian food, which Chapter 4 analyzes. According to this urban myth, ethnic Chinese attempt to make low-quality, Italian-style food on Italian soil. However, they fail because of the timely interventions of skillful Italian entrepreneurs with inimitable product expertise. The Italians are also depicted as displaying utmost devotion to protecting the reputation of Italian culinary arts. The cultural discourses that coalesced around this alimentary stereotype rhetorically assuaged some Italians' concerns about adaptation to rapidly changing Italian identities at individual, company-specific, sector-wide, national, and international levels, many of which were perceived as negatively influenced by Chinese capital, labor, and migration. However, recent media and cultural examples have positively evaluated China-Italy collaborations on the production and circulation of specific foods for which Italy is globally known: olive oils and coffee. I demonstrate that authenticity in Italian food is relational to Italian food expertise articulated in several dimensions, including technology, knowledge, entrepreneurship, company management, and branding.

Chapters 5 and 6 provide the first extended cultural analysis of Chinese consumers' Italian gastronomy tourism in China and Italy. In Chapter 5, I examine how, in elaborating their Italian culinary tourism since the 1990s, middle-class Chinese with considerable educational, economic, or cultural capital have deployed two hegemonic culinary repertoires. A culinary repertoire provides cultural resources (e.g., interpretive frames, perspectives, and arguments) for individuals to narrate their food-related experiences in texts. Through experiencing "authentic" higher-end Italian restaurants such as fine dining and trattorie (homelike, hearty, family-style restaurants), some middle-class Chinese consumers embraced the Made in Italy culinary repertoire. Focused on Slow Food, Italian food entrepreneurs in the country have enthusiastically promoted this culinary repertoire since the 2000s.

Many more middle-class Chinese consumers, however, have drawn upon an American-influenced culinary repertoire nurtured by Pizza Hut China since the 1990s. This repertoire stressed both pragmatic Italian food hybridity and conscious accommodation of Italian foodways to local Chinese palates. The two prevailing culinary repertoires helped the Chinese nation begin to feel cosmopolitan. Thanks to the uniquely widespread presence and longtime engagement in China, Italian and Italian-inspired food cultures have been vital to fashioning this cosmopolitanism in post-reform China.

Chapter 6 treats Chinese foodie travelers in Italy. During the 2010s, middle-class Chinese consumers' Italian food–assisted cosmopolitanism, as analyzed in Chapter 5, was conditioned and enhanced by their culinary tourism in Italy. Accustomed to a fast-paced lifestyle in China and lacking time to travel slowly in Italy, how did Chinese gastronomy tourists in Italy view Slow Food so pervasively and variably practiced and promoted by the country's gastronomy sector? Food-assisted Chinese cosmopolitanism has had an ambivalent relationship with Slow Food. I demonstrate this thesis by interpreting influential Chinese food journalism, initiatives, and documentaries that exhibit both appreciation and skepticism toward Slow Food. The majority of Chinese tourists in Italy during the 2000s–2010s used food-focused tourism websites with features that embraced a fast-paced consumerist style to approach Italian food. The narrative of a major 2010s Chinese film shot in Italy strongly recalls that of the American classic *Roman Holiday* (William Wyler, 1953), part of a group of Hollywood movies that helped rebrand Italy as an attractive tourist destination for American leisure tourists during the 1950s. The Chinese film features Italian cuisine and uses it to stage a symbolic emulation of China with the United States in terms of culinary tourism and cosmopolitanism.

ONE

Chinese Migrants' Food Entrepreneurship and Italians' Culinary Tourism, 1962–2020

Milan's first formal Chinese restaurant—La Pagoda (The Pagoda)—opened in October 1962. The Italian writer Dino Buzzati wrote a review of the inaugural dinner for *Corriere della Sera*, Italy's foremost daily and largest-circulating newspaper.[1] As Buzzati admits, Chinese food was "a total novelty" for him. In his opinion, most guests' maladroit but persistent attempts to eat the food with chopsticks constituted a "traditional tourist number" of sorts. The writer also praises how the group of prestigious Italian guests bestowed an impression of "official solemnity" on the elaborate banquet. This was the beginning of Milanese social elites' Chinese culinary tourism, which also occasioned the first extended Chinese restaurant review in *Corriere della Sera*.

More than thirty years after the publication of Buzzati's account, in 1996, a frustrated Stefano Bonilli, founder of Italy's revered food and wine magazine, *Gambero Rosso* (*Red Shrimp*), lamented in *Corriere della Sera* about

Chinese food, which was now widely available in Rome. The critic believes that migrants in New York City and London made Chinese dumpling fillings much more expertly than those living in Rome. For Bonilli, "in order to understand true flavors, even without going to China, [. . .] one ought to have eaten at least once in London, New York, or San Francisco in one of the great Chinese restaurants."[2] In other words, the quality of Chinese food in Rome was nowhere near that of other major Western cities with large Chinese diasporic communities.

Some twenty years later and almost a year before Milan became the epicenter of the COVID-19 epidemic in Europe, in April 2019, Allan Bay, a frequent contributor to food journalism in *Corriere della Sera*, blogged about the restaurant Gong in Milan, praising its innovative food practice.[3] The restaurant's culinary style is informed by "a profoundly Chinese soul which is contaminated by Japanese techniques, Italian creativity, and attention of French haut cuisine." As such, Gong represents the "force of cuisine in Milan today: the reality of having an utmost vast offering at all levels, with an additional, fundamental, and powerful contribution by haute cuisine, indeed by all the haute cuisines in the world." At the end of the 2010s, Chinese food could serve as a core ingredient in Milan's haute cuisine experimentation.

The three snippets about Italians' Chinese culinary tourism prompt this chapter's research questions about food mobilities and food-circulated cultural dynamics. What has transpired between 1962, when Chinese food was accessible only to the elites, and the widespread presence of Chinese food that enabled Italians' Chinese culinary tourism starting in the 1980s? What cultural and political agendas did opinion makers have in the 1980s and 1990s when claiming that Chinese food in Milan and Rome—Italy's two undisputed cosmopolitan food capitals—was poor in quality compared to that made in Western cities with more established Chinese migrant communities? What did it mean for food writers to highlight that Chinese and Italian cuisines could join forces in creating new and stimulating luxury food in the 2010s?

This chapter offers a first taste of the complexity of studying transcultural China-Italy food mobilities, in which migration, tourism, and media circulation intersect across countries and cultures. I analyze how Italians' Chinese culinary tourism developed in close interaction with Chinese migrant-managed food entrepreneurship in Italy in the last six decades. In the Italian-Chinese migrant context, the two have been intimately interdependent. On the one hand, without migrant entrepreneurs and workers' involvement in the Chinese restaurant sector, there would have been no Chinese culinary tourism for Italians to enjoy on Italian soil. Without the Chinese food businesses' tactics to survive competition within the restaurant sector, there might not have been various ways of accommodating Italy's local palates, economic circumstances, and political and cultural milieus. On the other hand, Italians' Chinese culinary tourism has not only made many Chinese migrants economically established but also helped the Chinese migrant community construct a more nuanced identity for itself.

For Lucy M. Long, culinary tourism means "the intentional, exploratory participation in the foodways of another—participation including the consumption, preparation, and presentation of a food item, cuisine, meal system, or eating style considered to belong to a culinary system not one's own."[4] Long qualifies "foodways" by referring to "the total cookery complex, including attitudes, taboos, and meal systems—the whole range of cookery and food habits in a society."[5] Importantly, for Long, the perceived alimentary "other" is distinguished from the "self" by way of "culture, region, time, ethos/religion, and socioeconomic class," as well as gender and age.[6] It was through such participation in foodways and food-assisted differentiation that Italian public perceptions about Chinese food and migrants became sharpened. Chinese migrants' own self-identity construction also crucially benefited from these sociocultural processes.

To understand these dynamics, I begin this chapter by providing a concise historical account of the most consequential empirical conditions about Italy's Chinese migrants and their restaurant sector from the 1980s through the 2010s. A comprehensive social scientific or historical account of this sector, which began in the 1940s, is lacking in any language. Additionally, most existing literature on specific dimensions of this sector in history, anthropology, sociology, and geography is written in Italian. This existing literature is slim in numbers. Despite such a critical gap, my goal is not to produce a comprehensive history of the subject. Instead, I equip the reader with the historical context and the general parameters of ongoing cultural conversations on the subject, paving the way for my subsequent chapters. Thus, my narrative goes beyond a mere summary of existing research findings to accentuate gender and race dynamics, which the social scientists I quote often gloss over but are highlighted in Chapters 2–4.

While Italians' Chinese culinary tourism is not well-captured by existing empirical studies, mainstream Italian media extensively covered it. The news media framed the Chinese foodscape in Italy in specific ways that I discuss incrementally in Chapters 1–4. In this chapter, I examine the first major example of these news framings. I analyze how, during the 1980s and 1990s in particular, *Corriere della Sera* repeatedly covered Italy's Chinese cuisine with reference to American food. On a minor scale, Chinese cuisine was favorably viewed compared to American fast food in Italians' culinary tourism. More important, Italian Chinese cuisine was often discussed in relation to Chinese cuisine available in the United States. American fast food and American Chinese food became foils against which to signal a significant cultural role played by Chinese culinary tourism: the news construction of Milan and Rome as cosmopolitan food capitals that could aspire to match New York City.

Using this method that draws from both empirical and media studies, I intend the research findings in this chapter to mirror a central critical concern that Krishnendu Ray articulates in his monograph titled *The Ethnic Restaurateur*.[7] Why was Chinese immigrants' cuisine turned into "ethnic food" even when this food has had a long-standing and substantial presence within contemporary Italy's foodscape? Is it true that Chinese cuisine consumed in Italy has not changed our fundamental beliefs about the "Italian" foodscape? In other words, how and in what ways does Chinese food in Italy become recognized as "Chinese" food? How and why is the taste of Chinese food perceived as such, especially when it is discussed together with Italian food? How does the Chinese restaurant sector negotiate the Italian socioeconomic milieu? I consider these questions by highlighting the role of cultural work.

Chinese Migrations to Italy

Since the 2000s, the Chinese have been the fourth largest migrant community in Italy, trailing Romanians, Albanians, and Moroccans.[8] The number of officially registered Chinese migrants in Italy increased from about 8,500 in the late 1980s to nearly 280,000 in the early 2020s.[9] This growth indicates that, among continental European countries, together with France, Italy has received the highest percentage of contemporary migration from China since the implementation of China's Open Door policy, which created opportunities for Chinese nationals to migrate beginning in the 1980s. While Chinese migrants in Italy have diverse geographical origins, most came from Wenzhou and its surrounding counties in Zhejiang Province in eastern China. Wenzhounese labor migration to Italy began during the 1920s in small numbers and has continued since then, despite disruptions from the 1950s through the 1970s owing to China's isolation policy. In more recent decades, labor migrants from other Chinese regions also moved to Italy. However, their numbers remained much smaller and their influence on the community's public socioeconomic life was much less felt. Partially because of the dominant presence of Wenzhounese migrants, the Chinese community in Italy was often perceived to have higher cohesion in cultural outlooks and business practices.

Two features of this labor migration are often said to distinguish the Chinese from other migrant groups in Italy: a migration agenda focused on entrepreneurship and the employment of an ethnic Chinese labor force. Many first-generation migrants became entrepreneurs with their own import and export companies; service businesses, including hair salons and travel agencies; garment factories; and restaurants, coffee bars, and other catering services. They mostly hired co-nationals as workers in these businesses, but some wealthy and forward-looking Chinese business owners also employed European Italians and non-Chinese migrants.[10] Unlike their co-nationals in other parts of Europe, Italy's Chinese specialized in fast fashion, accessories, and leatherwear, as such production drew on Italy's manufacturing and design strengths. Service businesses that were initially developed to cater to Chinese clientele included, for example, grocery stores that offered Chinese vegetables, supermarkets that sold merchandise imported from China, (bubble) tea salons, gadget and telecommunications stores, and hair salons. Chinese migrants' management of Italian coffee bars also became widespread in Italy, a business type intended for Italian customers.[11] But some Chinese migrants worked for Italian companies, including manual labor, such as stonecutters in the Piedmontese villages of Bagnolo Piemonte and Barge.[12] The so-called second-generation Chinese migrants or Chinese Italians enjoyed a wider variety of professions, including professions in arts and academia.[13] The number of such cases remained minuscule compared to Italy's Chinese migrants' more traditional areas of employment.

The Chinese tended to reside in major cities (e.g., Milan, Rome, Turin, and Naples) and specialized industrial districts (e.g., Prato). Milan's Via Sarpi, Prato's Via Pistoiese, and Rome's Piazza Vittorio were well-known Chinese neighborhoods that served as the community's service and commercial centers. But because the Chinese lived across many districts in the three cities and because migrants were never confined to those neighborhoods, critics believe that it is erroneous to label them "Chinatowns," which incorrectly recall those in North America.[14] As an example of community life for migrants, two Italian cities hosted prominent Chinese Buddhist temples: 普華寺 (*Pu hua si*)/Tempio Buddista Pu Hua Si in Prato (Pu Hua Si Buddhist Temple, created in 2009 by local Chinese migrants), and 華義寺 (*Hua yi si*)/Hua Yi Si Tempio Cinese Italiano in Rome (Hua Yi Si Chinese Italian Temple, founded in 2013 by a Taiwanese temple association). Both temples catered to the large ethnic Chinese populations in the two cities, although the level of local engagement is difficult to ascertain. Many more Chinese migrants were Christians belonging to associations such as the well-organized 基督教意大利华人教会 (*Jidujiao Yidali huaren jiaohui*)/Chiesa Cristiana Evangelica Cinese in Italia (Chinese Evangelical Christian Church in Italy), which was founded in the early 1980s with branches and devotees in many Italian cities.[15] In Prato, there were also several other Christian churches specifically serving the local Chinese population.[16]

Chinese migrants were relatively well-organized in their community activities, including their own media outlets. Both print and digital media, often published in Chinese, connected them to Italian society, as well as to Chinese communities in Europe and to mainland China. Their media clout in the Italian media landscape was on full display during three significant events: the 2007 riot in Milan's Via Sarpi district caused by popular Chinese discontent with Italian traffic policing; the controversies over fast fashion and Made in Italy in Prato, particularly in the initial period when these emerged, during 2005–2012; and the 2012 march in Rome organized by the Chinese following the public assassination of two Chinese migrants. During the 2010s, migrant-generated news communications increasingly moved to social media platforms, such as those hosted by WeChat, mainland China's powerful instant messaging, social media, and mobile payment app developed by Tencent in 2011.

Other Chinese migrations to Italy also existed on smaller scales, especially during the 2010s, including those of students and highly skilled expatriates. Despite a scarcity of research on the topic, some broad observations can be made, which can help form a holistic picture of the multiple routes and histories of Chinese migrants living in Italy. Thanks to inter-governmental agreements, the Marco Polo and Turandot programs funded a steady flow of Chinese students to study at Italian universities. Many Chinese students also utilized private funds. While students pursued undergraduate and graduate degrees in various subjects, fashion, design, music, the arts, and engineering were popular. At the end of the 2010s, with a little over 8,000 enrollments, Chinese students made up approximately 10 percent of the non-European Union student body in Italian universities.[17] Some students were then employed by Italian or Chinese migrant companies, or they married Italians, thereby becoming long-term migrants or naturalized as citizens in the country.

Professional expatriates followed China's direct investment in Italy in areas such as banking, mobile communications, apparel, food, and energy. While in Western Europe, China has focused on the United Kingdom, France, and Germany for investment, more projects could come to fruition in Italy in the 2020s.[18] For example, majority stakes of Pirelli, Italy's giant in tire manufacturing, were acquired in 2015 by the state-owned China National Chemical Corporation (ChemChina). As part of China's Belt and Road Initiative, the two countries signed a nonbinding "Memorandum of Understanding" (MoU) in 2019 to deepen their collaborations in various sectors. An example is the intention to revitalize Trieste's port following the successful Chinese redevelopment of Athens' Port of Piraeus.[19] Giorgia Meloni's government withdrew from the MoU in 2023 but continued to maintain a good relationship with the Chinese government for trade and investment.[20] The short- or long-term migration of these high-mobile transnational workers and managers can ebb and flow according to the vagaries of Chinese outbound investment and Italy's China policy.

Italy's Chinese Migrant-Managed Food Entrepreneurship: Opportunities and Crises

FROM THE 1980S TO THE 2002–2003 SARS OUTBREAK

According to Federica Redi, the first Chinese restaurant in Italy opened in Rome in 1949, when the People's Republic of China was founded.[21] Subsequently, Chinese establishments appeared in Milan and Florence during the 1960s and in Venice in the mid-1970s. Initially, these eateries often sourced ingredients and condiments required for Chinese cuisine from London or Paris, hired Hong Kong or Taiwanese professional male chefs already present in Europe for high salaries, and catered to Chinese and other Asian tourists and businessmen in addition to Italian customers. The menus were created with input from these migrant chefs from more established European Chinese communities. They already had substantial experience in addressing local customers' eating habits and altering dishes to suit such a palate.

As migrations from mainland China to Italy grew exponentially in the 1980s and 1990s, the restaurant sector also transformed. This is visibly reflected in the number of Chinese restaurants in major Italian cities. Pierpaolo Mudu's research shows that Rome had 6 Chinese-managed establishments offering Chinese food in 1977, 72 in 1987, 184 in 1997, and 237 in 2005,[22] a situation that likely provides a reasonable analogy for Milan. In a *Corriere della Sera* article, we read that there were 50 Chinese restaurants in the country in 1987 and 287 in 1994, while another article from the same newspaper indicates that 90 Chinese restaurants existed in Milan in 1988.[23] These figures should be viewed as approximate, particularly for more recent decades. Counting has been difficult, and discrepancies in various sources can be interpreted as differences in selection criteria. For example, Mudu discusses whether eateries that Chinese migrant entrepreneurs financed and managed but where the cuisine was not Chinese or not exclusively Chinese should count. The above-cited figures he provides refer to Chinese-managed restaurants that exclusively offered Chinese cuisine. This type of Chinese-managed restaurant is also what I am most concerned with in this book.

What is clear from these sources is that the 1980s represented the decisive decade in which Chinese restaurant businesses began booming. Restaurateurs often borrowed capital from a network of relatives, friends, and acquaintances, usually without interest, a system that has been at the heart of the financial infrastructures of Italy's Chinese migrant entrepreneurship. Despite the significant growth of the Chinese restaurant sector, the quality and variety of food offered were lacking. Using an oral history provided by Daniele Cologna, Nicoletta Bressan notes that during the 1980s, Chinese restaurants in the Province of Milan mostly offered standardized menus of simple dishes, owing to a migrant labor market where very few trained cooks were available.[24]

The mid- to late 1990s marked a watershed moment for Italy's Chinese restaurant sector as professionalization, differentiation, and specialization emerged. First and foremost, these changes responded to the needs of a dramatically expanded base of Chinese migrant customers. Second, Chinese visitors, international tourists, and Italian residents also helped engender change. According to Bressan and Cologna, the Chinese culinary scene in Milan was vibrant and competitive in the mid- to late 1990s. There were restaurants focused on either evening or daytime meals. Some offered both Italian and Chinese food, while others featured pan-Asian fusion cuisines. Still others specialized in seafood. The more elite restaurants hired professional chefs and carefully designed their ambiance, occasionally for the purpose of hosting visiting officials from China. Descendants of Chinese migrants also began innovating in the sector, as they paid more attention to interior decor that went beyond commonplace Chinese motifs to embrace generic modern Western styles. Unlike in previous decades, when canned food had been widely used in the Chinese kitchen, the new crop of restaurateurs tended to use fresh and higher-quality ingredients. They also offered more refined and inventive food choices. Analogous to what occurred to Italian Americans during the 1920s and 1930s, the Chinese food and restaurant businesses in Italy in the 1990s not only provided "community self-sufficiency" but also "created a unique pathway for the formation of an immigrant middle class," to use Simone Cinotto's words.[25]

Rome is a better-studied example of the exponential growth and internal diversification of the Chinese restaurant sector in the 1980s and 1990s. According to Mudu, Chinese eateries there expanded from the historic center and the Vatican City, where they catered to foreign tourists and Italian workers, to service centers for lunchtime clerks in areas such as the administrative and business district of EUR (Esposizione Universale Roma, or Universal Exposition Rome). Later, establishments appeared in the capital city's periphery, such as in Torpignattara, where foreign migrants and their descendants became the majority of the clientele. Chinese eateries also sprouted in Rome's outlying suburbs, where European Italian residents remained the main customers.

That Chinese restaurants served such a diverse Roman clientele was a story of fortuitous circumstances and planned accommodation. In Italy, eating in restaurants became normalized in the 1980s. Work arrangements for Italians in cities caused them to eat lunch nearby rather than return home, as they had traditionally. Moreover, as Mudu notes, the concept of (Chinese) ethnic restaurants became fashionable in Italy when they became associated with the more "popular" and, therefore, working-class and lower-priced eateries in the city's foodscape. By then, the neoliberal economy was elevating to an exalted standing in both "traditional" trattorie (offering family-style food) and osterie (serving simple food and drinks), which purportedly made "authentic" Italian dishes. Mudu also argues that in the Italian imagination, lower-quality Chinese food was comparable to lower-grade Italian-style food worldwide because both were viewed as migrant cuisines. For the critic, Italian public discourse promoted this notion while actively disparaging the Italian diasporas and conveniently forgetting Italian colonialism.[26]

Further, Chinese owners ethnicized their identities by perpetuating popular perceptions of their foodways, thereby helping cement the hierarchy of fancy and working-class cuisines. On his ethnographical visits to Chinese restaurants where he also dined, Mudu observed furnishings and red lanterns that would meet the expectations and imaginations of the locals about Orientalist exoticism. The same rings true for the association of Chinese food with low prices, which occurred partially because of brutal competition within the Chinese restaurant sector. Usefully, the food critic Massimo Alberini documents in *Corriere della Sera* that at the closing of the 1980s, a complete meal cost 8,000 lire on average. Redi informs us that an average lunch, including service, would cost 9,000 lire in the mid-1990s. Mudu offers figures for the prices in the mid-2000s: a meal consisting of a starter and a main course cost roughly eight euros.[27] Industrialization of foodstuffs such as pre-cooked and frozen food also made the low prices in Chinese restaurants possible.

The expansion of Chinese migrant cuisine during the 1980s and 1990s had important implications for enlarging Italians' gastronomic and cultural horizons. The widespread availability of Chinese cuisine occurred before the full emergence of other "ethnic" restaurants. According to Redi, for Italian diners during this period, Chinese cuisine was the premier international food option with an accessible price range, an appearance of exoticism, and reasonable accommodation to local tastes. Many menus presented Chinese dishes following a typical Italian meal sequence, from appetizers to first and second courses and desserts. Moreover, Redi believes that Chinese migrant cuisine provided many Italian customers with the opportunity to enrich their culinary knowledge of non-Italian food. For the critic, Chinese food entrepreneurs were tasked with addressing the difficulty of sourcing fresh ingredients (which in the 2000s became more available, partially through home-grown Chinese vegetables on Italian soil[28]), the lower-level professionalism of cooks in the 1980s and 1990s, and Italians' thin knowledge of cuisines other than their own. Nevertheless, continues Redi, the Chinese fared well with the presentation of dishes, Chinese-like decor that met diners' expectations, and the welcoming demeanor of restaurant waiting staff. However, Redi mentions a few popular stereotypes about Chinese culinary and hygienic practices already circulating among Italians in the 1990s. Fried odors lingered in restaurants' interior spaces. Customers could not watch food preparation, which supposedly guarantees food's freshness and authenticity.

The increasing popularity of Italy's Chinese restaurant sector was upended by the 2002–2003 outbreak of severe acute respiratory syndrome, or SARS, which closed a significant number of restaurants. The outbreak created alarmism among Italian customers, whose most extensive contacts with the Chinese migrant community were food-related. Stereotypical associations of Chinese food with disease and poor hygiene also resurfaced powerfully, further making Chinese food an unappetizing thought. But, as Mudu notes, SARS was not the only factor contributing to a major crisis in the sector in the Rome metropolitan area in the mid-2000s. Other causes include Italy's economic crisis, competition with other ethnic restaurants, and saturation in the Chinese food catering industry.

FROM POST-SARS TO THE 2020 ONSET OF THE COVID-19 PANDEMIC

When the SARS outbreak subsided and normal life resumed in late 2003, new entrepreneurial diversification and creative solutions in the sector ensued. Many restaurants in Milan that survived the SARS period moved away from Chinese cuisine, possibly reflecting a general trend in Italy. Some Chinese migrant food entrepreneurs opened Japanese and Korean restaurants, while others switched to Italian pizzerie, trattorie, or coffee bars. Many adopted an "all you can eat" formula, serving Asian and Italian food in large spaces, often near industrial areas that employed large numbers of Italian and migrant workers.[29] Smaller numbers of establishments targeted other ethnic groups, such as Latin American migrants. According to Bressan's informants, Chinese restaurant owners employed non-Chinese Asians and Latin Americans but not European Italians. Other research shows that European Italians occasionally were also employees and collaborators in Chinese-managed restaurant businesses.[30]

The racial economy of this period's Chinese food entrepreneurship in Italy can be appreciated through three aspects that existing literature mentions. In his study focused on the Veneto region, Livio Zanini claims that the success of Chinese-managed Japanese eateries can be partially attributed to many Italians' naivety about East Asian cultures and their inability to tell Japanese and Chinese cooks apart.[31] The Chinese exploited the Italians' ignorance, according to which Chinese food was oily, unsanitary, and cheap, while Japanese cuisine was refined, healthy, and expensive. Moreover, through business connections forged within Asian ethnic communities, some Chinese restaurants in Venice operated in a niche market that had special arrangements with travel agencies. Organized tours have brought Chinese travelers since the 2000s and Korean, Thai, Indonesian, and Malaysian tourists since the 2010s to eat in these Chinese or other pan-Asian restaurants.

However, migrant restaurateurs had more difficulty breaking the glass ceiling of offering exclusively Italian food. For example, Zanini mentions the failure of a Chinese-financed Italian establishment in Vicenza, which the owner attributed to the Italian customers' racially biased criticism of the Italian dishes made there, even though the cooks and the servers were white Italians.

In this regard, things appeared to be changing in the late 2010s and early 2020s, at least on mainstream television. Aspiring Chinese Italian male chefs who cooked exclusively Italian food were participants in various cooking competition shows, including Chang Liu in *Hell's Kitchen* on Sky, Federico Liu in *Antonino Chef Academy* on Sky, and Rong Hao Wu in *Bake Off—Dolci in forno* (Bake Off: Desserts in Oven) on Real Time. Although their biographies on the shows' websites often mentioned their previous experiences working in their parents' Chinese restaurants, on the shows their culinary skills were exclusively applied to Italian dishes. Through the demonstration of acquired culinary capital, these television representations endorsed the widespread conviction that younger generations of Italians of Chinese heritage were able to bridge both cultures. In this mediascape, two women who cooked Chinese or Chinese-Italian fusion food stood out: Angela Lei Han Zhen in *Cuochi d'Italia. Il campionato del mondo* (Italy's Chefs: World Championship) on TV8 and Yilan Anna Zhang, who won first place in the 14th edition of *MasterChef Italia* (Sky).

Several management and employment patterns consolidated during a Chinese restaurant boom after the SARS outbreak. According to Mudu's research, during the 1990s and 2000s, many restaurants were individual companies, as opposed to limited partnerships (Sas), general partnerships (Snc), and limited companies (Srl).[32] For Bressan, since the early 2010s, management in Milan's Chinese restaurants can be divided into three types. First, traditional nuclear family enterprises invested in a single commercial activity within the sector, such as a restaurant or an import and export firm. Second, transnational family enterprises engaged in multiple business activities in the restaurant and food sector, and many invested in both Italy and China in this and other unrelated sectors. Third, migrant entrepreneurs in managerial enterprises purposefully owned interests in both the restaurant and other unrelated sectors to diversify their investments.

Turning to employment patterns, most cooks and workers during the 2000s and 2010s were not professionals, and most worked with no contracts. Working in the sector was often viewed either as a survival strategy in the migrants' initial settlement in the country or as a stepping stone toward other trades or realizing their own entrepreneurial aspirations. Indeed, the mobility of Chinese restaurant workers in Milan was extremely high, owing to their relatively easy access to Chinese networks, as well as to the availability of informal job announcements, such as those distributed in public spaces in the Chinese migrant commercial centers in Milan, Prato, and Rome, as well as through social media. Interestingly, Bressan's fieldwork in the early 2010s indicates that some Chinese either preferred or aspired to work in Italian restaurants, thanks to a perception that they would receive better salaries and working conditions from Italian employers. But, according to the critic, the percentage of Chinese migrant cooks and servers in Italian establishments remained minuscule, and such expectations were not always met.

According to Bressan's findings, the choice to enter the restaurant business can be markedly gendered.[33] In one instance, the family's parents helped their son own a coffee bar, which they believed was an important opportunity for the family's financial success. In the informant's account, who was the daughter of this family, she profoundly understood Chinese parents' gendered bias when supporting their sons more readily than their daughters. But she believed in and verbalized an old adage to the interviewer: behind every successful man, there is a strong woman. In contrast, Bressan documents the story of a young woman who was emotionally invested in opening a restaurant. Her dream was realized with the support of her father and brothers because they trusted her managerial ability. Moreover, we learn from Bressan's study that female food entrepreneurs and workers had different experiences in the workplace. Some entrepreneurs said they were highly independent and self-controlled when running their restaurants. Some workers were dismissed by their employers because of pregnancy, and in one case, the individual did not receive her last month's pay and therefore took her employers to court. At one point during an interview, at the researcher's insistence, the subject finally revealed that, apart from work experiences and education, her employers also considered her physical attributes and demeanor as criteria for hiring her as a waitress. While Chinese women are commonly known to be waitresses and owners, I have not yet unearthed a case where a woman is celebrated as the chef of a Chinese establishment in Italy.[34] The gap points to the dichotomy between the professionalization of Chinese cuisine in Italy as a masculine affair and the extensive female labor employed in the home Chinese kitchen.

During the 2010s, Italy's Chinese restaurants also considerably enlarged their customer base and food offerings. They began catering to increasing numbers of leisure and business travelers from many parts of the world, including mainland Chinese and people of Asian descent from English-speaking and other countries. Many Chinese students who studied in Italian universities also frequented the eateries. Non-Chinese foreign migrants in Italy, moreover, ate Chinese food and had some notion of American Chinese food in their cultural repertoires. Menus from the 2010s, often written in Chinese, Italian, and English, accommodated this highly mobile, cosmopolitan, and varied clientele in Milan, Florence, Rome, and other major tourist cities. Restaurants have also significantly broadened their food offerings beyond simplified versions of stereotypical (American) Chinese dishes to embrace current culinary trends in mainland China. Occasionally, they also experimented with Italian-Asian fusion food and with financial co-partnerships.[35]

Here, I examine official menus and Tripadvisor.com reviews of two successful Chinese restaurants in Milan to illustrate some of the communicative strategies that Chinese establishments adopted in attracting clients, especially in the digital space. The choice of writing about Bon Wei and Mao Hunan is not driven by an intention for them to represent the variety of Chinese eateries now existing in Milan. Rather, the two restaurants tellingly illustrate a contrast in the current Chinese foodscape in Milan between self-consciously high-style cuisines and cuisines said to possess a mass appeal. This contrast helps me account for textual, visual, and discursive differences between the restaurants' menus and other self-presentations. This case study opens up a discussion about restaurant and food communications, which complements this section's geographical, anthropological, and historical literature.

Since its 2010 opening at 16/18 Via Castelvetro, Bon Wei has become representative of high-style Chinese cuisine in the Lombardy capital. It claims to be the first in the city to offer dishes from all of China's eight major regional culinary traditions. The publicity materials drawn from the restaurant's website intend to capture more elite consumers of Chinese food. From the online introduction to the restaurant, we learn that Bon Wei aims to offer "a culinary experience that is as 'high' as possible, devoid of misleading clichés, with a view to allowing Italian diners to appreciate authentic Chinese cuisine."[36] The website dedicates extensive sections to the main chef, Zhang Guoqing, who migrated to Italy in 1989 and initially worked in Prato's restaurant sector, and to the Chinese-inspired but generic, modern interior design by Carlo Samarati. The carefully designed menu downloadable from their website first presents specialty dishes from the eight traditions.[37] Each tradition has a concise introduction in Italian and recommendations for three typical dishes, with names accurately written and translated into Chinese, Italian, and English. The rest of the menu is more predictable, consisting mainly of Chinese, American Chinese, and Southeast Asian food. The menu also mixes dishes familiar to non-Asian diners with less common ones that mostly target Asian customers, such as frog and crab meat-based items.

Bon Wei's menu covers an impressive range of culinary traditions, underscoring its intention to please a customer base equipped with sophisticated palates and a sense of culinary adventure. To be sure, several specialty dishes carry names that diners without a firm knowledge of Chinese history and specific historical figures would struggle to understand or relate to. Often, these names indicate only the main ingredients, not the spices used or the cooking methods. For example, in the section dedicated to Zhejiang's regional cuisine, the name "Jiaohuaji—Pollo del mendicate—Beggar's chicken" appears without any explanation of how the chicken is prepared or why it is nominally associated with beggars in the local tradition.[38] Nevertheless, the accurate translations throughout the menu, concise introductions to each of the eight regional cuisines, and full descriptions of ingredients, spices, and cooking methods for the majority of dishes mentioned conjure an impression of a restaurateur and a chef with rigor and expertise. This textual and discursive appearance encouraged the diner to order with confidence. Judging from the pictures that customers shared on Tripadvisor.com, the presentation of food on white plates was equally well-executed. Although the diners' judgments of the food and the service as revealed by the many reviews were mixed, approximately 70–75 percent of total reviews at the time of my research rated their experiences as "excellent" or "very good."[39] Interestingly, many reviewers expressed their frustration and even a sense of injustice at the small portions, a possible reference to the widespread perception that Chinese food tends to come in large sizes. This detail would indeed be the kind of stereotypical views that the restaurant's menu says it sets out to combat.

Bon Wei's projection of an image of self-importance, higher prices, and sophisticated decor is thrown into relief by Mao Hunan restaurant, located at 5 Via Nicola Antonio Porpora in Milan. Mao Hunan represents a boutique-style approach to Chinese restaurants, which centers on offering good and unapologetically spicy food in an intimate and friendly dining space. The restaurant's generous food portions, accessible prices, and noisy and convivial ambiance fit into the stereotypical Italian perception that Bon Wei assiduously avoids. The food project was initiated by three young foodies, including a European Italian, a Chinese Italian, and a Chinese migrant from Hunan. Opened in 2015, the restaurant specializes in the cuisine of Hunan, the home province of Mao Zedong, whose Cultural Revolution became the inspiration for its menu design and dishes. Some dishes are described as originating from Sichuan, but most of them are spicy, according to the two provinces' culinary traditions.

During the COVID-19 lockdown in Milan, in the takeaway menu posted on the restaurant's Facebook page on May 9, 2020, which simulates the format of their one-page paper menu, we witness humor and irreverence relating to Maoism.[40] On the menu's first page, Mao is said to be "Grandpa Mao," who cares about his people's diet, which presumably justifies the eatery's presentation of basic, hearty, and peasant-origin dishes. The menu ends with two pages dedicated to "specialties that you would never choose (but we put them here anyway)," referring to dishes that employ pig kidneys, pig feet, intestines, pig's ear, and duck heads. Unlike Bon Wei, Mao Hunan actively encourages Italian diners to experience exoticism and adventure. Mao Hunan's ironic take on Maoism through its menu presents novelty for Italian culinary tourists who are tired of seeing the archaic Chinese motifs of pagodas, dragons, and vases. The restaurant does not appear to be as critical of Maoism as some Westerners and Chinese may. Instead, the focus is on postmodern playfulness, showing a stark contrast between the Maoist dictum of cherishing food and the current neoliberal consumerist approach to food. Such a restaurant design and ethos must have resonated with the diners, as the Tripadvisor.com rating, based on 921 reviews, was as high as 4.5/5 at the time of writing. Indeed, the restaurant has also been popular among Chinese students residing in Milan and with Chinese visitors, some of whom left reviews commenting on how the place had a convivial atmosphere that reminded them of being back home.[41]

The profound and creative diversification of the Chinese food scene in Italy since the SARS outbreak brought the number of Chinese-owned restaurants to a record high at the dawn of the COVID-19 pandemic in early 2020. According to the Milan-based, center-left Italian newspaper affiliated with the Roman Catholic Church, *Avvenire*, in early 2020, approximately 2,000 Chinese establishments operated in Italy, 1,300 of which were located in Milan. These numbers likely included both restaurants and hotels because the newspaper cites the Camera di Commercio di Milano (the Chamber of Commerce of Milan) as a source, which considers restaurants and hotels as a single category for data collection.[42] With most Chinese restaurants closed down, the lockdown months of 2020 witnessed a dramatic surge in delivery services transporting Chinese groceries and food in Milan. Popular delivery platforms and apps included the multinational companies Deliveroo, Uber Eats, Foodora, and Glovo, as well as 呱呱到家 (*Guagua daojia*)/Guua Now, an app developed by Chinese migrants based in Milan in 2015 and now available in select European countries.[43] While Chinese food delivery had existed since the 1980s, the 2020 lockdown expanded its role on several fronts: meeting hygienic standards, mitigating the effects of restrictions on residents' mobility and their food and grocery needs, and supporting restaurant and catering businesses when physical distancing was necessary. Italy's Chinese food industry is bound to evolve in a new way following the COVID-19 pandemic.

Italians' Chinese Culinary Tourism: Acquiring a Taste through America

When surveying *Corriere della Sera*'s coverage of Italy's Chinese cuisine from the 1980s and 1990s—when the Chinese restaurant sector boomed for the first time in Italy before its major setback due to SARS—a recurring communicative pattern emerged. Chinese food reviews were frequently framed as relating to contemporary American foodscape, particularly American fast food and American Chinese cuisine. As the following analysis shows, the American connection is as much a surprising ingredient as expected in the commerce between Italians' culinary tourism and Chinese migrants' food entrepreneurship. My analysis deepens Fabio Parasecoli's remarks on how "the analysis of tourism can uncover the political, social, and cultural relevance of food," in particular culinary tourism of foreign food.[44] Studying this news frame foregrounds the ideological and reputational agendas of Italian journalism on Chinese food, which resonate beyond China-Italy issues.

SIMPLE CHINESE FOOD VERSUS AMERICAN FAST FOOD

In a 1985 *Corriere della Sera* article, Roberto Della Rovere encapsulates many of Long's points on culinary tourism by lauding the benefits of eating in a Chinese restaurant in Rome. Chinese cuisine "offers pleasant, economic dishes, and allows you to indulge in fantasy and to spend a pleasant evening with friends. This is in contrast to alienating fast food, which instead is pure and rushed nourishment."[45] This comparison asserts the superiority of old-world, homemade Chinese food over modern and industrialized American food. The structure of this contrast also gives the impression that Chinese food is slow food, thereby rhetorically making it closer to a conventional notion of Italian cooking. Why was simple Chinese food recommended as a superior choice over American fast food during the 1980s when Italian culinary tourism, both within and beyond Italy, boomed?

The contrast in Della Rovere's review has implications for ideologically driven food tourism. The familiarity of Italians with American fast food, which the reviewer assumes as the basis for his Chinese-American culinary comparison, was achievable only through tourism outside of the country, in other European or Western countries. Italy's first McDonald's restaurant opened in Rome only a year after the publication of Della Rovere's review, in 1986, much later than the establishment of the American food chain in most other Western European countries. Slow Food was then a burgeoning movement institutionalized with an express goal of resisting the imminent opening of the Roman McDonald's and the industrial food homogenization the chain was thought to represent.[46] Against this backdrop, Della Rovere's review can be interpreted as inviting Italian eaters to stay in their home country and to enjoy a culinary detour into the exotic and (supposedly) slow-cooked Chinese food, rather than to travel for trendy American fast food only available abroad. Implicit in this suggestion was a sympathy for Chinese migrants as underdogs from a Communist country and a distaste for vulgar American capitalist expansion.

Further, this contrast illustrates Jack Goody's discussions of homogenization and differentiation in the globalization of American and Chinese food in Europe in this period. In his view, whereas McDonaldization came to symbolize American-style industrialization of food, Chinese and Indian cuisines were part of the process of "multicultural globalization," presumably "enriching industrial cultures by giving them a global dimension."[47] Indeed, for the critic, Asian cuisines helped "offset the homogenization of world cultures brought about by the mass production of industrialized foods."[48] Food journalism in Italy about simple Chinese food versus American fast food, therefore, aptly articulated both ideological dynamics influenced by the Cold War and the increasing pressure of globalization on local exigencies.

To appreciate the 1980s narrative nuances of Chinese culinary tourism in Italy just relayed, it is useful to refer to Buzzati's 1962 *Corriere della Sera* review of La Pagoda mentioned at the outset of this chapter.[49] This is an important precursor to later Italian food journalism about Chinese food, and it was produced when the Cold War was raging. Although La Pagoda offered high-style Chinese food, quite unlike the simple one described by Della Rovere, basic tenets about narrating Chinese culinary tourism were held. Indeed, although formulated differently from Della Rovere's article, both the adventurous and politicized aspects of culinary tourism inform Buzzati's review.

As relayed above, for Buzzati, Chinese food was "a total novelty," and the attempted use of chopsticks by most guests resembled a "traditional tourist number." What Buzzati missed most as a culinary tourist was seeing more Chinese faces as waitstaff, cooks, guests, and hosts in the restaurant. The writer laments catching sight of only a few Chinese "with almond-shaped eyes" and only one petite Chinese woman (*cinesina*), who was the half-white, half-Chinese Alberta Jang, "daughter of one of the prominent figures of the [Chinese] colony [in Milan]." Such expressions focused on the supposedly characteristic shape of Chinese eyes and a preferred physical size for Chinese women place Buzzati's review within the Western Orientalist literary tradition that exoticizes the Chinese often during migration and other exploration-related mobility events.[50] Chinese food and foodways are unsurprisingly gendered and exoticized in this account of Chinese culinary tourism, part of the "fantasy" to which Della Rovere refers in his review.

Like Della Rovere, Buzzati also displays a high degree of ideological and political awareness when describing his interactions with Chinese food and Italian guests on the restaurant's opening night. He praises how the prestigious Italian guests bestowed an impression of "official solemnity" on the elaborate banquet. He lists names including Giuseppe Trabucchi, then the minister of the economy; the (unnamed) ambassador of the Republic of China (Taiwan) in Rome; Carlo Martani from Milan's archbishop's palace; Giuseppe Cereda of San Gioachimo parish; and Giuseppe Sironi from Via Canonica-Via Sarpi parish. For Buzzati, this list was a welcome departure from the usual "high society" business elites who attended similar restaurant openings in Milan. Buzzati further muses on the significance of the presence of the Taiwanese ambassador: Does this mean the co-owners of La Pagoda declared political allegiance to Taiwan rather than to the People's Republic of China? Or was the ambassador there to "simply solemnize that appetizing family feast"? Buzzati even seems to refer to the same Chinese-American culinary comparison as understood by Della Rovere: the lavish presentation of eleven courses at the dinner conjured "a refined cuisine with slow penetration, instead of a cuisine bent on frontal assault."

Buzzati believes that La Pagoda played an important role in cementing the city's cosmopolitanism in its perennial rivalry with Rome. Chinese culinary tourism in Italy during the Cold War delighted guests looking for food exoticism and helped them make food-channeled comparisons of political cultures against American-led capitalist expansion and globalization in Western Europe. Fittingly, when Buzzati's review was reprinted in *Corriere della Sera* in 2014, it was meant as evidence for claiming that Milan was the best Italian city in which to taste Chinese cuisine.[51] Culinary cosmopolitanism meant not globalization-induced homogenization but multicultural super-diversity.

CHINESE CUISINE MADE IN ITALY VERSUS AMERICAN CHINESE CUISINE

Buzzati's 1962 review begins by elucidating the significance of the opening of the first Milanese Chinese restaurant: "We can now breathe: Finally, Milan has the right to be considered a metropolis of an international profile, which until last Sunday was denied to her." He continues, "As the provincials, we will no longer be annoyed by the accounts of friends who come back from New York, Chicago, Hong Kong, or even Beijing [about their culinary experiences there]."

Almost thirty-five years later, in 1996, as relayed at the outset of the chapter, Bonilli lamented in the same newspaper that Chinese migrants in Rome did not make dumplings as expertly as those living in New York City and London. For him, "in order to understand true flavors, even without going to China, [. . .] one ought to have eaten at least once in London, New York, or San Francisco in one of the great Chinese restaurants."[52]

Fast-forwarding twenty years to 2017, writing for *Corriere della Sera*'s "Cuisine" section, the journalist Alessandra Dal Monte recounts how she initially discovered the beauty of Chinese soup dumplings in New York City's Chinatown. "But in order to eat them, there is no need to have to go to New York. In Milan, which is by now homeland to Chinese restaurants and to dumplings, there are numerous choices." Dal Monte then goes on to introduce six such eateries.[53]

The three examples of Italian food writings drawn from a lengthy time span point to a recurring communicative pattern, in which an adequate understanding of Chinese cuisine in Milan and Rome was said to be achievable through experiencing that which was found in major American cities with large communities of Chinese migrants, particularly New York City. Chinese foodscapes in other European capitals, including London, Paris, and Amsterdam, were occasionally referred to in *Corriere della Sera*'s journalism on Italy's Chinese cuisine. But the more constant and widely mentioned yardstick against which the quality and variety of Chinese migrant cuisine was judged remained the American experience. While other American cities may be mentioned or omitted, New York City always appeared on these lists. Depending on the critics' opinions and the time period, Italy's Chinese food may be positively or negatively viewed against its American counterpart. Most often, these narratives became a vehicle for Italian food journalists to praise "authentic" and expensive food over hybrid and popular food offered by Chinese migrants in these countries. Ultimately, the relevant news stories in *Corriere della Sera* from the 1960s through the 2010s have produced a cultural narrative about how Italy's Chinese cuisine gradually gained sophistication, helping Milan and Rome, as the country's cosmopolitan food capitals, to finally aspire to rival migrants' ethnic foodscapes in cities like New York City.

When Buzzati covers the menu served on the opening night of La Pagoda, he accidentally leaves evidence of the co-presence of "authentic" Chinese cuisine and hybrid American Chinese dishes. The writer uses both generic terms and proper names to identify the dishes presented in the following order, which I paraphrase or cite: prawn and meat spring rolls, *marosta* shrimp, prawns with peas, duck meat seasoned with various spices, chicken with cashews, meat with bamboo shoots, sweet and sour sauce fish, "Chinese Restaurant-style" stir-fried rice, fish soup with mushrooms, swallow's nest, Chinese fruits, and an Italian dessert. Thus, the presentation of the dishes followed the typical Italian meal sequence by progressing from appetizers to desserts. Meanwhile, the dinner exhibited a formal Chinese meal's customary focus on serving rice and soups after the main meat and fish dishes.[54] The vague terms that Buzzati applies to some of these courses leave us uncertain about the exact composition of ingredients and cooking methods. For example, what meat was used in the spring rolls? How was the duck meat seasoned? What Chinese fruits were served?

On the one hand, Buzzati's reference to a range of meat and fish dishes and the swallow's nest makes us think that the owners of La Pagoda showcased some higher-class dishes commonly available in China, which can be therefore considered genuine Chinese cuisine. Mentioning chicken with cashews (an almond chicken type of dish?) and the so-called Chinese Restaurant-style stir-fried rice (possibly a version of what is more widely known as Cantonese fried rice), on the other hand, would seem to indicate

Chinese dishes that were either invented for an American palate (the former) or popularized in North America (the latter). According to Buzzati's article, one of La Pagoda's two chefs came from Hong Kong. He might have included American Chinese dishes based on his experience catering to European customers. The journalist also refers to conversations that he had with two Italians who supposedly had a deeper knowledge of Chinese cuisine: one thanks to his friendship with an "Indo-Chinese" colleague and the other having spent four years in Beijing. However, Buzzati only mentions their highly subjective and undefined judgments on specific dishes. In general, the writer does not show explicit awareness of American Chinese and other hybrid overseas Chinese culinary traditions. The slim and imprecise evidence gleaned from Buzzati's review nonetheless allows us to peek into an underlying mobility story of American Chinese recipes and dishes available in Italy as early as the 1960s.

By the mid-1980s, thanks to the widespread distribution of Chinese eateries in major cities, increasing numbers of ordinary Italians had become familiar with Chinese culinary choices. Restaurant reviews more frequently referred to and complained about simpler and more economically priced Chinese restaurants in Italy. A major concern was the presence of Chinese American dishes and other popular Chinese fare readily available in America and in Chinese diasporic communities. In 1986, Monica Paternesi of *Corriere della Sera* covered a request-only service called "China Cena" (China Dinner), which delivered Chinese food to Italian families in Rome. Its menu contained shrimp toast and chicken with almonds (now identified as such), which originated from the American Chinese culinary tradition.[55] In 1988, when reviewing newly opened Chinese restaurants in Rome and Milan in the same newspaper, food critic and one of Italy's most celebrated food scholars, Massimo Alberini, lamented the uninspiring conformism that plagued menus of the country's Chinese restaurants. According to a common public perception that he reported, eateries only offered spring rolls, sweet and sour pork, Cantonese rice (named as such), and dishes made from canned food, all of which had a mediocre quality.[56]

For an example from the 1990s, in his detailed 1992 review of La Grande Hai Cheng, located at 41/43 Via Lucrezio Caro in Rome, food journalist Bruno Vergottini duly mentions the "the super-classic cuisine that one usually makes in Rome in Chinese restaurants," including, for example, fried wontons, shrimp chips, Cantonese fried rice, sweet and sour pork or beef, and canned fruits.[57] But Vergottini highlights a typical American Chinese takeaway food dish which, according to him, was slightly different from how it was usually prepared: "The lemon chicken at Gampiero's is gracefully served with candied fruits."[58] But the real novelty for Vergottini was Tung's ambition to make food that would use Western ingredients and Chinese cooking methods and presentation, drawing from his experience studying and working in Italian restaurants in Los Angeles and Rome.[59]

Food journalists such as Alberini and Bonilli, and to some extent, Vergottini, critiqued the poor quality and the small variety of dishes offered in what was presumably a large number of Chinese eateries in Rome and Milan. For them, this situation painted a negative portrait of Chinese food in Italians' imagination. Recent scholarship on Chinese cuisine in Italy makes similar points. Through a survey of menus and interior decor of Chinese restaurants from the early 2000s, Parasecoli reveals the stereotypical and inauthentic image of Chinese food that they perpetuated.[60] Scarpellini also recognizes that experiences offered by Italy's Chinese restaurants can be inauthentic and even act as "vehicles that reinforced the racial and cultural stereotypes and biases held by their customers."[61]

However, from the perspective of this section's analysis, 1980s and 1990s food writings can also be interpreted as implicitly critiquing the cheap Americanization of Chinese food in Italy, which took the form of offering American Chinese dishes and other simple dishes widely available in America's Chinese restaurants (e.g., fried wontons, spring rolls, and fortune cookies). Both types of dishes were perceived as low-quality and fake Chinese cuisine. Della Rovere's review of the values of simple Chinese food versus American fast food represented a minority voice in this foodscape. The same can be said about the alternative voice of the Chinese-Italian writer and fashion model Bamboo Hirst, who, in her 1988 cookbook, *Il riso non cresce sugli alberi* (Rice Doesn't Grow on Trees), praises the simplicity of Chinese and American Chinese dishes and their contributions to wellbeing and to reliving her family memories.[62]

Since at least the late 1990s, Italian food critics have demonstrated more consciousness in making sense of Italy's Chinese food scene through the lens of American Chinese food. In 1997, Allan Bay, a frequent food writer for *Corriere della Sera*, claimed that the widely available dish in Italy, *chop suey* (a meat and vegetable stir-fry), was an American Chinese invention. Bay believed this was understandable because most Chinese migrants in Italy came from Guangdong Province (Canton).[63] Bay is correct mainly about *chop suey*'s culinary origin but erroneous about the origin of Italy's Chinese, the majority of whom came from Zhejiang Province. *Chop suey* is arguably American Chinese cuisine's most iconic dish.[64] Haiming Liu states that, while Chinese restaurants in the United States transformed their food to adapt to popular tastes, they also shaped the American diet, for example, through the wide availability of *chop suey* throughout the United States from the 1900s to the 1960s.[65] Bay's straightforward statement about *chop suey* signaled a conscious attempt to acknowledge the hybridity of the Chinese food offered by Italy's Chinese migrants. Buzzati, Paternesi, Alberini, Bonilli, and Vergottini did not acknowledge such a fact, even as their writings repeatedly described this phenomenon. The concerns of Alberini and Bonilli, in particular, mostly focused on gauging authenticity in cuisine based upon a tourism- and class-related notion of Chinese food in America. Through this assessment, the authors asserted that Milan and Rome still needed to play catch-up to achieve the true status of cosmopolitan food capitals. As Dal Monte's quote mentioned at the outset of this section shows, during the 2010s, journalists self-assuredly, but perhaps exaggeratedly, claimed Milan as a capital of Chinese cuisine on par with New York City. By this time, the focus has switched from a need to critique the Americanization of Chinese cuisines made in Italy to a desire to praise the culinary variety and innovations in Italy's Chinese foodscape. This latter point will be further examined in Chapter 2.

The news frame discussed in this section illustrated the journalists' awareness of Chinese ethnic food discourses as facilitating public claims about culinary cosmopolitanism in Italy's two largest immigrant-receiving cities, Milan and Rome, where other processes of globalization were also most visible. American fast-food chains and Chinese migrant culinary experiences in the United States became two key channels through which to narrate the pains and joys of Italy's growing multiculturalism, of which the Chinese migration has been an indispensable component. My analysis shows that

China-Italy food mobilities were not limited to commercial and narrative transactions exclusively between the two countries. American popular culture and American Chinese experience played a crucial role in these exchanges. To appreciate this point effectively, in addition to analyzing migrants' food entrepreneurship and culinary tourism in their empirical dimensions, we ought to consider the media circulation of these dynamics and their cultural agendas.

■

As this chapter's analysis has revealed, empirical and media analyses are needed to approach the complexity of Italy's Chinese restaurant sector and its weighty role in Italians' culinary tourism more broadly. Both Chinese migrant food entrepreneurs and Italian food journalists were deeply invested in communicating specific interpretations of Chinese cuisine to their white Italian audiences. Economic gains were a primary goal in most of such public promotions. But we can also boil down the texts' communicative agendas to sociocultural identity-making of Italian culinary tourists and Chinese migrants involved in food businesses. When one scans the current scholarship in the field, it is difficult to find another migrants' food entrepreneurship in Italy that has influenced Italians' culinary tourism through such a long evolution, in such a multifaceted way, and with such wide-ranging socioeconomic and politico-cultural implications. Chinese food has fundamentally changed many food writers' and culinary tourists' perception of the contemporary foodscape in Milan and Rome, although Chinese food has remained stubbornly ethnicized and kept outside of the cities' "Italian" foodscape.

TWO

Romantic Waitresses vs. "Kung Food" Workers:
Gendering the Chinese Restaurant

Two notable 1980s Italian popular films were set during the first significant growth of Chinese food businesses in Italy. Both refer to "the Chinese restaurant" in their titles: *Delitto al ristorante cinese* (Crime at the Chinese Restaurant, Bruno Corbucci, 1981) and *Sotto il ristorante cinese* (Under the Chinese Restaurant, Bruno Bozzetto, 1987). The definite article in these titles signals an archetypical space then associated with the Chinese in the mindset of Italian viewers. Both films' titles also stress crime narratives. The former uses the term "delitto" to indicate a homicide storyline, and the latter points to an underground area of the restaurant in insinuating seedy affairs. The films' creative teams conceived the Chinese restaurant as both a criminal space and a stand-in for the Chinese community.

For contemporary Italians, Chinese restaurants are the most recognizable and widespread symbol of Chinese migrant communities and identities.

From the 1940s through the 1970s, restaurants were often the exclusive tangible marker of the Chinese migrant community in the consciousness of Italians. In the late 1980s, Chinese eateries expanded rapidly in Italy, prompting, on the one hand, a popular impression that they grew like mushrooms and, on the other hand, an appreciation for the culinary novelties that they brought to the country.[1] Due to this geographical expansion, Chinese establishments are far more visible on Italian streets than leather and garment workshops, another socioeconomic space often associated with Chinese nationals in Italy. Chinese restaurants are also much more widely distributed throughout the Italian peninsula than are concentrated Chinese neighborhoods, the most famous of which are located in Milan, Prato, and Rome, with the former already well-defined in the early 1980s and the latter two by the 1990s. Since the 1980s, most general-interest news coverage, novels, nonfiction, and films concerning Italy's Chinese migrant communities have examined restaurants to varying degrees. Discourses on the Chinese restaurant as a sociocultural space have significantly shaped the Italian public's knowledge of the Chinese.

Food studies scholarship also views restaurants as a productive space to investigate the intersection of food and popular culture. For David Beriss, "Restaurants provide a context in which questions of popular culture can be especially well focused."[2] He shows that, over the past two centuries, restaurants have changed from markers of elite status to sociocultural spaces expressing the rise of consumerism and the ascendancy of the middle class. For the critic, the growth of immigrant-managed or "ethnic" restaurants was integral to a reconceptualization of race and ethnicity in Western society. Beriss's case studies indicate that, historically, restaurants that offer the food of migrants may be either viewed with suspicion over their health standards or lavished with distinction by the adventurous (white) customer. In Beriss's assessment, these public perceptions occasionally lead to controversies that the media helps amplify, as is the case for laws proposed to prohibit "foreign" restaurants in the historic centers of certain Italian towns, notably including Lucca in Tuscany. But in another case mentioned by Beriss, we witness the role played by films such as *My Big Fat Greek Wedding* (Joel Zwick, 2002) in increasing the possibility of wider societal acceptance of ethnic restaurants.

In this chapter, I analyze the evolution of the images of Chinese restaurants since the 1980s in influential Italian films and graphic novels. I contend that in the recent four decades, mainstream Italian fictional representation of Chinese restaurants has enjoyed a cultural logic largely detached from the realities of the relevant foodscape, which, however, corresponded closely to the gradual accumulation of discursive and social power of Chinese migrants. I emphasize the necessity of explaining why, from the 1980s through the early 2000s, fictional depictions of Chinese restaurants evolved in a way that scarcely reflected reality, as relayed in Chapter 1. In the 1980s and 1990s, in particular, cultural production conjured the Chinese community through the lens of organized crime. According to a prevailing cultural script, Chinese restaurants were places where migrants made a profit through organized crime, which used food businesses as covers. Such criminalization was further encouraged by mainstream Italian media's tendency to associate crime with the country's foreign populations more generally. The images concerning the Chinese restaurant have played an important role in channeling this cultural frame of interpreting Italy's Chinese.

I also show why we need to address both the emergence of pro-Chinese migrant cultural production and the change in mainstream Italian news media about Chinese migrant-managed restaurants during the 2000s and 2010s. The restaurant-crime-migration frame was gradually destabilized in this more recent cultural work, which became vocal about viewing Chinese restaurants, at least select ones in Milan, as contributing to the city's cosmopolitanism befitting neoliberal economy. Although no typical reception studies are conducted in this chapter, my analysis shows that many 1980s and 1990s cultural discourses were debated, reinforced, and challenged in more recent decades.

In the cultural accounts that I analyze, the establishment, consolidation, and contention of the restaurant-crime-migration frame have occurred crucially through considering gender roles or positions assigned to Chinese migrant men and women. In my interpretation, European Italian and Chinese Italian creative teams debated this issue by consciously deploying both negative and positive stereotypical diasporic Chinese American masculinities and femininities. I use "Chinamen" and *cinesine* (petite Chinese women) to refer to the Italian revisions, adaptations, or updates of these Chinese American stereotypes, which exhibit a variety of specific characters, as will be clear in subsequent analyses. To take some characters from my analysis as examples, a cruel Chinaman can be a Fu Manchu reincarnation that controls Chinese migrant food entrepreneurship, while a heroic Chinaman can be a Bruce Lee figure who helps ameliorate neighborhood (food) businesses. A submissive *cinesina* is a Chinese migrant woman who resorts to white Italian men to escape her Chinese world, which is often symbolically represented as a Chinese restaurant. In contrast, a dragon lady-like *cinesina* claims her own space in defiance of both Chinese and Italian patriarchy. Chinese restaurants either constrain or enable her acts of identity-making. Gender has become an important discursive battleground for enacting cultural contentions about Italy's Chinese restaurants and communities.

When selecting from a sizeable cinematic and literary production for the chapter, I only consider key examples of popular cinema and graphic novels, which, with one exception, were created by European Italians. I leave out Chinese-language texts published in Italy, documentary cinema, and migrant-authored novels, among others, all of which merit separate studies that this chapter does not allow. Nevertheless, the texts chosen for analysis include comedy and romantic films and graphic novels, which are among the most popular contemporary Western visual narrative mediums. Considering these popular cultural genres helps me better analyze the long-term competition among various cultural scripts about the Chinese restaurant as a sociocultural space. I am not claiming that the body of cultural texts discussed in this chapter was influential to the point of shaping many people's attitudes about Chinese food. Rather, I insist on how they shaped cultural scripts and discourses that were perceived as viable and stimulating, given that they existed on the cultural market and reached a fair number of audiences. My selection of examples is useful for scanning important Italian cultural symptoms about Chinese migrant food in the four decades to understand the cultural purchase it has made in public discourse. My research in this chapter lends more credence to recent scholarship on how food and food-related practices are intimately related to forming individual and group identities, including such dynamics during migration.[3]

Criminals and Fools

What specific interpretive frames and cultural scripts about Chinese migrant restaurants and food became influential in the 1980s and 1990s? And what did these food discourses articulate about the migrant community? Answering these questions helps set the parameters of discussions about the 2000s and 2010s cultural contestation connecting the Chinese restaurant with specific gender dynamics in the rest of the chapter. A restaurant-crime-migration frame with a comic touch was applied to the ostensible narrative subject of Chinese migrants in this section's texts. Cultural scripts, such as how Chinese migrants are criminally organized or minded or how Chinese food is ridiculous, derived from this frame.

In *Delitto al ristorante cinese*, the Chinese migrant chef is a protagonist who generates narrative energy on his own terms. In contrast, *Sotto il ristorante cinese* only features Chinese migrants as minor characters who are insignificant to the main plot. Unlike the news media or documentary films, the two films are not concerned with depicting the social reality of Italy's Chinese community. Instead, these entertainment-oriented movies ultimately examine Italian-centric issues by drawing from diverse Italian and American cinematic genres. As a crime comedy in a film cycle focused on an Inspector Nico Giraldi, *Delitto al ristorante cinese* exploits the comic talent of the actor Tomas Milian, which is the pseudonym of the Cuban-born American and Italian citizen Tomás Quintín Rodríguez, a favorite of Italian B movies. *Sotto il ristorante cinese* can be best described as a fantasy-comedy film. Its director, the filmmaker and cartoon artist Bozzetto, is known for his animated shorts and features. As such, the two films' representational ethics vis-à-vis migrants are framed with reference to the directors' exercise of artistic license. No effort is made to seriously think about how the media ought to host migrants within its narrative and representational space in a Western country like Italy, where the majority of the population is white.

Consequently, the representations of Chinese restaurants and foodways in the two films are meant to activate specific genre requirements. The film genre in question is a lighthearted and comedic version of the Italian *poliziesco*, or crime film. While *Delitto al ristorante cinese* is framed in this tradition, *Sotto il ristorante cinese* refers to it in crime scenes. As Peter Bondanella relates, the Italian police film was shaped by the period from the 1960s to the early 1980s, when both extreme-left political terrorism such as the Red Brigades and *Cosa nostra*-led violence caused considerable social and economic unrest in Italy. In the critic's assessment, the kind of violence depicted in this film genre is closer in spirit to the spaghetti Westerns than to another popular Italian genre—the giallo, or the thriller—which prefers a psychosexual type of violence.[4] By the early 1980s, as Roberto Curti notes, popular Italian cinema, including the *poliziesco* films, faced a decisive decline. Important factors contributing to this decline included the dominance of television, the gradual decrease in movie attendance in Italy, and the larger market share of American films. For Curti, "Such a genre with a high degree of violence as the *poliziesco* no longer has citizenship at the cinema, at least not in Italian cinema."[5] However, Bondenella mentions that already during the 1970s, the initial neorealist treatment of violence had given way to comic parodies. Some films in this strand touch upon Chinese themes, including *Ku Fu? Dalla Sicilia con furore* (Kung Fu? From Sicily with Fury, Nando Cicero, 1973), which stars the popular comic Franco Franchi, and *Piedone a Hong Kong* (Flatfoot in Hong Kong, Steno, 1975), part of a series of popular films starring Bud Spencer as the Inspector "Flatfoot" Rizzo.[6] *Delitto al ristorante cinese* and the reference to crime in *Sotto il ristorante cinese* belong to this last category of films, which spoofs the more self-important depictions of violence in mainstream Italian crime films.

The Chinese elements in such films are unambiguously staged as exotic spectacles or forms of diversion. Concurrently, Chinese restaurants in these films are merely portrayed as tourist destinations for Italians, which are "inscribed in circles of anticipation, performance, and remembrance" of eating rituals and dining experiences, to borrow John Urry and Jonas Larsen's words.[7] As such, the two films may be viewed as either confirming Italian viewers' previous real-world encounters with Chinese establishments or inviting them to experience Chinese cuisine. But as I contend, behind the benign façade of culinary tourism is the popular cinema's reinforcement of the cultural frame that interprets Chinese migration through the metonymy of Chinese restaurants and through the lens of organized crime. I also suggest that the restaurant-crime-migration frame draws from American cinema that perfected discourses on the "Yellow Peril" and yellowface techniques. The Italian news media also played a crucial role in strengthening the cultural frame that linked the so-called Chinese mafia to Italy's Chinese migrant community.

Set in Rome in the early 1980s, *Delitto al ristorante cinese* presents general conditions of the Chinese restaurant sector in line with the previous chapter's discussions. The fictional location of the restaurant at number 3 on Vicolo del Forno, near the Trevi Fountain, illustrates the expansion of Chinese restaurants in Rome's historic core. The emphatically Chinese decorations that characterize the exterior and interior would meet the expectations of Italian customers who sought exoticism. In a period when mainland Chinese migrants were not yet numerically significant, the staff was seen waving Republic of China (Taiwan) flags and the new cook arrived from Hong Kong. The diegesis also tells us that the restaurant has existed there for thirty years, which indicates a plausible opening date since the first Chinese restaurant was established in Rome in 1949. The Taiwanese reference also makes sense because some Chinese migrants already living in Italy at the time of the 1949 founding of the People's Republic of China (PRC) chose to declare political allegiance to the governors of the Republic of China, who eventually settled in Taiwan.

Whereas the main context seems plausible, the food-centered plot and characters are fanciful creations that play on emotional contagion through caricature, surely a hallmark of popular cinema. Milian plays two roles in the film: the assistant cook named Ciu Ci Ciao, who recently arrived from Hong Kong, and the Inspector Giraldi, who is in charge of investigating the film's main criminal.[8] Ciu Ci Ciao is depicted as a cartoonish buffoon when he first appears onscreen at an airport in Rome. Dressed in a vaguely Japanese-inspired robe with a bow tie, the white actor dons an exaggerated hairstyle, which is thick on two sides with a lock of hair tied up in a knot in the center that points upward. Milian's eyelids are glued together to simulate the infamous almond-shaped Asian eyes, a yellowface technique that is enhanced by the character's self-proclaimed Mongolian heritage. Ciu Ci Ciao speaks Italian in a way that popular imagination often associates with how the Chinese speak Italian, notably using only infinitives and not conjugated verbs, and replacing "r" with "l." Milian's intentional verbal tic, an "oh" sound in many sentences, and his unpleasantly high pitch in a flat and unmusical tone also bestow clownish effects upon the character. Stereotypical images and extradiegetic sounds of an imagined ancient China further cue the character's filmic presence. The filmmaker knowingly exaggerates Ciu Ci Ciao's absurdity through these traits to achieve audience disidentification.

The most distinguishing feature of Ciu Ci Ciao's bizarre Chinese-like identity involves food. In a close-up, he prepares his so-called specialty dish, namely, rice grains stuffed with ants: a rice grain is cut open, an ant is put in, and then the grain is sutured using a thread. After showing the initial operation in detail, the film immediately repeats the same gesture in the next sequence using a fast-motion camera technique. In the rest of the film, the same food preparation is repeated several times to stress its association with Ciu Ci Ciao. These camera movements and this editing recall what Laura Lindenfeld and Fabio Parasecoli observe as features of the genre of "food film."[9] In deploying such techniques, to be sure, *Delitto al ristorante cinese* tries to convey a host of conventional ideas about Chinese workers more generally. For example, the movie may refer to how Chinese work obediently like ants. But to my mind, above all, the episode underscores the Chinese cook's ridiculousness. Indeed, this film is an early example of how Chinese food is satirized in Italian cinema with no outlet in the diegesis for redemption.

Through the film's other Chinese character, the filmmaker expresses the theme of mafia-infiltrated Chinese restaurants found in the *poliziesco* and in crime films more generally. Chinese food is the catalyst for the murder referred to in the film's title. An Italian customer is found dead in the restaurant, and the cause is determined to be the arsenic contained in the food he ingests. Subsequent speculation and investigation ultimately lead Giraldi to the owner of the restaurant, named Chan Zeng Piao (John Chan), who assassinated the customer. As a secret agent, Chan believed that the man was about to execute him. Indeed, an indication of Chan's criminal association is already evident when at the airport, Ciu Ci Ciao greeted him by kneeling down before him, kissing his shoes, and treating him as a key figure within the (presumably) human trafficking or smuggling and financial network that brought the cook to Italy for work. While it is not clear from the narrative whether Chan works for Taiwan or the PRC, the film references the ongoing political jockeying between the two, especially between the 1950s and the early 1980s. In this early representation of the rapidly developing Chinese restaurant sector in Italy, a criminally laden discourse is projected onto the ethnic Chinese migrant community, be it Taiwanese or PRC in origin, through Chinese food and restaurants.

Overall, Chan's storyline, which begins and closes the narrative, is perfunctory, while Ciu Ci Ciao's characterization is one-dimensional. Such inconsistency and incompleteness may be viewed as symptomatic of how a belief about the criminal nature of Chinese restaurants and migration in Italy was still taking shape within Italian popular culture in an unfocused way. More important, the symptoms can also be interpreted as a broad cinematic tendency to overemphasize the outwardly visible Chinese restaurants and the inwardly veiled Chinese criminality in the diegesis as a metacommentary on the lack of transparency of the burgeoning community to the outside world. This point will be amply demonstrated by the films that I examine in the next section, but for now we can also observe it in *Sotto il ristorante cinese*.

Set in the late 1980s, when the Italian economy flourished, Bozzetto's vision of Milan is, however, bleak. The Italian protagonist, Ivan (Claudio Botosso), accidentally becomes involved in a bank robbery. As he flees the scene, he stumbles upon a Chinese restaurant. The Chinese community is represented solely through this restaurant, of which the viewer is only able to see two parts in some detail. First, its storefront is located in a rather dilapidated cul-de-sac, filled with garbage and noise, where a large sign "Go Home" is written on the adjacent walls. Second, a dark underground cellar is lit with blue and black colors to emphasize its secrecy. The cellar, however, conceals a door that leads to a parallel world, where Ivan's subsequent adventures will unfold on a sunny and beautiful beach. This representation first confirms and then destabilizes a commonplace stereotype of the Chinese community: Chinese restaurants symbolize disgust and abjection, but they conceal the entrance to something extremely desirable for Italians. The beauty in ugliness, however, is a secret only accessible to Ivan and not to the Chinese; only Ivan has the capacity to operate the remote control for the secret door in the cellar.

In the cellar, a brief encounter between Eastern European robbers and Chinese migrants can be interpreted as highlighting organized crime in both groups. While aiming for Ivan, the robbers accidentally shoot a soft drink bottle in a basket carried by a Chinese individual. The Chinese man announces the price of the drink that the robbers have broken and demands compensation. Although the robbers have guns, they occupy the bottom of a stairway. Meanwhile, a group of weaponless Chinese emerge from the backlit top section of the stairway, towering above them. As the Chinese begin to descend menacingly, the robbers promptly produce more banknotes than necessary. This scene may indicate the robbers' knowledge of *kung fu*, which would supposedly overwhelm their modern weapons. It may also refer to their knowledge of Chinese criminal groups that control these restaurants, which they would do well not to disturb. The film is not explicit about the criminal association of the Chinese restaurant. Rather, the main Chinese migrant character is depicted as only interested in money and in work.

In interpreting the restaurant-crime-migration frame in the two films' representations of Chinese food and restaurants in the 1980s, we would do well to consider specific American cinematic precedents. To start, both films illustrate their American inspiration through car chases, a classic trope of Hollywood cop movies and action films in general.[10] In *Sotto il ristorante cinese*, the first time we encounter the Chinese restaurant in a dilapidated corner of the city is by way of a car chase through Milan's busy historic center with its august-looking architecture. In *Delitto al ristorante cinese*, the car chase is staged against the backdrops of the Roman countryside and a neighboring industrial district, places that convey their Italian character as opposed to the Orientalist Chinese decor of the restaurant. Thus, in both films, the mise-en-scène of the two car chases, in itself an American cinematic trope, becomes domesticated to indicate Italianness, which then is contrasted with the stereotypical Chinese milieu of the restaurants. In these instances, we already notice the contrast between neat-looking Italian locales and Chinese places in disarray, denoting a clear spatially articulated moral stance.

Another American cinematic trope that the two Italian films restage and adapt to the local Italian contexts is the use of Chinese restaurants as generic places of secrecy and crime. The image of the "Yellow Peril" proliferated in nineteenth- and twentieth-century English-language journalistic accounts and fictional representations of the Chinese. Fu Manchu was the most representative figure of the "Yellow Peril." This character enjoyed an active life in both literature and cinema, with both demonizing the Chinese diaspora as a destructive and invasive enterprise that aimed to eliminate the white race in the West.[11] The iconic American film *The Mask of Fu Manchu* (Charles Brabin, 1932) introduces the character to the big screen for the first time. In the film, the main characters find opium dens and torture rooms in the inner quarters behind a Chinese eatery. Thus, in Brabin's film, the Chinese restaurant provides an entryway to examine the supposed cruel and dissolute lifestyle of Chinese migrants and their descendants, exposing at once this race's brutality toward Westerners and its doomed destiny owing to a lack of proper morality.

To be sure, in *Sotto il ristorante cinese* and *Delitto al ristorante cinese*, their representations of Italy's Chinese migrants and restaurants are devoid of the extremely racist premise of *The Mask of Fu Manchu*. Moreover, the two Italian film's postmodern irony and playfulness, as well as their entertainment-oriented agendas for audiences from the popular classes, make their authorial intentions fluid and multidirectional. However, as I will discuss shortly, cultural texts about Chinese migrant food, kitchens, and restaurants from the 2000s and 2010s clearly took issue with the enduring cultural force that connected Chinese migrants to crime of many kinds. Thus, in the domain of cultural contestation, participants in later cultural debates about the representational ethics of Chinese migrants took this fundamental lesson taught by the American cinematic trope of the "Yellow Peril" and its more recent, postmodern iteration as a primary target. To remediate this situation, cultural producers often conveyed a comparable sense of community within the contexts of Chinese migrant kitchens and restaurants, which is positively depicted in some American films, notably including *The Joy Luck Club* (Wayne Wang, 1993).

Finally, we can pinpoint specific yellowface techniques—dialects and accents, makeup, posture, and costuming—that both *Delitto al ristorante cinese* and *Sotto il ristorante cinese* deploy, owing to their debts to the "Yellow Peril" discourse in Hollywood cinema. Similar to how blackface represents African Americans, yellowface is predominantly used by white actors who portray Asian characters using degrading caricatures. As Krystyn R. Moon analyzes in the context of nineteenth- and early-twentieth-century American musical theater, mainstream American audience came to expect Asian American actors to replicate yellowface caricatures.[12] Milian's chef character in *Delitto al ristorante cinese* has semi-closed eyelids, a yellowface technique first developed for the American film *The Good Earth* (Sidney Franklin, 1937). His costuming and hairstyle also indicate a confusion of Chinese and Japanese cultural motifs, reminiscent of a similar occurrence in a 1973 Italian-directed Spaghetti Western film, *Il mio nome è Shangai Joe* (The Fighting Fist of Shanghai Joe, Mario Caiano, 1973), which in turn was inspired by an American martial arts Western television serial, *Kung Fu* (1972–1975, various directors), starring a yellowface actor in the lead role as a Shaolin Temple monk. Moreover, the interchangeability of East Asian actors in casting may be viewed as bordering on yellowface. The Chinese restaurant worker featured in *Sotto il ristorante cinese* is played by the Japan-born actor Haruhiko Yamanouchi, sometimes credited as Hal Yamanouchi, who appears as the Chinese criminal boss archetype in several films about Chinese migrants in Italy. His angular facial features and caricatural voice acting conform to the archetype.

While these Orientalist tropes promoted by the two films frequently appeared in 1990s Italian news coverage, none illustrates the American-inspired restaurant-crime-migration frame better than a story from the March 27, 1994, Roman edition of *Corriere della Sera*, Italy's most widely circulated newspaper.[13] The article about the murder of two Chinese migrants covers almost an entire page of the newspaper. The coverage is a mixture of the above-mentioned ingredients. A photograph of the storefront of the Chinese restaurant where the murder is said to have occurred is the only evidence of the scene. The image of an octopus with a Fu Manchu-like head is printed alongside the article to signify the "Chinese mafia," recalling a widely understood metaphor for the mafia.[14] The page also displays a film still with a caption explaining that it depicts Chinese migrants in Los Angeles in Alan Parker's film "*Come to Paradise*." In reality, this is an image of Japanese Americans taken from a recent American drama, *Come and See the Paradise* (Alan Parker, 1990), which depicts their internment experiences during the Second World War.

As this example from the news media shows, apart from the American-Italian cinematic intertextuality, the Chinese representations in *Delitto al ristorante cinese* and *Sotto il ristorante cinese* amplified a prevailing interpretive frame that 1980s mainstream Italian news media was nurturing. As I have analyzed at length in a previous book, the "Chinese mafia" became part of the Italian news media's lexicon during that decade through covering both the *Cosa nostra*, the Sicily-centered organized crime syndicate, and (alleged) Chinese organized crime in the United States.[15] In the late 1980s and early 1990s, the "Chinese mafia" began to be regularly invoked to depict Italy's Chinese community in the news media because of a confluence of factors. An exponential increase in the Chinese population in Italy gave news outlets a novel topic. The news media increasingly covered all migrants by focusing on their crimes, and the Chinese through their economic crimes in particular. Italian crime reporting also grew more sophisticated thanks to intense coverage of the Italian mafia, which induced some journalists to view the "Chinese mafia" as a parallel. The writing style of much Italian crime journalism further became blurred with Italian crime fiction.

Under this discursive construction of Chinese migration to Italy, the Chinese restaurant sector, being the most widespread and publicly visible Chinese-owned business activity, was singled out by journalists to illustrate the supposed veracity of the news frame of migration crime. According to a major line of argument within this frame, given that we do not clearly see how Chinese food was financed, sourced, and prepared, and given that this food tradition's nutritional and cultural values were not properly explained to us, we can only infer that something unhealthy, seedy, and bizarre was going on behind the scenes. Moreover, if we do not know where migrants obtained the capital to open so many Chinese restaurants in such a short period (recall that the 1980s was the sector's first booming decade), then Chinese criminal organizations must have provided the finance, just as we read in the media about their human trafficking and money laundering. Indeed, in addition to the American-Italian cinematic intertextuality, this Italian media milieu functioned as another major premise for Corbucci and Bozzetto's films. Both conditions helped Italian viewers at the time grasp the simplistic East-West crime theme and related comedy.

In 1990s news media, Chinese restaurants continued to function as a backdrop for illegal activities within the Chinese community, such as extortion and abduction.[16] Media reports frequently speculated about restaurants' direct involvement in organized crime. Dino Martirano's 1992 article in *Corriere della Sera* is a prime example, which is prominently featured in the general news section.[17] Together with an infographic about the "Chinese mafia," the text covers a full half page. According to Martirano, through two restaurants located in Rome, namely, Su Zhou on Via Nomentana and Hang Zhou on Via San Martino ai Monti, a person named Chu Xang laundered money for the "Chinese mafia." Although the journalist describes these details with gusto, he admits that they were not verified by the police. Moreover, the news account palpably conveys the concerns and Sinophobia of certain owners of Roman *trattorie*, who believed that their businesses were being taken away by the cheaper-priced Chinese eateries, which, for them, infested the city's historic center. Strong emotions, which are based on both the perceived threat of the Chinese and the tangible fear of the Italian Romans, add verve to this instance of Italian articulation of the "Yellow Peril." For another example, Gianfranco Ambrosini's 1992 coverage in the same newspaper argues that following their trafficking by the "Chinese mafia" to Italy, Chinese migrant workers were forced to work without pay in leather workshops and restaurants.[18] Many subsequent articles throughout the 1990s pursued the same association of Chinese restaurants with human trafficking and smuggling, illegal employment, labor coercion, extortion, money laundering, and other economic crimes.[19] The restaurant-crime-migration frame was thus firmly established as an integral part of what elsewhere I call the Italian-Chinese migrant cultural repertoire, which both enabled and constrained media discussions about Chinese migrations to Italy.[20] Thanks to their economic and ethnocultural importance for Italy's Chinese migrant communities, the Chinese restaurant as a sociocultural space significantly facilitated the functioning of this cultural repertoire.

Romantic Waitresses: Three Shades of "White and Yellow"

Since the 2000s, many Italian fiction and feature-length documentary films have examined Chinese migrations to Italy. Many highlight Chinese restaurant owners and workers in their narratives. I do not discuss nonfiction cinema here, as elsewhere, I have argued that it pursues representational agendas quite different from those of narrative films.[21] The 2000s, in particular, was the most fertile decade for fictional film production about Italy's Chinese, with the most popular films either released or conceived of during this time.[22] Here, I analyze three such narrative films. While differing significantly in cinematic genres and moods, they all feature Chinese migrant women in restaurant milieus, most often as waitresses, to channel some aspects of Chinese criminality. I shed light on how the restaurant-crime-migration frame gained representational complexity and communicative force in 2000s Italian popular culture through portraying such women's interracial romances with white Italian men on screen. Such romantic affairs are self-consciously racialized as pertaining to the color combination of "white and yellow."

The moody crime film *Gorbaciof* (Gorbaciof, Stefano Incerti, 2010) revolves around the vicissitudes of the daily life of its titular character (Toni Servillo) and addresses the effects of the *camorra*, the Italian organized crime syndicate from Naples and the surrounding area, on the local community. The first time Gorbaciof is seen visiting a Neapolitan Chinese restaurant, he walks by the cashier, through the kitchen area, and into the storage room, where the Chinese restaurateur and other Italians are playing poker for money. Although we witness a brief scene in which the female protagonist, Lila (Mi Yang), washes vegetables in the kitchen, we mostly associate the restaurant space with gambling and physical aggression. Lila's father (Hal Yamanouchi) goes into the kitchen when his hand is hurt, possibly because of a fight. When Lila is being harassed by several local thugs at the counter area of the restaurant, Gorbaciof helps her fend off the aggressors. Purposefully out-of-focus shots of diners and scenes of Chinese food being served or packaged flash by. Lila, the restaurant's waitress, seems tense every time she brings drinks to the gambling table, suggesting her sense of being out of place. The restaurant is the space where the filmmaker amasses images of illegal deeds, transactions, and people associated with Chinese migrants.

Gorbaciof's plan to save Lila from this space is a modern version of a recurring narrative pattern in the West's encounter with the East: a white man rescues his Asian victims out of harm's way. Indeed, as Gina Marchetti remarks with reference to Hollywood cinema on interracial romance, "Salvation stories posit the white hero or heroine as an irresistible moral force that 'saves' the Asian lover from the evils or excesses of his or her decadent culture."[23] Lila's inability to utter a word in Italian in the film's diegesis ironically underscores this basic formula, although the director, Incerti, intends this detail to help articulate the couple's mutual recognition because of their shared sense of being trapped in life. From a meta-communicative perspective, this is precisely the lingering cultural rationale that underpinned the Italian media's repeated denunciations of the deeds of Chinese organized crime "bosses," in particular during the 1980s and 1990s. (This is not to say that journalists were not serious about stamping out organized crime, nor to say that Chinese victims did not deserve rescuing.)

The white savior narrative and the depiction of Lila as a helpless victim have both American and Italian popular cultural precedents with deep roots in Western culture. Contemporary Italian narrative cinema has become a medium to draw from, imitate, adapt, and update previous American representations of the Chinese diasporas and previous Italian popular Orientalism. In American cinema, according to Renee Tajima-Peña, the submissive, quiet, and weak "Lotus Blossom Baby" often serves as a love interest for white men. In contrast, the dangerous, deceitful, and treacherous "Dragon Lady" engages in frequently illicit interracial affairs and is often played by Asian actresses with Caucasian-like physiognomic features.[24] Analogously, in Italian culture, two types of Asian women are depicted in two of Giacomo Puccini's most well-known operas focused on interracial love relationships. Cio-Cio San in *Madama Butterfly* (Madame Butterfly, Luigi Illica and Giuseppe Giacosa, 1904) is the teenage Japanese wife married to, and exploited by, an American naval officer. As the Chinese princess in *Turandot* (Giuseppe Adami and Renato Simoni, 1926), which is set in Beijing, Turandot intends to select her own mate but eventually succumbs to the authority and love of Calaf, a Central Asian prince.[25] The Cio-Cio San versus Turandot dichotomy in fiction finds concrete expressions when *Gorbaciof* is compared to the lighthearted comedy film *Questa notte è ancora nostra* (The Night Is Still Ours, Paolo Genovese and Luca Miniero, 2008).

In *Questa notte è ancora nostra*, a scene set in a Chinese restaurant is crucial in establishing the circulation of illicit money and unethical commercial and sentimental transactions involving women within the Chinese migrant community. In this scene, a singer dressed up as a geisha is entertaining a group of middle-aged Chinese men and women who have come to the restaurant to socialize and dance. The conversation in the foreground revolves around the steep debts that the parents of the female protagonist, Jing (Valentina Izumi), owe to Lao Wang (Hal Yamanouchi), who seems to be a major creditor in the community. Wang suggests that Jing marry his nephew to help settle the debts. This detail is primarily about Jing as a conduit for her parents' generation's sordid business, which suggests the family's success in migration takes precedence over personal sentiments. But a viewer versed in pervasive 1990s mainstream media discourses on the Chinese migrant community would associate the episode with tales of debt bondage facilitated by the "Chinese mafia."[26] A Chinese migrant-managed restaurant and entertainment space, not the family dinner table at Jing's parents' place, which makes an onscreen appearance later in the film, is where the film's most explicit remark on Chinese criminality is made.

Subsequently, the film tries to lessen the impact of this ambiguous narrative detail on its view of the Chinese migrant community by telling the framing story about an interracial romance that ends in assimilation. In so doing, Genovese and Miniero adopt another formulaic storyline from Hollywood cinema on Asian-white interracial romance. As a progressive, feminist, and "second-generation" Chinese Italian woman, Jing criticizes both suitors: white Italian Massimo (Nicolas Vaporidis) for his womanizing and racial stereotyping, and recent Chinese migrant Banlong (Shi Yang Shi) for his excessive theatricality. First, Jing succumbs to her Chinese family's pressure and agrees to marry Banlong, and then she changes her mind out of her love for Massimo. The ending credits champion hybridity by alluding to the combined skin colors of Massimo and Jing. They "will make a child who is a little white and a little yellow" and live in a "rosy future, finally full of colors." Thus, the film's basic plot aligns with what Marchetti terms "assimilation narrative" in the context of American cinema. In such narratives, "the nonwhite lover completely relinquishes his or her own culture in order to be accepted into the American bourgeois mainstream, usually represented by the creation of a 'typical' nuclear family."[27] While both women are victims of Chinese criminal networks that Chinese restaurants help foreground cinematically, unlike Lila, who is in need of rescue by the white masculine society, Jing's domineering attitude must be tamed and subsumed into the white heteronormative mainstream society.

The poetic drama film *Io sono Li* (Shun Li and the Poet, Andrea Segre, 2011) explicitly refers to the restaurant-crime-migration frame through the main motivation of the plot. The protagonist, Shun Li (Tao Zhao), is coerced to work first in a garment workshop in Rome and then in a Chinese-managed Italian osteria/bar in Chioggia, near Venice, to settle the debts accrued from her trip to Italy and from her permit to stay. The forced labor will then lay the foundation for her to bring her son to Italy. As I have argued elsewhere, this plot is an ambivalent directorial choice that merits a sharp critique.[28] Consider that the film hints at significant Chinese organized crime in Italy that determines the life courses of several key Chinese migrant characters in the narrative. Moreover, a detail in the diegesis verbalizes a popular perception of this connection: when Bepi (Rade Šerbedžija), a long-term Italianized migrant from the former Yugoslavia, embarks on a romance with Li, a local man uses the term the "Chinese mafia" to remark how it forces Chinese women to marry old Italian men in order to seize their inheritances. Thus, Segre's story does not merely refer to a generic situation of exploitation of migrant workers, which is a much more prevalent worldwide phenomenon. A tangible outcome of the film is indeed an impression of the close association between Chinese crime and migrant workers. The remarks of several film reviewers and critics of *Io sono Li* confirm this understanding.[29] From a broader point of view, these problems make Segre's film fall in the same category as the previous two films in reinforcing the prevailing restaurant-crime-migration frame.

Nevertheless, I analyze how a careful reading reveals the nuances that the film lends to the frame by differentiating between two types of Chinese-managed restaurants in Italy. This differentiation is also assisted by a conscious choice not to Orientalize Li's femininity in the film. Li is the main character who motivates the plot on her own terms, unlike Lila and Jing, who serve their films' ultimately Italian-centric narratives. Li works as a waitress in a Chinese-managed Italian neighborhood osteria, which also has a coffee bar. Chinese entrepreneurship in Italian coffee bars is a relatively recent phenomenon that began in the 2000s and has taken root across the country. This environment necessitates Li's acculturation as she learns the trade and interacts with local customers. Indeed, a primary objective of the film is to examine the integration of the Chinese into the social and economic fabric of the little town. The osteria/bar is thus reasonably depicted as both a place riddled with daily obstacles in Li's job, including racism and bullyism, and a springboard for her romance with Bepi. To use one narrative thread as an example, Li's co-worker (Zhong Cheng) makes *canocchie*, a type of Mediterranean Sea shrimp, as snacks for the locals. The Italians perceive Chinese-made Italian food as inferior to that which is prepared by Italians themselves, commenting that the Chinese prepare their own food well but not these *canocchie*. Later, the film hypothesizes that food chauvinism by the locals is also applied to Italian food items from elsewhere, such as the *mozzarella di bufala*, rumored by the locals to be produced by cows that eat toxic garbage in Campania, the main region that manufactures this iconic Italian food. Only Bepi appreciates the shrimp, signaling his future connection and romance with the Chinese woman. Indeed, a significant portion of their initial interactions takes place at the osteria/bar, initially around the counter area of the bar, cinematically posing as both a barrier and a bridge, and later at a dining table in the osteria section, thereby indicating a closer and more intimate relationship.

In contrast, the Chinese restaurant is constructed as a purely Chinese world. It is the realm of Li's enigmatic male employer (Guo Qiang Xu), who refuses her request to take a half-day break and who cautions her to abandon her relationship with Bepi, or else he will increase her debts. Moreover, whereas chopsticks are used in preparing the *canocchie* and coffee and other drinks are machine-made in the Italian café, no substantial scene involving Chinese food is depicted onscreen, a lack that adds another layer of secrecy to the place. However, located in the back of the restaurant is also Li's dormitory room, where she writes letters to her son, recuperates from work, and befriends Lian (Wang Yuan), who the narrative implies helps Li settle the debts so that she can reunite with her son. Thus, the Chinese restaurant is deployed both as a cover for alleged migrant labor bondage and as a haven for migrants' initial settlement in a period of tremendous uncertainty. Only later does Bepi's fishing hut become Li's preferred place of refuge. Overall, *Io sono Li* aptly illustrates Jane F. Ferry's observation on food communication on different scales, "Food communicates intra-personally, interpersonally, nationally, and cross-culturally."[30]

Interpreted in this way, we can begin to appreciate Segre's proclivity for using restaurants to argue both sides of a controversy.[31] For example, Segre seems to pose the questions: What exactly is a Chinese restaurant? Is it a Chinese-owned restaurant or a restaurant that offers Chinese cuisine? How are Chinese restaurants related to the Chinese migration: through the "Chinese mafia" or through its place as a safety net for newly arrived migrants? Should Li's food preparation in the osteria/bar be ethnicized as an Italian, Chinese, or Italian-Chinese practice? Moreover, regarding waitresses in Chinese restaurants, Segre asks whether they must possess immediately recognizable Asian beauty, as demonstrated by Lila and Jing's gracious and athletic bodies. Li's makeup limits the viewer's ability to appreciate her face, and her sartorial choices disguise her body's contours. Whereas actors Yang and Izumi's onscreen presence in general, and in restaurant scenes in particular, are meant to attract the viewer's attention, Zhao's performance in the plain-looking osteria/bar seeks to minimize the camera's intrusion into her character's mundane life. *Io sono Li*'s restaurant scenes illustrate self-introspective ways of considering opposing arguments that the restaurant-crime-migration frame engenders.

In all three films analyzed in this section, the restaurant is represented as a socially significant space where Italians and *cinesine* negotiate their power relations. Consider how the films highlight female agency and the role of female migrant labor in the restaurant sector through devising episodes involving local bullies. Each film addresses the situation differently, providing cinematic solutions for the characters and the other Chinese migrants around them when they face discrimination and racism from Italians in public workplaces. In *Io sono Li*, when Li asks Devis (Giuseppe Battiston) to pay the debts owed to the osteria/bar, he threatens her with simulated Chinese or Japanese martial arts moves and then orders a coffee. She is taken aback by his aggression, but she keeps her composure and makes the coffee for him, knowing that she must endure the ordeal head-on. In *Questa notte è ancora nostra*, when Jing dines with Massimo in a Chinese restaurant, several Italian customers at a table assume that she is a waitress. When they begin insulting Chinese women and characterizing them as prostitutes, Jing confronts the men with her superior *kung fu* skills. She takes this action after Massimo fails to properly intervene to stop the verbal abuse. In the Chinese restaurant depicted in *Gorbaciof*, when a customer picks up a spring roll and asks Lila if she would perform oral sex on it as if it were his penis, Gorbaciof hits the bully and saves her from the harassment. Be it silent endurance, active self-defense when challenged, or Italian-led salvation, the methods depicted in these films provide a window into the fundamental role played by gender in expressing migrant agency. In proposing these cultural formulas to moviegoers, the three films substantiate the restaurant-crime-migration frame, reinforcing and critiquing it by turns.

"Kung Food" Workers: Culinary and Masculine Capital for a Cosmopolitan Milan

The 2000s reinforcement of the restaurant-crime-migration frame in Italian popular culture, of which the films analyzed above were key proponents, prepared the groundwork for counternarratives in the subsequent decade. Elsewhere, I have examined Chinese migrants and pro-migrant Italians' challenges to various prevailing interpretive frames applied to Italy's Chinese, as the tension played out in the news media, documentary and fiction films (made for both the silver screen and television), and literature of diverse genres.[32] Building upon this previous work, in this section, I address the pro-migrant agenda of performing extremely positive representations of Chinese restaurants in which waiters, chefs, and entrepreneurs thrive.

The second booming decade of Italy's Chinese restaurant sector, the 2010s, which ended with the COVID-19 pandemic, was far removed from its previous boom in the 1980s when Chinese food was significantly criminalized and ridiculed in media and popular culture. Two important Italian graphic novels articulated a strong desire during the 2010s to narratively mobilize Chinese cuisine as valuable culinary capital in supporting Milan's ambitions to become a European city with a cosmopolitan lifestyle. The two cultural accounts I analyze also endorsed the view that men embodied the successes of Milan's Chinese restaurant sector, thereby intimating valuable human capital in the form of Chinese Italian masculinities for Milan's cosmopolitanism.

Published during 2013–2014 in twelve self-contained episodes, the comic book series *Long Wei* (Diego Cajelli) rehearses many of the same details about Chinese restaurants and food depicted in previous cultural works or relayed in previous scholarship. *Long Wei* also moves away from past negative stereotypes and becomes more precise in demonstrating Chinese culinary knowledge and various social functions of Chinese restaurants. The protagonist Long Wei's primary contact in Milan is Uncle Tony, the owner of a Chinese restaurant. Echoing the Chinese father's plotline in *Gorbaciof*, at the beginning of the narrative, Uncle Tony has lost all his assets in a gambling hall in an effort to raise money to save the eatery from bankruptcy. A master of *kung fu*, Long Wei helps him regain financial independence by fighting injustice that has led to the bankruptcy. But the migration-restaurant-crime association stops here. Indeed, although the overarching narrative of the graphic novel focuses on the conflicts between the good and the evil factions within Milan's "Chinatown," the Via Sarpi area, as well as those between Long Wei and Italian and migrant criminals, the storyline pertaining to Chinese organized crime is no longer attached to Uncle Tony's restaurant.

Instead, first and foremost, the Chinese restaurant stands as a symbol of Long Wei's success as a neighborhood hero for young people, such as in episode 5, and for those whose lives are afflicted by crime, which is the main theme in most episodes. In the final episode of the series, upon completing his final mission, Long Wei symbolically leaves the host society, as the ending creates a fake death for him to exit the series narratively. He enjoys the acknowledgment of his contributions to the Chinese community in Milan from behind closed doors in a room located above the restaurant on Via Sarpi. The restaurant becomes the focal point for commemorating his legacy. A panel offers a bird's-eye view of the storefront, where many flowers are left at the entrance in his honor. Indeed, set in Milan's Via Sarpi district, formal features of the exterior and interior designs for Uncle Tony's restaurant are taken directly from *Delitto al ristorante cinese*. However, while the newly arrived Ciu Ci Ciao is a caricature of Chinese culture, Long Wei becomes the true hero of the comic strip. The Chinese restaurant functions as an archive in which episodes about Long Wei's masculine heroism can be deposited. In this way, the values of both the restaurant and his masculinity enhance one another.

When interpreting the character's heroism by considering stereotypical Chinese American men, Long Wei can be primarily identified with Bruce Lee. The two figures' heterosexual masculinity is achieved by engaging in violence with other men and by showing the advantage of their smaller but nimbler bodies over often larger and brutish Western ones. Similarly, despite their muscle-bound hyper-masculinization, Bruce Lee and Long Wei's masculinities are subdued because they are rarely overtly contrasted to homosexual men, despite occasional homoeroticism.[33]

Further, related to Bruce Lee through *kung fu*, the Chinese American character Shang-Chi from 1970s Marvel Comics is portrayed as the Chinese villain Fu Manchu's estranged son. Long Wei inherits some character traits from Shang-Chi, as he was trained as a *kung fu* monk in China but left the temple to pursue a career in acting. He finds his true vocation in the Via Sarpi district as a defender of the victims of local Chinese and Italian criminals. Like Shang-Chi, Long Wei is scripted as an unambiguously heterosexual young man who commits patricide when fighting an older generation of Chinese criminals and, to some extent, fratricide when confronting young Chinese criminals for the benefit of both his ethnic group and the wider receiving society.[34]

Apart from a place of public commemoration of Long Wei's masculine heroism, the Chinese restaurant provides insights into his private life, evoking his feelings of home, nurturing, and friendship, but especially romance and sex, as it is partially the case for Li in *Io sono Li*.[35] In several episodes, after the main plot ends, Long Wei relaxes in the dining area, joking, conversing, and eating with his adoptive family. He also works in the kitchen and waits tables in several episodes. In episode 5, while eating, Long Wei confides frustration with his *kung fu* actor career to Vincenzo, his new Italian best friend. Initially, a mutual attraction seems to emerge between Long Wei and Uncle Tony's daughter, Maria, who works as a waitress in the restaurant. But his real love interest turns out to be the white Italian inspector Ilaria De Falco.

De Falco's enjoyment of Chinese food is the harbinger of her *kung fu* fighting, professional collaboration, romance, and sex with Long Wei. De Falco's consumption of Chinese dishes in *Long Wei* is comparable in narrative function to Bepi's instructions to Li on how to make coffee with liquor. Consuming and making food or drinks together sets the stage for later emotional and romantic bonding. Indeed, as Elspeth Probyn argues, "the sensual nature of eating" is a primary lens through which to probe how relations between sex, gender, and power are negotiated.[36] Long Wei and De Falco's interracial romance, to follow Probyn's line of inquiry, is crucially channeled by the "viscerality of life" that Chinese food served in a Chinese restaurant helps bring forth in the characters' senses. In episode 8, the couple consummates their mutual attraction in the novel's only explicitly erotic scene. De Falco is the active partner who initiates the sexual encounter, whereas Long Wei has always held any sexual interest in check. Consider the graphic design of the panels to appreciate this point further. The first panel of the sex scene depicts the female cop almost forcing Long Wei into the act, and the final panel, which is also the episode's final panel, frames the couple in lovemaking face-to-face with her on top of him. As per the graphic novel's design, the final panel of each episode shows a Chinese-looking motif, often placed at the four corners of the page, which recalls a decoration drawn from the Chinese restaurant's counter area and its windows on the exterior. This is also the same decoration that frames each episode's title page and its next page, titled "Menu of the Day," in which each narrative's characters are introduced. Thus, the final panel of Long Wei and De Falco's intimate scene is meant to recall the overall milieu of the Chinese restaurant, reinforcing the intimate sex-food connection.

In the private sphere, then, Long Wei's masculine identity recalls that of the asexual and self-effacing Chinaman figure Charlie Chan. According to Jachinson Chan, this archetype of Asian Americans as good citizens and a model minority group was specifically created to counter the negative Fu Manchu figure.[37] Charlie Chan is typically depicted in American novels and films as a much-rewarded collaborator with the host society's prevailing masculine order. He lacks physical aggression and enjoys a large family composed of several children. He is steeped in a "stereotypical cultural stoicism that promotes a submissive male identity that is content in spite of systemic racial discriminations."[38] While Long Wei defies many of these characteristics, his law-abiding and heteronormative behavior, as well as his humbleness, is line with mainstream societal expectations.

Moreover, Long Wei's heroic masculine role is typecast as athletic, compassionate, and only slightly sexually desirable and available. To be sure, such a depiction of Long Wei recalls the puritanical sexual attitudes of the ideal male heroes in the Chinese *wu* tradition (originally, martial valor, but also, athletic ability), which the novel's Italian creators may have referenced by using Hong Kong martial arts action movies as their inspiration. For Kam Louie, Western audiences are unlikely to appreciate a restrained Chinese character's subtler sexuality.[39] Because Italian readers would be unlikely to readily or fully appreciate this context, *Long Wei* ends up sustaining the long-standing Western prejudice against Asian men's sexuality and desirability in fictional representations.

Finally, in addition to Long Wei's public heroism and private enjoyment, whose storylines the Chinese restaurant helps frame or advance, the space is also posited for education on Chinese cuisine, especially for Italian customers who are not yet as familiar with the menu as Vincenzo. Long Wei's Italian best friend is often seen eating Chinese food with relish in the restaurant. This detail recalls the comic acts of an Italian customer in *Questa notte è ancora nostra*. In episode 9, we learn about Uncle Tony's idea, executed by his son, of a Chinese-Milanese sweet and sour sauce, rice noodle *cassoeula* (a typical Milanese winter dish with cooked meats and vegetables). Thus, the restaurant also becomes a laboratory for hybrid or fusion cuisine combining Chinese and local Milanese traditions, which was trending in Milan in the early 2010s, according to the news media.[40] Milan has a high concentration of immigrants and what is often considered Southern Europe's largest "Chinatown." Chinese-Milanese and other Chinese fusion foods championed the city's claims to Italy's foremost cosmopolitan food capital. *Long Wei*'s depictions reflect this buoyancy despite the ongoing problems that Chinese food entrepreneurs faced in growing and keeping their businesses, as relayed in Chapter 1.

Indeed, during the 2010s, Milan's Chinese restaurants were featured in *Corriere della Sera* not as anecdotes or representations of Chinese migration but rather as a lifestyle topic of their own, often appearing in sections dedicated to cuisine and city life or in articles about Milan's self-proclaimed status as the most culinarily cosmopolitan city in Italy. The 2010s was a period in which Chinese food tended to be assessed for its quality and culinary merits rather than in relation to the Chinese migration that the reader was urged to judge negatively. Consequently, coverage of Chinese restaurants also became more nuanced and wide-ranging. Food journalists explored regional differences and varieties of the same item, such as the many kinds of dumplings within China.[41] They also educated Italian readers about new ways of eating Chinese food, including dim sum, *baozi* (stuffed steamed buns), and the hotpot.[42] At the end of the 2010s and before the COVID-19 pandemic began, the restaurant-crime-migration frame was no longer the hegemonic way of covering and representing Chinese restaurants in mainstream Italian media culture, at least for the Milanese case. Chinese cuisine, as represented in popular culture and in influential newspapers, was viewed as contributing to Milan's cosmopolitan milieu in the increasingly intense competition between world cities to attract greater investment and human capital.

The 2010s praise of Chinese culinary capital in fashioning a cosmopolitan Milan was not limited to that decade's foodscape. Ciaj Rocchi and Matteo Demonte's graphic life writing titled *Chinamen: Un secolo di cinesi a Milano* (Chinamen: A Century of the Chinese in Milan, 2017) reminded Italian readers about the origin of the city's Chinese gastronomical adventure. The graphic novel argues that high-style Chinese culinary tourism suitable for both Italian and Chinese elites was made possible thanks to Chinese migrant men's entrepreneurial efforts. In the third chapter of *Chinamen*, the narrative embarks on a positive story about La Pagoda, the first formal Chinese restaurant in Milan, which opened in 1962 (see also Chapter 1). In an extremely celebratory mode, mimicking the appearance of a video sequence, the narrative relates the entrepreneurial successes of several male migrants who financed the restaurant. The first few pages of the chapter are focused on the various migration trajectories of these men, thereby clarifying La Pagoda's financial support and cultural importance. Then, the chapter enacts its didactic agenda by displaying chopstick etiquette in steps and by listing typical ingredients for the lavish Chinese dishes served at the restaurant's opening, ingredients that were difficult to procure at the time. In a panel that covers two full pages, the reader sees a dining space decorated with Chinese red lanterns and fit with Italian-style long tables; the tables are set with Italian cutlery and glasses, as well as Chinese plates and chopsticks. The narration then describes how La Pagoda became a place of socialization for politicians, ecclesiastical representatives, journalists, intellectuals, and entertainers, showcasing its symbolic value for mainstream Italian society. Subsequently, the authors introduce the prominent male chefs from Hong Kong who worked in other Chinese restaurants in Milan,[43] and they end the chapter by considering the legacy of La Pagoda.

The book's highlight of the inner workings and social values of a restaurant from the 1960s omits much of the empirical complexity of the Chinese restaurant sector since then. The narrative is also predictable as a cultural script set in an epideictic mode, and its tone is reverent vis-à-vis elite migrants and their migration successes. However, a merit of the book lies in expressing a strong counterargument to the charge that Chinese restaurants were shady places and a cover for organized crime by explicitly describing the restaurant's finances and management. Moreover, although cooking in behind-the-scenes or backstage panels is largely missing from this book, the range of information that it does contain is impressive. The creators detail the sourcing of ingredients, ways of eating the food, and prominent Italians' appreciation of the place, mirroring the generally favorable appreciation of Chinese restaurants in the Italian press since the beginning of the 2000s.[44] Both Italian eaters' culinary tourism and the Chinese migrants' desire for entrepreneurial success beyond the immigrant community itself were met at La Pagoda's inauguration dinner.[45] What emerges from the restaurant section of *Chinamen* is a dignified image of high-quality Chinese cuisine served in a tastefully decorated restaurant. According to the graphic memoir, this identity construction is fitting for seeking legitimacy for the elite group of Chinese migrants from mainstream Italian society through food-facilitated cultural diplomacy.[46] This argument is set in stark contrast to the previous ridicule and criminal associations applied to Chinese food and restaurants in popular films and other media and cultural texts.

A combination of Charlie Chan and Bruce Lee's characteristics informs the depictions of Chinese food entrepreneurs in *Chinamen*. The title uses the old-fashioned and offensive English term—Chinaman—but subverts its semantic meanings. One of the novel's creators, Demonte, is a biracial, third-generation Italian of Chinese heritage who intends the book to commemorate and celebrate the centennial Chinese legacy in Italy and individual stories to represent entire generations of predominantly male entrepreneurs. The story concerning La Pagoda praises the collaboration of various owners whose strengths in management and networking successfully attracted an elite group of Italians to the establishment. This story illustrates a positive model of Chinese Italian business masculinity, which is anchored to the businessmen's managerial abilities and entrepreneurial aspirations. In the quasi-hagiographies that relay the owners' backgrounds, we learn about how they ventured from tie and leather workshops into other businesses in the 1960s, thereby helping Chinese migrant communities gain a reputation, social status, and cultural legitimacy, which La Pagoda's opening night dinner most clearly embodied. These men's entrepreneurial efforts can be interpreted as an update of Bruce Lee's martial arts skills, and the men's fervent desire for acceptance into mainstream Milanese society mirrors Charlie Chan's model minority image.

As previously analyzed in relation to the two 1980s films, Chinese migrant men employed in or associated with Chinese restaurants are either criminalized or ridiculed. In contrast, their counterparts in the two 2010s graphic novels are dignified characters with relatable stories. Further, while cinematic Chinese migrant femininities helped strengthen the restaurant-crime-migration frame during the 2000s, Chinese migrant masculinities in 2010s graphic novels were used to combat the negative consequences of this frame. Whereas the Chinese woman portrayed in cinema is a conduit for expressing some aspects of migrant crime, on the page, the Chinese man is a public medium for exhibiting migrant success. Thus, the range of archetypical Chinese American masculine identities that I contend *Long Wei* and *Chinamen* perform further shows the discursive technology with which pro-migrant Italian artists challenged the negative restaurant-crime-migration frame. The graphic novels also critiqued the images of Chinese male criminals and fools that were common in popular cinematic culture from the 1980s through the 2000s. However, similar to *Gorbaciof, Questa notte è ancora nostra* and, to some extent, *Io sono Li*, the graphic novels also inherited the same problematic cultural baggage from their American predecessors, which they negotiated with varying degrees of awareness. To borrow from Térésa Faucon, such are the nuances of "kung food," Italian style.[47]

■

Food discourses have played a key role in fashioning public narratives about the country's Chinese migrants since the 1980s. While the cultural narratives occasionally aligned with historical realities relayed in Chapter 1, they strived to account for their own medium-specific exigencies and origins. These fictional representations interacted with Italian mainstream news media, resulting in overlapping interpretive frames and narrative scripts about Italy's Chinese migrants. Foremost in its lasting power over the Italian public, the restaurant-crime-migration frame interpreted Chinese migration to Italy through its most visible entrepreneurship—the restaurant sector—and in the lens of socioeconomic criminalization. During the four decades examined, this frame was aptly articulated through gender bias and Orientalizing, Italian style. Italian popular culture customized both negative and positive Chinese American gender archetypes for its own understanding of recent Chinese migrants to the country. In the exemplary cultural texts examined in this chapter, the Chinese restaurant is the crucible in which these discourses contended with one another. This phenomenon was symptomatic of a cultural need to differentiate Italian "natives" starkly apart from Chinese migrants that cannot always be effectuated in everyday economic and social life. The next chapter examines another formulaic cultural mechanism in this regard—racialization—and I expand my analysis from a focus on the Chinese restaurant as a sociocultural space to one on food consumption in this space.

THREE

The Chinese Who Eat Dogmeat: Racialization of Chinese Food Consumption

In April 2020, in the midst of the COVID-19 pandemic, the Italian fashion designer Elisabetta Franchi ignited an online controversy when she campaigned to ban China's dog-eating festival in the city of Yulin, set to take place in June.[1] Although Franchi's crusade against Yulin's festival began several years ago, the timing in 2020 proved different. According to *Jing Daily*, an English-language newspaper that specializes in covering the luxury goods sector in China, some Chinese customers harshly criticized Franchi.[2] The newspaper covered an example of such criticism drawn from Sina Weibo, China's most popular microblogging service. Attaching screenshots of Franchi's "controversial posts and deleted comments" as evidence, one Sina Weibo user blamed the designer for claiming on her brand's official Instagram page that as many as 15 percent of the Chinese population eat dogmeat and that "China spread the [COVID-19] virus abroad." This user also indicated that the brand's page immediately blocked individual users who rebutted Franchi's remarks. According to the same *Jing Daily* article, "thousands of boycott posts under the #ElisabettaFranchi# hashtag" appeared in mid-May that year, apparently in reaction to the circulation of this and other similar Sina Weibo posts with the same content.

At the time of writing, it is difficult to verify the exact claims attributed to Franchi as covered in *Jing Daily* because no digital traces remain on Franchi's official social media channels. Moreover, the complexity of interpreting mainland China's current digital culture and censorship vis-à-vis foreign products and cultures goes beyond the scope of this chapter. Nevertheless, we can still identify the core of the controversy as communicated in popular media. The fundamental issue pertains to what some Chinese perceived to be Franchi's smear that a large number of Chinese people eat dogmeat and her provocative correlation between such consumption and the global spread of the COVID-19 virus from China.

The Franchi incident was a recent reenactment of the most enduring negative stereotype concerning Chinese food in Italy: it accuses migrants of eating unhealthy dogmeat dishes and offering them in restaurants, habits said to be characteristic of the Chinese overall.[3] To be sure, dogmeat-eating is the most pernicious and long-standing alimentary stereotype associated with Chinese migrants in the West more broadly. The urban legend's pervasive presence in cultural discourse in the West may trap us in the habit of dismissing enunciations of it and attributing them to ignorance or irony. However, repeated public performances about this food consumption stereotype compel us to interrogate the specific sociocultural agendas behind each case in the spirit of devising solutions to lessen the injury inflicted on subjects targeted by this cultural weapon. Moreover, those who are the target of this cultural formula may not always present themselves as victims or casualties when they have cultural outlets to express their opinions on the matter, a cultural phenomenon that prompts analysts to probe the reasons why.

Thus, I want to ask a few related questions about the Franchi incident that can guide this chapter's analysis. Why was the dogmeat-eating image such a sensitive topic for Franchi and certain Chinese Sina Weibo users? Why was a causal link made between a specific eating habit and a deadly virus? What were the stakes for the Italian fashion designer making such a correlation, or what did the Chinese Sina Weibo users stand to gain from claiming that she made such a correlation? Finally, why were the virus and the foodways so prominently racialized as Chinese in this controversy?

While it may be difficult to definitively answer these questions based on the Franchi incident, this chapter shows that similar questions can be asked about many more Italian cultural narratives from the 1960s through the 2010s that intersect food, diseases, and acceptance or exclusion of migrants. During the 1980s–2010s, in particular, the dogmeat stereotype endorsed the racialized demarcation of Italians from Chinese migrants within Italian sociocultural spaces. Through racializing Chinese migrants' foodways, the quintessential Chinese alimentary cliché helped sharpen, safeguard, strengthen, or refashion Italian identities as white and hegemonic. In Italy, this hackneyed stereotype enjoyed influential cinematic treatments during the 1960s and 1970s. Even in the 2000s and 2010s, this food taboo still resonated with content creators. However, as evidenced by an important example of migration literature and TikTok posts by Chinese Italians that I will analyze, the alimentary stereotype met with robust rebuttals.

My research probes a similar line of inquiry for Italy's Chinese migrant food as those David Beriss and Aliza S. Wong have employed for other migrant food and identity politics in contemporary Italy.[4] The two critics examine controversies over attempts to pass laws prohibiting ethnic restaurants in the historic centers of Italian towns during the 2010s. In their analyses of Italian stakeholders' efforts to restrict ethnic cuisines, emphasis is placed on the role of racialized concerns over migrant food hygiene. Wong argues that:

> The recent polemic on food politics, hygiene, and xenophobia is not so surprising as Italians' struggle with the transformation of their nation from a land of emigrants to a land of immigrants. Even as the depictions of immigrants of color in Italy become increasingly tainted by terms that emphasize race, difference, legality or illegality, so have the protectionist arguments and legal bans against ethnic restaurants become ever more intolerant and prejudiced. (43)

I study the dynamics Wong has mentioned as they are represented mainly through films and novels. Although Chinese migrant foodways and cuisines are certainly not the only foil against which Italian narratives perform the Italian-alien demarcation, they have so far provided a particularly powerful example that exhibits a broad range of food issues and approaches for Italian content creators to elaborate on. Thus, an analysis of dogmeat narratives provides an especially sharp view of the communicative frames and representational agendas of food-circulated discourses about populations with migratory backgrounds in Italy.

Dogmeat as a Food Taboo

Italian mainstream news media, while repeatedly referring to the dogmeat stereotype, never reached the same conclusions as it did for the migration-restaurant-crime frame examined in Chapter 2. A sampling of relevant coverage in *Corriere della Sera* from the 1940s to the present day indicates the persistence with which this food taboo was relayed.[5] During the 1990s, when *Corriere della Sera*'s coverage of Italy's Chinese restaurants mentioned the cliché, it consistently confirmed that this culinary practice did not exist in the country. For example, a 1994 article speculates whether the recent disappearance of Rome's many roaming cats and dogs could be attributed to Chinese restaurants and laboratories of pharmaceutical companies.[6] But the report only describes an investigation into seven Chinese restaurants and a Chinese food distribution company, where various sanitary standards were lacking but where no evidence of dog or cat meat materialized. Similarly, a 1996 article covers searches in several of the capital city's Chinese restaurants, underscoring that mice and cockroaches were found, but there was no trace of dogmeat.[7] Still, the journalist inserts this detail: a piece of meat found in the kitchen was initially thought to be rabbit, but was suspected to be cat or dog, given "Chinese habits." After consulting with a veterinarian, the meat was proved to be from a piglet.

The same narrative pattern recurred in *Corriere della Sera* during the 2000s, but the focus now was on restaurants in Milan's Via Sarpi district, which by then had been firmly established as the country's premier "Chinatown." Some articles also mentioned families that presumably killed dogs for consumption. Such journalism, however, became anecdotal, and only a very small group of journalists still employed the stereotype.[8] The newspaper did not seem to have covered the dogmeat image during the 2010s, as news about Chinese restaurants and food moved onto other topics mentioned in Chapters 1 and 2. Overall, *Corriere della Sera* has not used the dogmeat stereotype to demarcate Italians from Chinese migrants in a noticeably criminalized, gendered, and racialized way as the case involving the Chinese restaurant (Chapter 2) has been.

While coverage of the trope has petered out in serious news media, the rumor has actively circulated in popular Italian culture since the 1970s. Creative works are the cultural domain where the cliché has received the most extensive representation in terms of semantic sophistication and the range of critical food issues treated. According to anecdotes told in popular culture, which this chapter's films and novels reenact, Chinese migrants eat dogs that they kidnap from Italian owners, or they kill dogs for culinary pleasures, following a supposedly widespread practice among diasporic and mainland Chinese. Whether or not Chinese restaurateurs in Italy actually do such things is irrelevant to the authorial intent of these anecdotes, although such narratives frequently perform deductive reasoning to argue that these acts occur. More important, the stereotype makes an intense emotional appeal to Italians, who are urged both to feel angry at the inhumanity of the Chinese and to experience a sense of alienation toward the act of slaughtering man's best friends to eat.

Why do creative works in popular culture persistently deploy this trope in depicting Chinese migrants in Italy regardless of the empirical situation? I analyze these textual and discursive symptoms through the prism of dogmeat as a food taboo. In Mary Douglas's classic discussion of specific biblical dietary prescriptions, she argues that holiness functions as a "systematic ordering of ideas" or a "total structure of thought" that ensures bodily integrity and spiritual purity.[9] To be sure, Douglas's structuralist argument may be interpreted as suggesting an unchanging ordering of ideas that limits people's freedom in their (narratives of) food choices.[10] Douglas also considers dietary rules as irrelevant for the preservation of cultural identities.[11] This argument runs opposite to mainstream cultural studies of identity differences and their articulations, embodiments, and performances through material objects and intangible thoughts. Nevertheless, Douglas's highlighting of ideas of defilement and pollution in relation to food taboos in the religious context is instructive. Her stress on the ritualistic dimension of cultural approaches to food taboos is also illuminating. Indeed, as Sidney W. Mintz observes, "It is possible that many Westerners distrust Han Chinese cuisine precisely because it is so open, and so unfettered by particular taboos [. . . or by] any heavy food-connected emotionalism."[12]

Following these critics, I suggest that such a food-associated and widely circulated defilement idea as the dogmeat stereotype can only make sense within cultural and media climates that seek to demarcate Italians from Chinese migrants on racial grounds effectively. Since the 1960s, the stereotype has functioned as a mark of racialized, politicized, and moral differentiation between white Italians and Chinese migrants for purposes that varied according to sociohistorical contingencies that were often extraneous to food issues per se.

In discussing these points, I examine a 1970s film and a 2000s novel, as well as the larger cultural milieus and related texts from the 1960s and 2010s, which allow me to refer back to the historical evolution of the Chinese restaurant and food sector in Italy, relayed in Chapter 1. The Japanese restaurant episode in the cult film *Fantozzi* (Luciano Salce, 1975) was created at a time when average Italians had little direct knowledge of Chinese cuisine in the country. Instead, they relied on their knowledge of the food of diasporic Chinese elsewhere. Thanks to *Fantozzi*'s significant success at the box office and its sustained popularity in subsequent decades, the episode has enjoyed a lasting impact on Italian popular culture's portrayal of East Asian cuisines.[13] By the mid-2000s, the Chinese restaurant sector had taken root in the country, and its businesses had diversified after the SARS outbreak. Published in this period, Tunisian-born Italian writer Amara Lakhous's novel *Scontro di civiltà per un ascensore a Piazza Vittorio* (Clash of Civilizations Over an Elevator in Piazza Vittorio, 2006, abbreviated as *Scontro di civiltà* hereafter) is one of the most widely read examples of Italian migration literature. It features a storyline that resolutely critiques this alimentary stereotype.

Dogmeat among Other Unclean Animal Meats

The episode follows a simple story about Ugo Fantozzi (Paolo Villaggio) and Mrs. Silvani's (Anna Mazzamauro) date in a Japanese restaurant, focusing on pranks and comedic situations. Fantozzi, a married accountant employed in an Italian firm, invites his colleague and extramarital love interest, Silvani, to a newly opened Japanese restaurant. When they meet at the restaurant and make small talk, both are lighthearted and feign cosmopolitanism: he tries to make a good impression on her by pretending to be an expert on Japanese food and language, and she wears an Asian-themed silk coat and adopts an elaborate Asian-looking coiffure. Their carnivalesque masquerade fits in among the multiracial clientele at the restaurant. The exotic setting vaguely suggests a milieu frequented by international diplomats in Rome or by globetrotting businessmen in Milan, although the location of the scene itself is deliberately ambiguous.

At first glance, an analysis of the *Fantozzi* episode may seem odd in this section, as Chinese and Japanese cuisines have followed different paths in Italy.[14] The two Asian cuisines were occasionally discussed together in the press, but only increasingly so in the post-SARS period when Chinese migrant food entrepreneurs began operating more Japanese restaurants. These businesses flourished because of both the lingering social stigma associating SARS with Chinese food and the entrepreneurs' need to diversify their work in the food industry. To be sure, the mise-en-scène, the traditional furniture and interior decorations, the traditional costumes, and the Japanese(-sounding) words spoken in the *Fantozzi* scene unambiguously evoke a Japanese ambience. However, it is highly likely that these things would have suggested a generic, archaic "Oriental" atmosphere for the casual Italian viewer at the time. Consider how the confusion of Chinese and Japanese cultural and aesthetic elements in popular Italian culture of the era was not rare. It was part of a culture of Orientalist racialization. For example, Silvani brings her Pekingese dog to the restaurant to meet Fantozzi, believing the animal is fitting for the Japanese theme of the night.

Furthermore, the racialized Orientalist pastiche in *Fantozzi* is given a postmodern twist within the range of possible interpretations of the episode's narrative premise. Because the dog-eating stereotype is not commonly associated with Japanese cuisine in the Italian imagination, we may construe the Japanese motif as part of *Fantozzi*'s satire. The director may be viewed as using a supposedly close analogy, Japanese food, to obliquely critique the actual subject, Chinese food, thereby intensifying the episode's comedic irony for audience members with a basic understanding of the differences between the two culinary cultures. For one thing, as relayed in Chapter 1, in 1970s Italy, there was no broad base of Italians who ate in restaurants, consumed ethnic cuisines, or tasted Chinese food. Hence, there was no obvious reason for *Fantozzi* to deploy the dogmeat stereotype to tarnish the reputation of Chinese eateries in Italian cities. Such a need would become more accentuated during the 1980s when their "invasion" or "proliferation" was discussed in popular media.[15] For another, as I have analyzed elsewhere, various techniques of postmodern writing and filmmaking have been applied to depictions of Italy's Chinese community during the 1990s and 2000s, especially in relation to the "Chinese mafia," the presumed organized crime said to have provided finance and labor to a majority of Chinese migrants' businesses.[16] Such postmodern texts all had deeper motivations to depict the Chinese in critiquing Italian ills, including the *Cosa nostra* (the powerful Sicilian organized crime) and the mistreatment of migrants in the country, among others. *Fantozzi*'s depiction stands as a precursor to the later, more widespread, anti-realist trend of creative works that use Chinese migrant characters and plots as a foil to better deconstruct and interpret Italian-centric issues.

The most immediate Italian preoccupation here concerns the two protagonists' first-time consumption of Japanese food. Given this narrative setup, their sensorial and affective journey through Japanese food presumably illustrates (petite) middle-class Italians' unmediated reactions to this culinary world. Throughout the scene, Fantozzi and Silvani demonstrate emotions ranging from curiosity and pleasurable exoticism through uneasiness and reluctance to ultimately disgust, horror, and anger. Despite adopting exotic-looking garments, makeup, and feigned knowledge about Japan, the two diners cannot incorporate Japanese food and drinks into their digestive systems and bodies and, by implication, into their (food) culture. When a warm Japanese rice wine is served, Silvani takes a sip and immediately disparages it, calling it "melted lead." Meanwhile, Fantozzi initially pretends to enjoy the sake. But when we see the liquor steaming out of his ears, we understand that he suffers when he drinks it. The comedic pattern of exaggeration is repeated later in the scene. After a live red goldfish from a pool has been chopped in front of their very eyes in preparation for their consumption, Silvani examines it with a frown, remarking that it is raw. Her initial unease escalates to pure abhorrence as she makes intermittent gagging noises while watching Fantozzi devour several pieces of the raw fish. Momentarily, Fantozzi's stomach is visibly bloated because of the food, signaling indigestion. In this sequence, Silvani rejects the food outright, whereas Fantozzi, driven by bravado, ingests it and is then punished for his imprudence.

These episodes of minor food indigestion lead to the climax of the episode, which is reserved for performing the dogmeat stereotype. Much to their relief, a roasted meat dish finally arrives. But as the waiter removes the collar from the meat to present it to Silvani, she screams and angrily accuses Fantozzi of killing her dog. Previously, she asked him to have the staff feed the dog, and he communicated this idea to the Japanese waitress in intentionally broken Italian, presumably because he did not believe the waitress followed standard Italian. Fantozzi now exclaims: "There was a misunderstanding. [. . .] It is a misunderstanding resulting from Japanese cuisine." The viewer is led to infer at least four layers of meanings from this enunciation. First, the Japanese believed that Fantozzi was asking for the dog to be cooked. Second, his request was not surprising to the Japanese because of their dog-eating habit or similar past requests from other customers. Third, Fantozzi is a provincial character who would confuse the Chinese habit of eating dogmeat with the Japanese. As Francesco Ricatti argues about *Fantozzi*, the audience is not meant to sympathize with Fantozzi's pains and humiliation; instead, he is to be laughed at as a victim of consumerism and capitalism.[17] Fourth, the filmmaker may be mocking the failure of animal rights advocates to securely instill their moral standards in Italians such as our two protagonists. While Silvani is furious with Fantozzi's ineptitude, he is indignant at the Japanese culinary tradition for ruining his date. Neither of them, however, is explicitly shown as indignant at eating freshly killed raw fish and roasted dogmeat on the grounds of modern animal rights advocacy, which emerged in the 1970s.

What merits particular attention in the Japanese restaurant episode is not how *Fantozzi* restates that foodways such as warm liquor, raw fish, and especially roasted dogmeat are contrary to Italian dietary rules and gastronomic traditions. The moral discomfort toward eating dogmeat is also not as generic as an understanding based on the many positive roles that dogs play in human society. Instead, this 1975 film relied on an already well-defined and widely shared cultural precept about dogmeat as a food taboo to climax the pathos of Fantozzi's actions and emotions. Moreover, by the time the movie was released, the characterization of dogmeat consumption as Oriental or Chinese—a learned social ritual of racialized demarcation—was sufficiently well-established to elicit viewer disidentification efficiently.

If my diagnosis is correct, then what prevailing cultural scripts and forces made *Fantozzi*'s depictions of the dogmeat-eating habit, as well as the morally grounded emotions that this food prohibition elicits, readily comprehensive to average Italian viewers at the time? What major cultural resources were available for a typical Italian audience member to draw from to recognize eating dogmeat not only as a food habit to be avoided but also as an act that demarcated them from Chinese migrants and entitled them to discipline the offenders? What were, following Douglas, the guiding principles for this discourse about food- and mobility-related racialization? Admittedly, Western narratives of the Chinese habit of eating dogmeat and its uncleanliness have a long genealogy that exceeds the scope of my current analysis.[18] Here, I advance two hypotheses in attempting to answer these complicated questions. The communicative and rhetorical influences of two key contemporary texts made them the best candidates for explicating the cultural forces behind the *Fantozzi* episode's meaning-making process.

Similar to other initial Italian cultural interpretations about the country's Chinese migrants, the cultural codification of the dogmeat stereotype in Italy partially, but importantly, drew from the American context. As I have analyzed in *Migration and the Media*, the story of Chinese Americans was better known to Italian journalists than Chinese diasporas elsewhere. Italian discourses on the octopus-like, yellow-colored "Chinese mafia" clearly evoked their American cultural precedents.[19] The dogmeat stereotype in popular Italian culture appeared to have a similar American inspiration. In their studies of ethnic food in the United States, both Yong Chen and Robert Ji-Song Ku refer to the persistent urban legend of Chinese and Korean restaurants serving dogmeat dishes. As the two critics mention, at the beginning of the 1849 California Gold Rush, newspapers had already disseminated this myth about the Chinese.[20]

More specifically, several years before *Fantozzi*'s release, in 1971, Reuters, one of the world's largest news agencies, published a news story that contained most of the details of the dogmeat incident told in the film. The only differences were the setting in a Hong Kong Chinese restaurant and the Swiss nationality of the culinary tourists. Although this story was immediately questioned as a hoax, it was widely circulated in several American newspapers, including on the front page of the *San Francisco Chronicle*, one of the largest-circulating newspapers on the West Coast of the United States.[21] To be sure, despite the uncanny resemblance in detail between the Reuters story and Villaggio and Salce's use of dogmeat in *Fantozzi*, there is no direct correlation between the two cultural moments that can be proven at the time of writing. Nevertheless, *Fantozzi*'s dogmeat reference was congenital to the American hegemony in Italy when interpreting the food cultures of overseas Chinese.[22] As my analysis in Chapter 1 shows, since the 1980s, media and cultural narratives have often compared Italian Chinese food to American Chinese food. At the very least, both the American media circulation of the Reuters story and the American tradition of linking the eating of dogmeat to Chinese migrants were two powerful cultural resources for informed Italians like Salce and Villaggio when creating narratives on similar topics.

Apart from my hypothesis of the American influence on *Fantozzi*, I contend that the dog-eating stereotype partially gained rhetorical power from then-existing Italian public knowledge concerning the traditional Chinese habit of eating animal meats that are unusual for human consumption. This Italian and broadly Western discourse blamed people of Chinese ethnicity for consuming unclean animal meats, be they from domesticated animals such as dogs and cats or from wild species, including pangolins. A representative text in this regard that prepared the average Italian viewers for the dogmeat episode in *Fantozzi* was the influential international documentary and exploitation film *Mondo Cane* (A Dog's World, Gualtiero Jacopetti, Franco Prosperi, and Paolo Cavara, 1962). While *Mondo Cane* is rambling in its episodic narrative, its thematic foci on food and dogs are unmistakably relevant to *Fantozzi*. Italian-made *Mondo Cane*, along with its sequels, spin-offs, and imitations, has had significant followers in the West from the 1960s through the 1980s,[23] thereby helping disseminate misinformation about the (alleged) Chinese penchant for certain animal meats.

While *Mondo Cane* makes several points about dogs, the consumption of dogmeat is exclusively reserved for ethnic Chinese. In the Taiwan vignette, the camera intercuts between innocent-looking caged dogs and a man avidly eating what was presumably dogmeat to enhance the viewer's repugnance at this practice. The voice-over contrasts the West—as shown in an immediately preceding episode set in California, the United States—where dogs are said to be valued for their intelligence and loyalty, with Taiwan, where dogs are eaten. Further, people of Chinese ethnicity also enjoy the dubious distinction in *Mondo Cane* for consuming the widest variety of unclean meats. The episode set in Hong Kong depicts a wet market where crocodiles, toads, lizards, snakes, turtles, pangolins, and civets were skinned alive and sold on the spot. The close-ups of people in Singapore's Chinatown eagerly eating snakes further underscore their taste for various forbidden animal meats. A Malaysian scene features men with mutilated body parts collecting dried shark fins meant for export to China for its people's "vices," implying their sexual immoderation and craving for food that presumably enhances sexual potency. An attentive viewer of *Mondo Cane* would come away with the impression that ethnic Chinese are the people with the least care for food taboos. Even the New Guineans, who mercilessly slaughtered pigs, many of whom "ate human flesh," treated their dogs with respect, according to the film. As the film claims through these episodes, as far as food prohibitions are concerned, ethnic Chinese are the most extreme example of consumers of unclean meats.

Such a cultural script cannot evade the question of moral judgment. In an extensive installment set in Singapore's Chinatown, the film's racist commentary reaches a climax. Over a sequence showing a large variety of Chinese dishes at a night market, the voice-over criticizes ethnic Chinese for their obsession with money and for their physical laziness. Overseas Chinese are said to spend all their energy at the dining table and in bed, with both activities giving birth to throngs of children. But the association among food, nutrition, uncontrolled births, and the Chinese diaspora is a pretext used to highlight the main macabre phenomenon analyzed in this vignette: dying seniors were put in a "hotel" waiting for their final moment. The filmmakers adopt a cross-cutting technique to contrast the conviviality of people enjoying food during funerals with the deformed faces and bodies of the dying in the hotel, thereby remarking on the inappropriateness of these occurrences to Western eyes. Should grieving people eat? Should greedy desires for food and passions for procreative sex override proper grief for the dying and the dead? Do ethnic Chinese worldwide have no inhibition when eating any animal meat thanks to their instinct to propagate their race and their tendency to lead a barbaric way of life? The film seems to ask these ethical questions about ethnic Chinese through an ethnocultural lens[24] and from the perspective of Western dietary restrictions and decorum.

Some critics caution against a straightforward reading of the *Mondo Cane* movies as documentaries and against moralistic interpretations of them. Mark Goodall has acknowledged the shock value and the tendency for fake content in many *Mondo Cane* products, describing the 1962 original as a "shockumentary" meant to repudiate establishment priorities, such as a critical obsession with Italian neorealist cinema at that time.[25] According to this argument, the depiction in *Mondo Cane* of the eating habits of overseas Chinese should not be interpreted as a documentary per se but as a metaphorical transgression of conventional boundaries. Reaching a different conclusion about the franchise's sociocultural function from Goodall, Mikita Brottman claims that the *Mondo Cane* series can be viewed as "the 'other' of the mainstream horror film," with "its images understood as catalogs of nervous disorders and psychotic symptoms: the repressed complexes of the 'sanctioned' horror film narrative."[26] In this lens, *Mondo Cane* shows presumably "real" animal and human deaths, engendering a sense of horror in the audience, as opposed to classic horror movies that address obviously staged events. Following this line of inquiry, witnessing *Mondo Cane*'s Chinese-related depictions of broken taboos would urge Western audiences to consider reinforcing social taboos and maintaining social order when they leave the movie theater.[27]

Despite divergent interpretations of *Mondo Cane*, the film played a key role in rehearsing the racialization of the old Chinese dogmeat stereotype for Western viewers in the 1960s and later. The popularity of the film also strengthened the exclusive association of ethnic Chinese with unsanitary animal meats within Western screen culture at the time.[28] As such, in addition to the 1971 Reuters news story, the 1962 film became another important and popular cultural resource for *Fantozzi* to deploy when showing Fantozzi and Silvani's aversion to unhygienic and unsafe meat like dogmeat. From the perspective of ongoing migrant settlement, the discursive legacy of *Fantozzi* is how Fantozzi and Silvani's rejection of dogmeat and other food effectively mirrors the refusal of Italian society to integrate East Asian migrant communities into its body politic. Racialized difference in foodways is one way for Italian cultural producers to provide the broader Italian society with an easily digestible ground for excluding migrants from becoming full-fledged social actors in their host country. The American precedents about the dogmeat stereotype had a similar sociocultural agenda. For example, the Reuters story articulated the anti-Asian sentiment that followed the 1965 Immigration and Nationality Act. Chinese migration to the United States significantly increased because the Act relaxed the restrictions imposed by the 1882 Chinese Exclusion Act.[29] Racialized demarcation of migrants from Italians for the purpose of social exclusion unites the two hypotheses that I have made to explain the cultural milieu in which *Fantozzi*'s dogmeat episode became meaningful and impactful.

Minorities Talk Back

Lakhous's novel *Scontro di civiltà* is one of the most widely read and well-studied texts of Italian migration literature. It won the Italian literary prize Premio Flaiano in 2006 and enjoyed a film adaptation in 2010. While the novel's reputation is nowhere near that of *Fantozzi* or *Mondo Cane* in popular Italian culture, it is a prime example for analyzing migrants' act of talking back to mainstream Italian culture and society.[30] Set in a working-class building in the Piazza Vittorio area in Rome near the Termini train station, all the novel's characters are migrants in their own ways. Processes of (self-)racialization through foodways are frequent. The memorable opening chapter, focused on the Iranian political asylum seeker Parviz Mansoor Samadi, is centrally conceived through food metaphors. The character's hatred for pizza expresses his desire for an eventual return to his homeland and an escape from the injustice he encounters in Italy.

Food also mediates migrants' identity conversion narratives in Lakhous's novel. As Harry Kashdan argues, the novel presents "stories of migration as an elective and solitary phenomenon," which dissociate the migrants' current identities in the host society from their previous national identities.[31]

Amedeo, the novel's protagonist who turns out to be Ahmed Salmi, an Algerian refugee, gives up North African couscous in favor of Italian cappuccino, croissants, and pizza. His eating habits contribute significantly to his passing as a bona fide Italian native in the eyes of the building's multiracial residents. Food habits are but one instance of Amedeo's overall making of Piazza Vittorio into a transitive space. For Graziella Parati, through *Scontro di civiltà*, Lakhous creates a "textual transitive city" that can foster larger discussions of immigration, space, and literature.³² Concerning other examples of Italian migration literature, scholars have also examined literary representations of food and women with migratory backgrounds, such as those by Igiaba Scego and Laila Wadia, which help explain complex processes of writing and authorial identities.³³

Unlike previous critics, I draw attention to how Lakhous depicts Italians' attitudes toward non-Italian food. What Italian identities and issues do such food-related character studies articulate? The dog-eating stereotype in the novel is circulated by two European Italians: Benedetta Esposito, who is an internal migrant from Naples, and Elisabetta Fabiani, whose dream is to move to Switzerland to escape from Italy, which she perceives to be an uncivilized country. The possibility that Chinese restaurateurs kidnapped Fabiani's dog, Valentino, motivates the two women's speculation about its disappearance. After ruminating on Fabiani's hypothesis as relayed to him, Amedeo returns home and humorously imagines a scene that references *Fantozzi*, thereby exposing key cinematic precedence of the gossip as it is circulated in contemporary popular Italian culture:

> I wondered what would happen if I knocked on Elisabetta Fabiani's door and said to her: "I've just come back from the Chinese restaurant next door, and I had rice with some delicious meat; when I was leaving I asked the restaurant owner what kind of meat I'd eaten and he said, 'It's a dog we found one morning near our restaurant, he was wearing a collar that had "Valentino" written on it.'" I haven't laughed so much for a long time. (43–44)

In both *Fantozzi* and *Scontro di civiltà*, the discovery of the dog's collar signals a moment of horror and indignation at violating the rights of living things. Indeed, while the cruelty of eating dogs is the immediate reference in these moments, the violation of human rights is the real focus. The latter expresses the Orientalist idea of the dichotomy between Asian despotism and Western democracy. In *Fantozzi*, the discovery is prefaced by several depictions of white customers in the restaurant who are disciplined by Japanese guards dressed like samurais. When the customers hesitate to consume the food because of concerns over its foreignness, or when they use hands rather than chopsticks to pick up food, the guards strike them with their swords. In addition to the Asian-Western contrast, violation of human rights also refers to the antinomy between Southern and Northern Europe for their degrees of civilization. In *Scontro di civiltà*, Fabiani lists the rights of dogs as a criterion in proving that, as Switzerland is more civilized than Italy, Italy is still more civilized than China. She intends to move to a country where her right to raise her dog and the rights of dogs are respected. Occupying an intermediary and thus unstable position between Switzerland and China and between what is considered true civilization and barbarity, the Italian characters' estrangement from Chinese foodways is depicted to provoke strong forms of psychological afflictions and outrage. Such fury and pain, rather than characterized as personal emotions, are depicted as collective sentiments, which embolden the characters to slander Japanese and Chinese cultures as repressive.

Apart from *Fantozzi* and the Chinese dogmeat stereotype that it helped cement in popular Italian culture, Lakhous's novel instructs us to consider another origin that motivates Fabiani's malicious disparagement of the Chinese: her unhealthy obsession with crime journalism. In the chapter dedicated to Fabiani, based on piecemeal consumption of "*cronaca nera*," or the crime news section of print and television news outlets, she makes ludicrous speculation on the parallel between the disappearance of her dog and that of Amedeo. Fabiani then attributes the former disappearance to the kidnapping by Chinese migrants and the latter—being the main literary frame of the crime novel—to the kidnapping of Sardinian criminal groups. Both the migrants and the criminals are said to operate in Piazza Vittorio. Lakhous thus fictionalizes how a self-proclaimed civically minded Italian resident like Fabiani only applies the migration-crime-restaurant frame to the Chinese in a petty way in a situation involving her dog.

This critique of mainstream Italian crime reporting is key to the narrative design of *Scontro di civiltà*. As a crime novel, its framing story assigns the reader the role of detective. The reader must decide whether or not Amedeo, who has gone missing and is accused of murdering another resident of the building, is guilty. As almost all the book's characters insist in their point-of-view chapters, their beloved friend Amedeo would be incapable of committing such a crime. To make the detective's judgment, the reader is invited to assess the soundness of each narrator's perspective and the veracity of their evidence. In this way, Lakhous asks us to carefully consider whether the popular understanding of Chinese food and crime upon which both Fabiani and Esposito draw is legitimate.

To appreciate this literary mechanism, let us analyze how Lakhous structures Esposito's reasoning about why the Chinese are behind the missing dog and how he satirizes the ways in which the stereotype can be conveyed in daily oral communications. The rationale is presented with both a high degree of orality and notable characteristics of self-referentiality:

> I [Esposito] told her [Fabiani] that Valentino's disappearance raises a lot of suspicions. I don't have clear proof available, but what I see all around me tells me it was kidnapping.
> First. Recently a lot of Chinese restaurants have opened in and around Piazza Vittorio.
> Second. The gardens of Piazza Vittorio are the favorite place for Chinese children to play.
> Third. They say that the Chinese eat cats and dogs.
> After all those things I've told you, there is no doubt that the Chinese stole poor little Valentino and ate him! (39)

Esposito's exposition can be usefully viewed as a rhetorical speech directed at Fabiani and the reader of the novel. As Esposito admits in the first paragraph, no "clear proof" exists in favor of her argument. That is to say, to use a rhetorical line of thinking, no irrefutable fact—such as conclusive evidence about the Chinese kidnapping of the dog—exists that the speaker may deploy. Instead, Esposito's argument is built upon various artistic means of persuasion that the orator creates for the case. The principal means Esposito chooses here is reasoning that appears, to her, logical. Lakhous uses four freestanding paragraphs composed of declarative statements to accentuate her reasoning: three brief premises are given before she reaches a conclusion. The first two premises refer to signs of demographic and social transformations that can be easily accepted by Fabiani and by the average Italian reader. In the early 2000s, the Roman Chinese community was transforming Piazza Vittorio into their commercial hub by purchasing storefronts and setting up businesses.[34]

The third premise, however, is presented as hearsay, and its argumentation is predicated on probability. This unstable premise would need stronger discursive energy because it neither shows evidence of the Chinese actually offering dogmeat and cat meat in their restaurants, nor can it derive from the credibility of the speaker, who is a building concierge, nor do we know the identity of the people who utter the sentence that Esposito is reporting here. Rather, the premise exclusively gains legitimacy by drawing from a commonly accepted, formulaic cultural opinion about the Chinese in popular Italian discourse. Note how the novel informs us that this reasoning and its conclusion are compelling to Fabiani. Later in her monologue, we learn that she has taken Esposito's proposition to heart and fantasizes about calling on the Chinese embassy in Rome to intervene, hoping to escalate the incident to an international diplomatic level. Thus, through this self-consciously logical reasoning delivered orally by Esposito to Fabiani, Lakhous poses the question of why the third premise, the dogmeat stereotype, is persuasive as such.

Apart from the cultural force of the stereotype, Lakhous's text indicates that the key to the rhetorical persuasion of Esposito's speech is brevity in content (i.e., three numbered, one-sentence declarations) and in numbers (i.e., only three premises). This textual phenomenon can be interpreted by referring to Christof Rapp's remarks on Aristotelian rhetoric: "It is a sign of a well-executed enthymeme [i.e., a deductive rhetorical syllogism concerning a contingent situation] that the content and the number of its premises are adjusted to the intellectual capacities of the public audience."[35] Neither Esposito nor Fabiani are intellectually sophisticated characters who are capable of handling lengthy oral inferences leading to fuller syllogisms that are required to warrant any sound claim. The concision that defines the verbal delivery exposes a populist way of reasoning that is dear to the two women. According to *Scontro di civiltà*, this instance of populist logic is nurtured by the circulation of the dogmeat stereotype between the news media, previous cultural depictions of influence, and daily conversations. Repeated oral enunciations of this stereotype among the Roman working class strengthen its apparent truth, as the novel excels at depicting the characters gossiping about their neighbors' public and private details.

The main literary weapon that Lakhous wields when treating the stereotype is humor that derives from multicultural and multiracial misconceptions. Amedeo's laugh at his conjuring of the collar-related moment presupposes its anticipated effects on Fabiani and ridicules her. Amedeo is also depicted as being amused by the absurdity of Fabiani's populist logic. Thus, through the dogmeat episodes, whereas *Fantozzi* satirizes petite middle-class Italians' feigned culinary cosmopolitanism in the aftermath of Italy's booming years of economic growth in the mid-1970s, *Scontro di civiltà* ridicules working-class Italians for their proud display of ignorance of Chinese foodways in the age of mass migration and globalization.

Likewise, during the initial months of the COVID-19 pandemic, some Chinese Italian TikTok users adopted a humorous or ironic approach to other users' provocations in this regard. In response to a remark that Chinese food products often were made under unsanitary conditions, wei_alessandro, who self-identified as an ethnic Chinese restaurant owner in Milan, rhetorically asked why his eatery had been open since 1998 if frozen cats and dogs had been consumed there. He ended his video by jokingly making an ominous face while referring to an image of a dog that he saw on the profile of the user who originally left the accusatory remark.[36] Others were more didactic in using humor to ask viewers to espouse moral relativism by showing respect for other people's foodways. Faced with the question "Do you eat dogs and cats?" from a white Italian-sounding account name, the TikToker dazibao explained that her only experience of eating dogmeat was in eastern Switzerland, not in China. Dazibao clarified the moral of her intervention by claiming that she would respect Swiss people who consumed dogmeat for the Christmas holidays.[37]

Despite the counter-narrative to the dogmeat cliché, Amedeo's laughter and Lakhous's humor are sympathetic to the Italian characters' conditions. As the novel intimates, Fabiani and Esposito are economically and socially marginalized Italians who must bear the effects of the neoliberal economic structuring of the country. During the 2000s, this meant, among other things, a rapid onset of globalization and migration, which bureaucratic responses were slow to mitigate its impact on ordinary lives. Through the dogmeat episode, *Scontro di civiltà* showcases certain working-class people's dogged belief in their right to remain deeply biased in an intuitive defense of their community, local, and national identities against the rapidly changing social reality around them. Lakhous contextualizes Fabiani and Esposito's visceral and racist defense as a coping mechanism available to the country's social underclass, who cohabit with migrants from a diverse range of cultures and countries in a neighborhood neglected by public authorities. In so doing, while not always agreeing with such Italian characters as Fabiani and Esposito, Lakhous nevertheless humanizes them in their daily struggles and existential plights. The dogmeat alimentary trope functions as a major literary mechanism through which the writer clarifies such a cross-cultural position.

Lakhous's representation largely works as a viable narrative solution to addressing the alimentary stereotype because, like *Fantozzi*, *Scontro di civiltà* presents no speaking subject who is of Chinese background, thereby necessitating no debate on the subject within the diegesis. But even in recent fiction featuring Chinese protagonists that are penned by migrant authors, the dogmeat or exotic animal meat stereotype has never been extensively treated.[38] It is simply not a serious subject for this body of work, whose intention it is to represent migrant identities and stories and to fight commonplace biases. In fictional works, the dogmeat stereotype falls within the purview of Italian-centric preoccupations with Chinese migrants, beginning with food taboos but extending to the acceptance of migrants. The 1970s and the 2000s saw their own distinctive social and cultural forces that molded the two works' approaches to the alimentary stereotype. This trope has been a prime example for registering differing modes and motives of Italian racialization of Chinese in diaspora, as well as minorities' contestation of such racialization. In creative works, this cliché provides discursive opportunities for artists to reinforce, question, or satirize acts of social exclusion by ordinary Italians toward their Chinese migrant neighbors.

■

Alimentary stereotypes evoke the visceral quality of food and its discourses in our society. Food intake becomes part of our internal corporeal and sociopolitical realities, and it helps regulate their vital mechanisms. According to Mimi Sheller and Urry, a theoretical influence on the study of mobilities concerns "the recentering of the corporeal body as an affective vehicle through which we sense place and movement, and construct emotional geographies."[39] Various examples in *Fantozzi* illustrate this point about food mobility. In this chapter, I have investigated the circumstances surrounding a quintessential hackneyed notion about the food and food entrepreneurship of Italy's Chinese migrants. In Italian popular culture, the dogmeat stereotype perpetuated xenophobia based on popular perceptions of predetermined sanitary and ethical guidelines. As such, the trope enacted racialized and social exclusion of ethnic Chinese from Italian society. As in Chapter 2, here I have also analyzed how Chinese Italians and pro-migrant authors responded to the stereotype through discursive disruptions of the dominant Italian-language depictions.

Over several decades, cultural workers in Italy have operationalized a racialized food taboo like dogmeat consumption as a fundamental cultural idea structuring interpretive approaches to Chinese food and migrants. Doing so has helped the culture industry identify major Italian social problems, debate their causes, adjudicate their moral stakes, and seek viable cultural solutions. The more influential representations on the subject negotiated almost exclusively Italian perspectives, and not Chinese ones in an interactive way, primarily owing to their focus on how Chinese migrations to Italy can help Italians address their realities. More broadly, the chapter concludes that certain aspects of Italian cultural identity-making can be effectively accentuated by its contacts with Chinese migrant cuisine. My analysis further demonstrates how China-Italy food mobilities in recent decades played a key role in negotiating issues not intrinsic to culinary transactions.

FOUR

Fighting "Yellow Mozzarella": Italians Safeguard Food's Authenticity

Widely produced in southern Italy, mozzarella is a signature Italian food. *Mozzarella di bufala*, made from the milk of Italian Mediterranean buffalos, is especially prized. The Italian region of Campania is particularly associated with this semi-soft white cheese, earning a trademark *"mozzarella di bufala campana"* ("Campania water buffalo mozzarella"). "Mozzarella gialla" (yellow mozzarella) is the nickname that Campania entrepreneurs use to refer to a mozzarella supposedly made by Chinese migrants in the comedy film *Mozzarella Stories* (Edoardo De Angelis, 2011). While not yellow in color, the Chinese-made mozzarella is perceived as "yellow"—referring to the supposed and pejoratively connotated skin color of the Chinese—by local Italians for its ethnicity and cultural value. The white and noble mozzarella denotes the white and morally superior identity of its owners, a stance sharpened by the "yellow" Chinese-made mozzarella presumed inferior in quality. Not surprisingly, in the film, Italian entrepreneurs are depicted as fighting the "yellow mozzarella" to protect their real mozzarella. This food-assisted racialization urges viewers to support the Italian entrepreneurs' safeguarding of the authenticity of an Italian food item against Chinese migrants' attempts to undermine it. The film's main storyline proves that Italian-made mozzarella is the only genuine mozzarella on the market and that various types of Made in Italy food-related expertise are the sole province of European Italians.

While *Mozzarella Stories* is fiction, as this chapter's analysis shows, Italian companies of olive oil, coffee, and rice have all made product advertising featuring diasporic or mainland Chinese food entrepreneurship through which to claim uncontaminated Italian authenticity of their foods. While this advertising was directed at Italian consumers, most of the companies I examine were transnational in their operations, and their customer base was highly globalized during the 2000s–2010s. These cases illustrate Emanuela Scarpellini's point about the impact of globalization on food: globalization can lead not only to the creation of foods that combine old and new culinary traditions but also result in harsh rejections of foreign foods in an effort to protect rediscovered or reinvented local traditions.[1] In Chapters 1–3, I have examined this impact by focusing on Italian depictions of Chinese migrant cuisine. Here, I consider this impact by inquiring into Italian representations of their own foods, especially those widely recognized as quintessentially Italian. These representations articulated an identity crisis that was intimately associated with Italians' economic well-being. In the last two decades, the rhetoric underpinning the representations often had a much more tangible real-world basis than the cultural formulas about the identities of Chinese food and migrants analyzed in Chapters 1–3.

In this chapter, by examining several 2000s and 2010s entrepreneurship-focused films and product advertising, I analyze a prevailing cultural script about authenticity and expertise in Italian foods and Chinese participation in the making of Italian foods. According to this cultural formula, ethnic Chinese attempt to make low-quality, Italian-style food—essentially fake Italian foods—on Italian soil. However, these attempts fail because of the timely interventions of skillful Italian entrepreneurs. Indeed, the Italians' food-related technical, artisanal, manufacturing, knowledge, management, and branding expertise—key areas that can be claimed for Italian food firms' expertise—is inimitable. Their devotion to protecting the reputation of Italian culinary arts is utmost. In the end, while such Italian food expertise cannot be copied, Chinese migrant and mainland Chinese entrepreneurs may be invited to invest their capital in Italian food firms, thereby forming joint ventures. In these cases, the Chinese may also supply unspecialized labor and unprocessed, or minimally processed, foods to Italian food firms, continuing to play a more conventional role in the business dynamics between the Global South and North.

According to this cultural script, then, labor, capital, and ingredients have been particularly vulnerable to Chinese influences since the 2000s for Italian food companies operating in a global context. As many cultural narratives under discussion in this chapter show, the use of Chinese labor, capital, and ingredients would help revitalize Italian food enterprises without undermining the foundation of Italian expertise in food. That core is said to be supported by specialized technology, knowledge, labor, work ethics, and branding, which white Italians alone can claim for themselves. The ultimate guarantor of authenticity in Italian foods is therefore the Italian food firms' expertise. More broadly speaking, this expertise refers to the "know-how" that Italian industry insiders, politicians, and journalists often repeat in public conversations about various Made in Italy products. Indeed, in his study on Made in Italy, Marco Fortis states that the maintenance of Italian entrepreneurs' individual, community, national, and international identities is, or ought to be, legally regulated in artisanal expertise, business practices, ecosystem management, and public image-making.[2] This chapter discusses how these dimensions of Made in Italy food "know-how" are articulated in cultural work to assert Italian food's authenticity against the foil of Chinese input.

Labor: Italian Entrepreneurs Fight Chinese Imitations

Conventional narratives about Made in Italy tend to focus on four sectors: fashion and personal accessories, furniture and home decor, automobiles and machinery, and food and agriculture. Beginning in the 2000s, media coverage of challenges to the Made in Italy industries intensified. As news outlets such as Italy's premier business daily *Il Sole 24 Ore* have regularly covered, diverse changes have been occurring in all four principal Made in Italy sectors.[3] Some changes have been painful, such as the influx of Chinese migrant labor and capital in Prato's textile and garment industry in tandem with the rise of fast fashion, which the media avidly covered.[4] Other changes have produced winners and losers within the same industry, as has been the case with the furniture sector. Some furniture enterprises began successfully exporting to China to cater to its burgeoning middle class, while others were forced to compete in China or third countries with Chinese-made furniture, some of which imitated Italian designs.[5] Indeed, fighting Chinese fakes of Italian originals has been the most significant aspect of the Chinese competition that Italian companies have been preoccupied with. This fear correlates to the financial and reputational losses that Italian companies or individuals likely suffer as a result.

In recent China-Italy exchanges, the controversy about imitations made by Chinese labor does not usually concern Italian food. But the Italian textile and fashion sector has been at the center of such debates, and it has received a range of cultural elaborations about such changing Italian identities. During the 2000s and 2010s, Prato's Chinese migrant-managed garment sector was routinely accused of mislabeling fast fashion "Made in Italy" and was said to have caused the decline of the city's Italian textile businesses. Marco Limberti's comedy film, *Cenci in Cina* (Rags in China, 2009), addresses this crisis by making an apt connection between fashion and food. The frame story concerns the imminent failure of a textile factory owned by two Italian men, Giachetti (Francesco Ciampi) and Pelagatti (Alessandro Paci), and its hopeful future revival thanks to the capital investment of a Chinese migrant businesswoman Li (Man Lo Zhang). The Chinese-Italian difference and specialization in this joint venture are tellingly illustrated by an episode about Chinese-made Italian food in the private kitchen.

In this episode, Li invites Giachetti to dinner at her house on the pretense of discussing a joint Chinese-Italian business venture. Meanwhile, Pelagatti secretly enters Li's bedroom, intending to uncover more about her planned purchase of the Italian company. Much in line with *Fantozzi* examined in Chapter 3, disgust and indigestion characterize the Italians' reactions to food prepared in the Chinese migrant's household, mirroring their equally palpable loathing of her business manipulations and the city's Chinese-managed garment sector. At the dinner table, Giachetti is confronted with a three-course Tuscan dinner Li's Chinese cook prepares in his honor: *crostini di fegatini* (liver on bread), *pappa al pomodoro* (tomato-based bread soup), and *bistecca alla fiorentina* (Florentine-style steak). Upon tasting the appetizer, he frowns, looks down to examine it, and swallows it with exaggerated difficulty. After having the first spoonful of the *pappa al pomodoro*, Giachetti exclaims, "Mamma mia," vocalizing his displeasure and disapproval. But Li seems to enjoy the soup and asks his opinion on it, further demonstrating Chinese people's supposed lack of good taste in food. In a previous scene, as Pelagatti sneaks into the house, he witnesses the cook and a Chinese helper debating in Mandarin how to make the *pappa al pomodoro*. Just as the cook displays his inadequacy in making the Italian specialty dish, the helper shows immoderation by suggesting that they add more pungent onions to the soup. By now, the film has established that the Chinese have questionable taste and ability to cook Italian food, a depiction that parallels similar traits in fashion making.

Next, the film seeks to strengthen its thesis about Italians' superior ability to cook their own food. Having suffered the Chinese cook's failed attempts to make the appetizer and the first course, Giachetti decides to take the matter into his own hands for the main course. He yells to the Chinese cook: "Wong, listen, get up from there. I am making the steak. You think about making the spring rolls. That's better. Let's go." This exclamation indicates that, in the film's food imagination, each ethnic group ought to cook its own food. The mention of spring rolls illustrates the low quality of Chinese food in Italian public perception, analyzed in Chapter 1. In contrast, in the film's next scene, Italian food conveys an authentic Italian identity, expertise, and artistry. Dressed in an apron and a cook's hat adorned with the Italian tricolor, Giachetti presents the steak to Li, who repeatedly compliments Giachetti on his culinary skills.

In this way, the major food episode in *Cenci in Cina* establishes Italians as consummate leaders in Italian food preparation and appreciation. The same argument is then applied to the fashion sector. In the film's final scene, Li, Giachetti, and Pelagatti announce their new Italian-Chinese company, which will apply Chinese capital and Italian expertise to textile manufacturing, thereby preserving the material and technical authenticity of Made in Italy fashion. This outcome essentializes Chinese and Italian strengths in this future joint venture: whereas Giachetti and Pelagatti contribute allegedly authentic Italian creativity and expertise, as well as masculine power and authority, Li brings global business competencies, which are trained through Chinese globalization, and her sexiness as a *cinesina*. While *Cenci in Cina* primarily addresses these fashion-related dynamics, the dinner episode plays a key role in cinematically disqualifying non-Italians' contributions of knowledge, expertise, and art to the various Made in Italy sectors. Mutual reinforcement between Italian food and fashion branding and industry identity construction finds an effective expression in *Cenci in Cina*.

Mozzarella Stories, the film mentioned at the outset of this chapter, reaches similar conclusions about Chinese migrants' inability to make genuine Italian food and about the injection of Chinese capital into failing Italian businesses. Set in Caserta in the Campania region, the film stages a tension between the famed *mozzarella di bufala* and a "mozzarella gialla" through intense racialization of their respective public reputations and social standings. Nicknamed Ciccio DOP (Giampaolo Fabrizio), the film's protagonist is the head of a local network of *mozzarella di bufala* factories. He believes that his consortium is on the brink of financial failure because of unfair competition from ethnic Chinese entrepreneurs. Ciccio learns from a television news program that, supported by a mainland Chinese company, Chinese migrant makers of the Tian Su brand sell their "mozzarella gialla" at half the price of his *mozzarella di bufala*. However, various Caserta locals interviewed during the program attest to the authentic flavor and shape of the Chinese-made mozzarella. Disbelieving such a description of the quality of Chinese-made mozzarella, Ciccio tries the product for himself. After taking a bite, he immediately spits it out and categorically criticizes the cheese as disgusting. But a fleeting change of his facial expression captured by the camera indicates how Ciccio has a moment of doubt when chewing the delicious cheese.

Although customers appreciate the genuine taste and lower price of the "mozzarella gialla," Ciccio finds the product profoundly lacking in authenticity. As an old friend's praise of Ciccio's achievements in the film's opening scene implies, bona fide *mozzarella di bufala* must have a specific *terroir* (the Campania region), a specific animal source (the buffalos from this region), makers of a particular ethnic identity (European Italian), and good branding and profits (for these same white Italians). Within this context, Ciccio is humorously referred to as Ciccio with a DOP—that is, a "Denominazione d'Origine Protetta" (protected designation of origin). Since the 2000s, this European Union-wide system has certified agricultural products made in specific geographical zones according to traditional specialties and regulations. As the Chinese-made mozzarella violates such criteria, Ciccio disputes its status as the authentic *mozzarella di bufala*. In the universe conjured by *Mozzarella Stories*, only Ciccio has the authority to both embody and perform the DOP mozzarella, which is conveniently conveyed through his round body shape, unlike the skinnier bodies of the film's Chinese characters. As Deborah Lupton remarks, food intake is about "containment, the exertion of the will over the flesh, the mind over the emotions, the striving towards the idealized 'civilized' body."[6] Ciccio's disavowal of the good-tasting mozzarella supposedly made by the Chinese articulates the self-control he must exert to uphold the culinary standards embodied by the mozzarella. A plot twist later in the film reconfirms these requirements for authentic mozzarella that Ciccio upholds and embodies. We find out that the Chinese actually buy the mozzarella they sell from local farms. The migrants are not capable of making genuine-tasting "mozzarella gialla" after all. They only package the cheese using self-Orientalizing designs and marketing schemes that create a media buzz and make people curious about their product.

The film's racialized depictions of the reputations of Italian and Chinese migrant entrepreneurs also reveal the interaction of culinary authenticity with a moral economy that is also highly gendered. According to Valeria Siniscalchi, the "moral characterization" of Slow Food concerns not only the action of the consumers and the environment but also the work of producers, which is assumed to fight unbridled free market capitalism.[7] In the context of *Mozzarella Stories*, we may further differentiate the Italian producers who adhere to high moral standards from the Chinese migrant investors and wannabe producers who resort to marketing schemes. Following Ciccio's death, his daughter, Sofia (Luisa Ranieri), inherits the buffalo mozzarella business and forms a new company with the Chinese. In this joint venture, not dissimilar to *Cenci in Cina*'s depiction of a garment company, the Italians offer artisanal expertise and specialized labor, while the Chinese provide the capital, nonspecialized workforce, and modernized factories. Further, the Italian leads are depicted as possessing the integrity to defend the authenticity of *mozzarella di bufala* and the ultimate prescience to collaborate with the Chinese for a renewed future. On the other hand, the Chinese entrepreneurs threaten, connive, and exploit the Italians' financial difficulties, infighting between companies, and the interference of the *Camorra*, the powerful organized crime organization centered in Campania.

Consider the first time that a Chinese migrant approaches Ciccio and proposes an acquisition plan to him. The Chinese businessman (Yoon C. Joyce) brings a plastic bag full of cash, which he says Ciccio can use to shore up enough capital to pay off debts. The Chinese man's Italian is perfect, but his demand is offensive and the tone callous: we pay you money, you give us the buffalos. Not surprisingly, Ciccio's reaction to the proposal is an emotional and total rejection. In this business sector, Ciccio embodies the hegemonic masculinity that can only accommodate men who worship him, such as his associates. He cannot accept the challenges of his masculine business authority from men who are thought of as subordinates because they cheat in business and buy off honest merchants. The Chinese-Italian mozzarella factory is created only when two women are involved: Sofia and Tian Su (Linda Chang), the executive of the Chinese mozzarella brand. Even here, the baseline moral comparison remains. Sofia understands that the future of the factor must accommodate Chinese capital, whereas Tian Su obtains the business deal crucially through the dishonest scheme involving the "mozzarella gialla."

To be sure, the director, De Angelis, seems to relish the idea of conjuring a peaceful coexistence of Chinese migrant and Italian entrepreneurs in his film. In an interview, the filmmaker first repeats familiar media tropes about Chinese migrants in Italy, especially their ardent entrepreneurship and close-knit community.[8] Then he claims that he developed the joint venture scenario so as to encourage Chinese migrants to invest in local businesses rather than sending money to China. This end would then become a cinematic "sharing of a community." But as my analysis shows, ultimately, *Mozzarella Stories* reinforces the racialized and moral divides, as well as the division of labor, between the Italians and the Chinese. The film lends legitimacy to Italian-Chinese joint ventures if the expertise remains in the hands of the Italians, who will supposedly ensure the authenticity and purity of the product for subsequent generations.

Undoubtedly, both *Cenci in Cina* and *Mozzarella Stories* employ what Àine O'Healy describes as "a playful, self-directed irony at the metanarrative level" in Italian films about migrations, which also characterizes some of the films examined in Chapter 2.[9] However, as I underscore in the preceding analysis, both directors ultimately praise the resolve of small- and medium-sized family-run Italian enterprises, which are the pillar of the Italian economy, to adapt to changing business environments. By keeping Made in Italy food expertise in-house, they also ensure both continued business viability and product authenticity. For Helene A. Shugart, in food films popular with white audiences, food "rhetorically manages contemporary anxieties around ambiguity and permeability as relevant to cultural identities prompted by desire for and consumption of Otherness."[10] Similarly, the two films argue that the Italian identity of the creators or manufacturers and their expertise is the only key to keeping the authentic identity of Made in Italy foods. According to this reasoning, the Chinese, as business or manufacturing collaborators in food production, are by default incapable of creating genuine Italian cuisine.

In most cases, this stance addressed the mismatch since the 2000s between the ethnic composition of a significant portion of the workforce and the reputation of Made in Italy specialty food products. The news media extensively covered the role played by migrants in the production of a wide range of traditional Italian food items. For example, as *La Repubblica* reports, in 2015, 166,000 migrants comprised a formidable workforce in the country's agricultural and food sector.[11] Migrant workers have been involved in the production of mozzarella, prosciutto, and parmesan cheese, for instance, which are some of the most iconic Italian foods.[12] In the case of Chinese migrants, whose entrepreneurialism was both admired and feared in Italy, cultural workers went further to depict them not only as diligent laborers but also as at once much-needed financiers of Italian firms and rejected experts of Italian food products. When suggesting ways to fight fake foods or food fraud (the misrepresentation of food), the two films' representations highlight the central role of preserving Italian food-related knowledge, specialized manufacturing, and company management expertise when significant unspecialized labor is delegated to migrants and important capital investment is sought from foreign financiers. This scenario represents a major cultural solution for Italian entrepreneurs and the general public to mitigate their discomfort about Chinese migrants' global mobilities and their localized entrepreneurship.

Capital: A Marriage of Italian Expertise and Chinese Investment

Both *Cenci in Cina* and *Mozzarella Stories* refer to investments made by Chinese migrants in previously Italian-owned companies so that Italian-Chinese migrant joint ventures can be formed. The latter film also depicts such an investment as partially backed by mainland Chinese businesspeople. A real-world example of the latter dynamic in the Italian food sector concerns Salov, the olive oil company based in Lucca, Tuscany since 1919, which includes the Filippo Berio line of products well-known in North America and in Britain. In 2014, Salov passed into the hands of the Shanghai food giant, Bright Food, which bought a majority stake from the Fontana family.[13] When interviewed by *Corriere della Sera* about the sale, Alberto Fontana provided a rationale centered on the well-being of the company and its workers, which is similar to those examined in relation to the two films: "Entering into a Chinese conglomerate is to begin a route to long-term development."[14] In China, Salov has been mainly focused on selling the Filippo Berio brand, which traces its origin to 1867 as a quintessential line of Italian oils for export. Chinese-language promotional materials highlight the authentic flavor and history of the olive oil product. Here the Chinese ownership is framed as a more engaged way for middle-class Chinese consumers to embrace a healthy eating regime based on olive oil and to appreciate Italy, a "land which, like China, is filled with gastronomic inspiration and creativity."[15] Compared to the Chinese-produced and Spanish-imported olive oil brands that are better known in the Chinese market, the Filippo Berio brand banks on the increasing customer appreciation for the Made in Italy cachet (added value and prestige).

In the best scenarios, this cachet can enhance product excellence and food-assisted international reputation for both Italy and China. In 2020, Xiangyu Coratina Oil won the top prize at the ATHENA International

Olive Oil Competition held in Greece.[16] The oil was produced in China's Gansu Province by the Longnan Xiangyu Olive Development Company using Coratina olives from Tuscany and Italian oil-making machines. This success followed a tradition of growing olive trees in Gansu thanks to a donation of saplings made by the government of Albania in the 1960s, another country in the Mediterranean where the production of olive oils is ancient.[17] Thus, in the case of Xiangyu Coratina Oil, the Chinese invested in the business that also grew the olive trees on Chinese soil. But the variety of olives was Italian-sourced, and the oil production relied heavily on Italian expertise in specialized machinery and other related areas. The name of the product bears this dual identity. Xiangyu Coratina Oil is not a Chinese imitation of an Italian oil. The oil also involves some specialized production by the Chinese company. But Italian expertise is called in to assist with the production. The financial investment in the product is exclusively Chinese.

The empirical and fictional examples of marriage between Chinese migrants' or mainland Chinese capital with Italian expertise in food that I have analyzed so far in this chapter refer to two important socioeconomic contexts. I relay the media conveyance of these contexts to set the stage for analyzing a series of Italian product advertising that goes against this tide of Chinese-Italian business collaboration. During the past two decades, the Italian media covered Chinese migrants' investments in Italy, particularly in labor and real estate markets. Already in the late 2000s, major Italian and international news media covered a model Chinese migrant entrepreneur, Xu Qiu Lin, whose garment company employed white Italian designers.[18] In 2013, Italy's premier news weekly *L'Espresso* published a cover story featuring a photograph of Francesco Wu. The story describes Chinese migrant entrepreneurs as investors in various businesses that employed European Italians.[19] Similarly, in 2017, *Corriere della Sera* covered a range of Chinese migrant-financed companies whose workforces included Italian employees.[20] Concurrently, since the late-2000s, the Italian media has intensified coverage of Chinese migrants purchasing properties from Italians. Purchases of previously Italian-owned workshops, warehouses, and industrial sheds by Prato's Chinese migrants were in the public eye for a relatively long time. But the news now focused on Chinese-managed coffee bars, restaurants, and hair salons that catered to the general public.[21] *Corriere della Sera* also covered the website vendereaicinesi.it, whose catchy name literally translates to "Selling to the Chinese." The website, launched in 2013, provided sellers and purchasers in Italy with a fee-based forum for posting announcements and therefore facilitating supply and demand.[22] *Mozzarella Stories* and the examples concerning Lavazza that I will soon examine wondered whether Chinese migrants would soon venture into Italian food companies and what consequences such entrepreneurship would entail.

Furthermore, since the 2010s, major Italian news outlets including *Corriere della Sera*, *La Repubblica*, and *Il Sole 24 Ore* have examined mainland Chinese companies' purchases of high-profile Italian brands, or majority ownership in important Italian companies.[23] Through this media coverage, we learn that since 2015, the majority of shares in the tire giant Pirelli have been held by a state-run Chinese company, ChemChina. Other examples include fashion brands such as Krizia, Cerruti, Miss Sixty, and GIADA; the Ferretti yacht company; and energy companies, including Cdp Reti (Snam and Terna) and Ansaldo Energia. The two soccer teams based in Milan were also partially owned by the Chinese at various points in recent memory. In 2016, Suning Holdings Group of China acquired the principal ownership of the soccer team Inter Milan. Between 2017 and 2018, another soccer team, A.C. Milan, was owned by a Chinese businessman, Li Yonghong, who eventually defaulted on his loans and left the club's ownership, which then passed into American hands. Chinese state companies also purchased around 2 percent of shares in Italian enterprises in the sectors of energy (Eni and Enel), insurance (Generali), telecommunications (Telecom Italia), automobiles (Fiat Chrysler), banking (Mediobanca), and technology products (Prysmian).[24] Examples in other sectors, which are too numerous to list here, were also covered in mainstream media.[25] In this wave of Chinese direct investment in Italy, Salov was the only significant example pertaining to Italy's agricultural and food sector and was amply covered by the media. The Chinese investment storyline in *Mozzarella Stories* also becomes meaningful when interpreted within this context.

In their common objective of both selling more to China's middle class and keeping Italian expertise at bay from contamination, some transnational Italian food companies, such as the Turin-based Lavazza company Lavazza, took a route different from Salov and *Mozzarella Stories*. As part of Lavazza's advertising campaign titled "Paradise," which began in 1995, the 2008 "Terracina" (Chinaland) commercial promotes Lavazza's "Qualità Oro" (Golden Quality) coffee, starring the comic duo Paolo Bonolis and Luca Laurenti.[26] Stereotypically, Chinese motifs pervade a Chinese paradise, including a dragon and a mandarin, who is portrayed as a Fu Manchu figure clothed in a Qing-style (the last dynasty of imperial China) coat with a long and thin beard. When the mandarin offers the two Italians a cup of coffee, he says that this is made with "Qualità Olo" coffee, replacing "r" with "l" as per the widespread belief that the Chinese are incapable of rolling the consonant. The Chinaman figure then sprays golden-color liquid onto the surface of the dark coffee, thereby prompting Bonolis's character to call it a disgusting, dirty thing. Bonolis then presents the authentic "Qualità Oro" coffee, a machine-made espresso with foam that gives the coffee a golden color. "You cannot imitate Lavazza!" is the commercial's final line. This commercial stresses how the Chinese are incapable of making genuine Italian coffee in a parallel to their relationship with the Italian "r."[27] As widely shared in the media and among the public, the espresso is seen as an expression of Made in Italy.[28] The advertisement acknowledges this widely known tenet of Italian coffee and spoofs the spread of Chinese migrant-managed coffee bars in Italy during the decade after the SARS outbreak.

Two 2017 Lavazza commercials promoted a coffee machine called Jolie Plus, featuring a character named Dr. Ping (Maurizio Crozza), who is either a transnational Chinese businessman or a Chinese migrant entrepreneur, as the context is intentionally ambiguous about his precise identity.[29] Dr. Ping always carries around a briefcase full of cash. As relayed above, *Mozzarella Stories* has a similar reference to the Chinese, who carry a plentiful supply of cash around. Dr. Ping is also always accompanied by his Italian lawyer, who speaks on his behalf, a mechanism that narratively deprives the Chinese man of a speaking role. In one commercial, the duo approaches Saint Peter with a proposal to buy the entire Lavazza company. But the saint resolutely refuses: "No, thank you, it's not for sale." When the lawyer suggests purchasing "Paradise," meaning both the soundstage for the commercials themselves and Saint Peter's home, the answer remains negative. Instead, as the spot suggests, what the Chinese businessman can buy from Italians is the coffee machine.

In a second commercial, the lawyer looks into the camera and speaks directly to the viewer about not skipping the commercial because if they do, then Dr. Ping will purchase Lavazza, "Paradise," their house, and even their dog. We are thus transported back to the dog stereotype once more, which is enunciated here by the presumably seasoned go-between. The commercials explicitly manipulate the audience's negative disposition toward any type of ethnic Chinese buyer. In doing so, they hope that Italian consumers would both empathize with food-related nationalist protectionism and revolt against food globalization. This act of lampooning cannot help but revert to the classic Hollywood yellowface ideology examined in Chapter 2: Dr. Ping is impersonated by an Italian actor dressed up as a "Chinaman."

In making sense of the Lavazza advertising's repeated performance of Italian product authenticity against the Chinese, I propose to also consider the company's recent expansion in China, its foreign holdings, and the challenge of global coffee giants as food for further thought. In April 2020, Lavazza announced its partnership with Yum China Holdings Inc., China's largest restaurant company, to form a joint venture in the country. Even with the advent of the COVID-19 pandemic, Lavazza opened a flagship store in Shanghai and twenty other stores in Chinese cities before the end of 2021.[30] Meanwhile, Antonio Baravalle, the CEO of Lavazza, spoke to *Corriere della Sera* to publicize how the company would continue to invest in its Italian facilities and workers.[31] Recently, Lavazza purchased foreign coffee companies, including the French company Carte Noire, the Danish brand Merrild, and the Canadian business Kicking Horse Coffee based in British Columbia. Indeed, a story on *Il Sole 24 Ore* compares Chinese investments in Italy and Italian "shopping" elsewhere.[32] A partial but significant reason for this spree of acquisitions was to offset the competition posed by the American company Starbucks and the Swiss multinational Nestlé in the booming global coffee business. Still controlled by its founding family, Lavazza's core strategy has been to increase its size in gaining an edge in what the media often calls the "coffee wars."[33]

Does selling in foreign markets enhance the necessity for Lavazza's publicity materials to heighten the brand's Made in Italy cachet discursively? Does gaining the reputation of a transnational company that owns previously foreign product lines impact narratives about Lavazza's Italian creativity and origins? These are worthy but difficult questions to which my analysis cannot provide definitive answers. What remains certain is that Lavazza's strategy in its advertising oriented toward Italian consumers in the 2000s and 2010s was to rhetorically safeguard its products' Italianness by ridiculing Chinese fakes of originals and debasing Chinese investors' money.

Compared to the widespread Italian preoccupation with Chinese fakes and labor, the injection of Chinese capital into Italian firms happens on a much smaller scale. But as the examples concerning Salov and Lavazza indicate, the deployment of Chinese investment in Italian food enterprises can be equally contentious because it has the (perceived) potential of damaging the genuineness of Italian foods. To add to this worry, when selecting products of olive oil and coffee, international consumers that Italian companies cater to are more likely influenced by larger-sized companies (e.g., the Spanish oil company Deoleo and the American coffee firm Starbucks) that enjoy more extensive business networks and clout in advertising. Under these circumstances, in their product advertising, the Italian oil and coffee companies tend to underscore even more strongly their expertise in food-related knowledge and technology. Their expertise in business management and entrepreneurship is also more likely to be praised as helping maintain the Made in Italy cachet. While Salov and Lavazza must accommodate transnational and even transcultural marketing needs, accounts of their various food-related expertise support their claims about providing genuine Italian food and lifestyle to middle-class consumers worldwide.

Ingredients: Chinese DNAs for Italian Foods

In 2023, Lavazza announced more sourcing of coffee beans from southern China's Yunnan Province and the planned creation of a single-origin Yunnan retail coffee.[34] Yunnan is located in a microclimate suitable for growing coffee plants and producing high-quality beans. According to an anecdote often mentioned by the media, the origin of Yunnan coffee cultivation can be traced to a certain French Jesuit missionary in 1893, who brought seedlings or saplings from Vietnam and taught the locals how to plant coffee trees and make coffee drinks that he craved.[35] While Yunnan's coffee plant cultivation took place on an industrial scale already during the 1950s and 1960s, the real impetus came in 1988, when Nestlé invested in coffee plantations in Pu'er City. In 2010, Starbucks signed a Memorandum of Understanding with the Yunnan Provincial Government to accelerate the company's investment in the sector. By the 2010s, global coffee companies' sourcing of high-quality and economically priced coffee beans in Yunnan was no longer a secret. Chinese media increasingly covered the desire of local entrepreneurs to create their own branding to become more than ingredient suppliers. During that decade, indeed, more Chinese businesses emerged to manage the processing of coffee beans.[36] However, the core identity of Yunnan coffee culture has remained that of an increasingly important player in the global supply of Arabica coffee beans, joining its African, Latin American, and Asian counterparts, all located in the Global South.

In addressing many of these coffee-circulated dynamics, Cristiano Bortone's film *Caffè* (Coffee, 2016) is billed as the first official China-Italy film co-production, following an official agreement signed in 2004, which took effect in 2013.[37] *Caffè*'s three intertwined storylines are set in China, Italy, and Belgium, the three countries that contributed to the film's co-production. *Caffè* analyzes the production of coffee beans in China, the trading of the roasted coffee beans through Italy, and the consumption of coffee drinks in Belgium. *Caffè* is exemplary in cinematically maintaining the basic structure of these rigidly assigned positions in the global coffee business. Such stasis, however, is contrasted with the film's negotiation of food mobilities. The coffee-centered plots explore the drama of the protagonists' involvement in migration, international trade, social inequality, and intergenerational struggle.

The Chinese story highlights the production of coffee beans in Yunnan. A Beijing-based manager, Ren Fei (Fangsheng Lu) is sent by his soon-to-be father-in-law to Pu'er to put an aging chemical factory back to work. After inspection, the factory is found to have tremendous structural defects that could endanger the environs of the valley in which it is situated if its outdated machinery were to malfunction. As the father-in-law urges Ren Fei to close the case quickly and return to Beijing to get married to his daughter, Ren Fei's sense of ethics is awakened. It turns out that he is from Yunnan, who has migrated to Beijing because he wants to escape from the poverty of his family. He also loathes his father's obsession with coffee drinks due to his job as a coffee plantation worker. Later in the film, Ren Fei meets an artist, A Fang (Zhou Tan), herself a Pu'er native who has returned from Beijing to work on paintings using coffee liquids as a base. A Fang's love for Yunnan and her sense of responsibility toward the coffee farmers and the type of coffee varieties and production there lead Ren Fei to rethink his future. At the end of the film, Ren Fei resettles in his hometown in Yunnan and heads a successful coffee plantation that exports to European markets.

The trade of coffee beans is a lucrative and exploitative globalized activity. Considered a precious and expensive type, Kopi Luwak is a variety of coffee made from the feces of civets who eat and digest coffee cherries. A coffee company in Trieste, Italy, imports several boxes of Kopi Luwak from Yunnan. Renzo (Dario Aita) is a coffee sommelier who is knowledgeable about the high price of this type of coffee. He suggests his friends and acquaintances, including an employee of the Triestine coffee company, steal the coffee beans one night. We learn that having recently lost their jobs, Renzo and his girlfriend, Gaia (Miriam Dalmazio), move from Rome to Trieste, where coffee culture is vibrant. The idea of stealing the coffee beans appeals to Renzo as they continue to struggle with proper employment in Trieste, and Gaia is pregnant. The robbery goes awry, and Renzo is the only person who escapes the police's search. Toward the film's conclusion, he reunites with Gaia and basks in the glory of seeing her and their baby.

Coffee is planted and traded and will ultimately be consumed as a drink. This takes us to the storyline set in Antwerp, Belgium. A French-speaking storeowner of Arab origin, Hamed (Hichem Yacoubi) owns and cherishes a coffee pot crafted in Baghdad that he makes coffee with daily. During a street riot, Hamed's pawn shop is ransacked, and the pot is stolen. Hamed manages to identify the robber, Vincent (Arne De Tremerie), and goes to his apartment to attempt to regain the pot. After a violent encounter, both Hamed and Vincent are wounded. Vincent's father then uncovers Hamed's true identity as an ex-soldier from the Iraq War. Despite Vincent's objections, his father intends to kill Hamed and justifies the potential execution as a righteous way to vindicate the people the veteran has killed during the war. As the group heads to a remote place for the execution, the truck crashes into another vehicle. The incident leaves Hamed and Vincent the sole survivors.

The film's final scene finds Hamed tasting coffee made with the pot that he bets his life on regaining.

This plot summary of the film points to several key dimensions of global mobilities, of which the global coffee business is a prime example. To take the Chinese storyline as an example, first and foremost, the need for modernization in China creates inequality between the geopolitical and symbolic North and South. This contrast is most well-articulated by the setup between investment and management teams originating from Beijing in agricultural and artistic Yunnan. Indeed, Beijing's exploitation of a faraway land shows how social morality deteriorates under the influence of quick and distasteful profit-making. Ren Fei's father-in-law exemplifies the indifference of the ruling business and political classes toward the underclasses in Chinese society, such as the coffee bean farmers. The intergenerational conflicts represented here pit a more brutal older generation against a more conscientious younger generation. The film also questions these power dynamics on the axis of the Global South and North. It designates China as where coffee beans are grown and Western Europe as where coffee is traded and consumed. These themes are some of the consequences of global mobilities that many other films have explored previously and successfully. The technique of discussing these issues using metaphors has also been extensively used in the past. In the China-Italy context, consider Gianni Amelio's *La stella che non c'è* (*The Missing Star*, 2006), in which a defective machine part becomes a metaphor for Italy's missed chances with globalization and China's disregard for globalization's negative influences on ordinary workers. The innovation of *Caffè* in this regard is to focus on food metaphors in probing other more complicated geopolitical and ethical questions.

Another innovative feature of *Caffè* is its choice of cities to stage the narrative's global-local events and the extremely hybrid business of the coffee trade. Pu'er, Trieste, and Antwerp are three notable border cities: Pu'er shares borders with Myanmar, Trieste with Slovenia, and Antwerp with the Netherlands. Border cities are characterized by multiethnic societies, and attentive viewers can also detect the subtle variation in regional accents within each film's national cast. From a meta-cinematic perspective, this mechanism meshes well with the film's ambition to become a border zone of sorts within the Italian film industry for international co-productions. Chinese and Italians both financed *Caffè* and collaborated on its screenplay. The film's webpage on imdb.com lists four writers: Bortone himself, Annalaura Ciervo, Minghua Shi, and Matthew Thompson. This working pattern manifests Bortone's Italian, American, and Chinese professional training or language competencies. He obtained his undergraduate degree in directing and film and television production at New York University. Upon return to Italy, Bortone founded the production company Orisa Produzioni, which has produced numerous feature, documentary, and short films since 1996. Setting the film in border cities helps strengthen Bortone's thesis about food mobilities and cultural hybridity, which the global circulation of coffee tellingly illustrates.

The world of *Caffè* values food-assisted cultural hybridization to which the Chinese contribute as qualified suppliers of minimally processed or unprocessed ingredients for Italian food companies. Lavazza also seemed to endorse this idea. But this is not always the case with Italian food firms that incorporate Chinese primary ingredients in their products. In 2017, the Italian rice company Riso Gallo (Rooster Rice) published an advertising campaign on the Internet and on television, in which the animated rooster takes on the role of "a station master, a Chinaman, a sportsman, a heartthrob as well as other characters," according to the official announcement of the campaign's creator, the Italian communications group Armando Testa.[38] In the animated commercial made for one of the brand's rice varieties, riso Venere (Venus rice), the rooster dons a conically shaped bamboo hat.[39] The hat, complementing the bird's yellow beak, is meant to signify a Chinese identity, indeed the "Chinaman" mentioned in the announcement. Similar to the design of Riso Gallo's brand logo, the rooster's appearance denotes Italianness: it has a green-colored body, a red comb, and a red wattle, while his name is always written in white. In the commercial, the rice rooster invites the viewer to taste an "exotic" grain, which is, however, "100% Italian." In Riso Gallo's 2020 commercial promoting both Venus rice and red rice, the same costumed rooster once again appears with a bamboo hat.[40] This time, accompanied by a stereotypically Chinese-sounding melody and a gong strike, he first imitates a Chinese accent, asking the audience whether they want to have "exotic rice," replacing the "r" with an "l." Then, throwing away the hat, the rice rooster switches to standard Italian, proclaiming that the two rice varieties are "100% Italian whole grains."

At first glance, the message directed at Italian consumers seems contradictory: if the Venus rice is completely Italian, how is it then exotic? The publicity ploy would seem to simultaneously legitimize the Italian soil upon which the rice is safely grown and the authentic Chinese DNA of this variety of rice. According to Riso Gallo's description, which I accessed in 2020, the Italian agricultural research center Sa.Pi.Se. gave birth to the Venus rice in 1997. We read from this description that currently the rice is cultivated predominantly in Vercelli and Novara in the Piedmont region.[41] However, the official narrative continued, the rice is an engineered hybrid of a variety of white rice from the Po River area in northern Italy and an Asian variety of black rice. While the specimen used by Sa.Pi.Se. was originally provided by the International Rice Research Institute based in the Philippines, the black rice was said to be revered by ancient Chinese emperors in this description.

However, in the updated 2022 description on the company's website, this narrative about hybridity was nowhere to be found. We only learn about "the original Italian aromatic black rice" through its "Made in Italy system of traceability" as it is "born, cultivated, worked, and packaged in Italy."[42] The name of Xue Ren Wang, the Chinese researcher who was instrumental in breeding the hybrid rice for Sa.Pi.Se., and whose contributions *Corriere della Sera* covered in the mid-2000s, was completely missing from any of Riso Gallo's publicity materials.[43] In such advertising, arguably the food staple most associated with China in the Western mind[44] became discursively domesticated as purely Italian.

The Venus rice advertising blatantly displays food chauvinism and protectionism that can be traced back to a fixation on *terroir*, the French term used to indicate the soil and the climate in which agricultural products and their derivative products are grown. To be sure, these discursive acts may be viewed as necessary moves to protect agricultural farms or as business ploys to increase product values in global markets.[45] More important, such enunciations reconfirm the necessity of narratively eliminating alimentary imports—ingredients included—into the Italian national diet to support a story about authenticity in Italian food. This issue of authenticity is also

Fighting "Yellow Mozzarella": Italians Safeguard Food's Authenticity   125

highly racialized in the advertisements. The Italian-identified rooster follows the yellowface tradition in donning a bamboo hat to indicate a relationship between black rice and China. Being ridiculed for his accent and antics, the "Chinaman" provides vulgar entertainment for the viewer. Relatedly, the name of the rice evokes the problematic colonial image of African women as "Black Venuses,"[46] implying that white Italians can taste exotic and sensual black beauty. These references to the "Black Venus" and the "Chinaman" show how public communications can become vehicles for legitimizing the offensive racialization of food items for the express purpose of asserting Italian alimentary authenticity and sovereignty.

■

Let us take stock of the Italian foods discussed in this chapter—rice, coffee, olive oil, and mozzarella—to consider the range of Italian expertise claimed in the cultural texts analyzed. These foods cover three of the four groups in the NOVA system for classifying processed foods, which is also adopted by the Food and Agriculture Organization of the United Nations. Within this system, rice can be unprocessed or minimally processed, coffee is minimally processed, olive oil is a processed culinary ingredient, and mozzarella is a processed food.[47] Processing is a generic term applied to any manipulation, ancient or modern, by hand or using machines, that renders the ingredients ready for consumption in some way. Mozzarella is processed using fermentation. Olive oil undergoes procedures such as pressing and filtering. Coffee requires washing and drying, which removes inedible parts, as well as roasting that enhances the sensory quality of the final product. Brown rice products are likely unprocessed, and white rice needs milling. Besides food processing, the primary ingredients of these foods—rice seeds, coffee beans, olives, and milk—also have their own specialized scientific and technological specificities. Italian expertise is claimed for both industrial and artisanal knowledge, as well as specialized manufacturing, for this processing of primary ingredients. Apart from its technological and knowledge-related dimensions, Italian food firms' expertise is understood to include entrepreneurship, company management, and branding.

In this chapter, I have examined several key entrepreneurship-focused films and product advertising from the 2000s and 2010s that reinforced a widespread perception of ethnic Chinese's presumed inability to make genuine Italian food and their propensity to influence Italian food enterprises through becoming laborers, investors, and ingredient suppliers. In attempting to preserve the Made in Italy cachet in such a diverse reality of business operations, Italian companies contrived narratives exalting the primacy of Italian food-related expertise in its many dimensions. Some of these cultural texts also promoted a heroic vision of certain Italian companies preserving their national identity in the face of an avalanche of investment by Chinese ethnic businesspeople in non-food-related Italian enterprises.

In reality, ethnic Chinese and Italian food firms have not interacted at the intense level depicted in the cultural production analyzed in this chapter. In fiction, including both fiction films and the fictional component of product advertising, such a hypothesis is entertained only to disavow its possibility. The Chinese element in relevant cultural texts efficiently helps Italian content makers sound a populist alarm that resonates with the Italian public: the authenticity of Italian food is being eroded, the Made in Italy cachet is under duress, and both are in need of safeguarding.

Overall, in Chapters 1–4 I have demonstrated how China-Italy food mobilities have amassed considerable cultural purchase in influencing Italian sociocultural identity-making. The next two chapters examine this dynamic by focusing on Chinese identity construction through Italian food cultures.

FIVE

Pizza Hut, Fine Dining, and Trattorie: Italian Gastronomy Tourism in China

On January 23, 2020, Wuhan—the first known place of the spread of the COVID-19 virus—began the first of a series of lockdowns. In February 2020, Pizza Hut China distributed a poster on the Internet in support of the city's fight against the coronavirus.[1] The center of the red poster shows a digitally rendered bowl of noodles divided into two equal parts: an Italian spaghetti dish on the left and a Wuhan specialty noodle dish on the right. Underneath this image, the poster claims: "Italian-style pasta with meat sauce cheers for Wuhan hot dry noodles." Pizza Hut China's poster drew inspiration from a series of images seen in a widely shared Sina Weibo post from January 31 that year, initially distributed by *People's Daily*, the Chinese Communist Party's official organ.[2] In it, nine regional dishes are said to "cheer for" (加油, *jiayou*, which literally means "to add fuel") Wuhan's signature noodles. Thanks to its political sensitivity to state-sponsored popular culture, this media campaign by Pizza Hut China—with its parent company being an American food business—was therefore timely in communicating a positive message during a major public health crisis.

What does the comparison between Italian pasta and Chinese noodles in the Pizza Hut China poster and wider Chinese popular culture say to middle-class Chinese? What key role has Italian-style food in China played in Chinese consumers' Western culinary tourism since the 1990s, a key period of "Chinese-style modernization"? During the 2000s and 2010s, when "authentic" Italian cuisine became more readily available in China, it provided middle-class consumers with more ingredients than ever before in Chinese history to recount, compare, and critique the country's "Italian" food with gusto and sophistication. Along the way, what sociocultural identities did Italian and Italian-inspired gastronomy tourism in China allow Chinese consumers to express? This chapter provides the first cultural-studies analysis of the Italian foodscape in China by considering these questions.

My main claim is that while the Pizza Hut culture influenced how China's rising middle class perceived hybrid Italian food starting in the 1990s, Italian migrants gradually helped cement the notion of "authentic" Italian cuisine during the 2000s. These two cultural patterns persist today in Chinese vernacular culinary culture concerning Italian food. These entrepreneurial and cultural efforts led to the prestigious reputation that Italian food enjoys among middle-class Chinese consumers today. The story of the wide recognition and commercial success of Italian and Italian-origin cuisines in China is a fundamental case study for understanding the formation of postsocialist China's heterogeneous culinary landscape. Comparable to Italians' dining experiences in Chinese migrants' restaurants that I have analyzed in Chapter 1, Chinese consumers' gastronomic tourism in Italian food has been an equally stimulating and diverse experience that they use to express cosmopolitanism.

A Tale of Two Culinary Repertoires

No reliable existing literature surveys the presence of Italian cuisine in China in the twentieth century, especially before the late 1980s. But some conclusions can be made by referring to sporadic evidence I have encountered in my research. French and British cuisines appeared in major Chinese cities soon after the first Opium War (1839–1842).[3] Italian food was served in some areas of the Republic of China (1912–1949). During the mid-1930s, a local newspaper in Tianjin mentioned an Italian chef who was working in the city's Italian concession at the Forum, an Italian-financed and managed sports and entertainment hub catering to both Chinese and foreign clientele.[4] As northern China's most significant industrial and financial center at the time, Tianjin had several foreign concessions, where the Qing government granted colonial powers full jurisdiction and extraterritoriality privileges. The city enjoyed a lively Western culinary scene serving the city's large foreign populations, as well as high-ranking Chinese officials and former aristocrats who retired there after leaving Beijing following the fall of the Qing dynasty.[5] From the founding of the People's Republic of China in 1949 through the 1970s, strict restrictions were placed on civil society's access to foreign imports. However, as a newsreel made by the Istituto Luce, Italy's national documentary company, proudly asserted in the late 1950s, Italian food such as spaghetti arrived in China via special trade arrangements.[6] While the newsreel does not mention who received these products in China, presumably they were used for educational displays or sent to select government officials. In much of the twentieth century, only an extremely limited number of foreign and Chinese elites had access to Italian cuisine on Chinese soil.

The first formal Italian restaurant was established in China in the late 1980s, approximately a decade after the 1978 Open Door Policy institutionalized by Deng Xiaoping, which opened Chinese markets to the West. Beijing's first Western fine dining restaurant after the end of the Cultural Revolution (1966–1976) was called Beijing Maxim's. Inaugurated in 1983, it became the first outlet of its French flagship location, Maxim's de Paris.[7] The Italians were the second to arrive on the fine dining scene in China. On April 25, 1988, the Milan-based El Toulà group (renamed Toulà Food and Dining Group in 2017) opened a restaurant in the newly completed Beijing International Hotel. The establishment primarily offered local cuisine in Treviso, a city in the Veneto region in northeastern Italy. Piero Pinto designed the art deco dining area. On the occasion of Toulà's opening, Italy's renowned food critic Massimo Alberini remarked on the difficulty of introducing the Chinese guests in the room to the *al dente* risotto with its slightly undercooked consistency. Alberini also specified the origin of the rice: the *vialone nano* variety grown in the Veneto.[8] Toulà is often considered Italy's first global fine dining franchise, and its name is attached to the master chef Arturo Filippini, who passed away in 2020 because of complications resulting from the COVID-19 virus.[9]

Both the placement of a high-end Italian restaurant within a luxury hotel and the association with a star chef have been replicated in more recent incarnations of Italian fine dining in China. The main difference between Toulà and the restaurants in the 2010s is their timing. The opening of Toulà had no resonance among ordinary Chinese, who were grappling with the inflation crisis in China in 1988–1989, following Deng's attempts to open commodity prices to the market.[10] In the 2010s, however, a significant number of upper-middle-class Chinese consumers were ready to enjoy the good life brought to them by Italian food entrepreneurs and chefs. Indeed, by that decade, Italian fine dining had secured its place as one of the handful of Euro-American culinary traditions to which Chinese consumers could properly assign national identities. Arguably the most popular Chinese website that hosts consumer reviews of restaurants, Dianping.com, or 大众点评网 (*Dazhong dianping wang*, literally, "public reviews net"), allows us to glimpse the 2010s widely shared understandings of "Western cuisines" (or 西餐 *xi can*), including Italian fine dining. Viewing Dianping.com's results for Shanghai, China's most international cuisine-conscious city, we notice that *xi can* is among the most prominently displayed categories of cuisine. In the second-tier categories, after we click on the "*xi can*" tab, we see an "Italian food" tab, together with "French food," "Spanish food," and "self-service Western food" tabs, among others. The last tab mentioned here does not specify a clear national origin.[11] It is reasonable to assume that this presentation highlights the most desirable Western cuisines by the visitors to the website and that the national cuisines identified refer to fine dining. If so, then Italian, French, and Spanish cuisines were the only three Western fine dining properly named and prominently displayed on Dianping.com in the late 2010s.

However, Italian fine dining is only part of the story of the forays that Italian restaurants have made into China by that decade. On Dianping.com, the "pizzas" tab appears adjacent to the "Italian food" tab. Why do these Italian-related food choices appear in a way that seems to suggest them as parallel categories? To be sure, the website intends to highlight both national cuisines and food items among the categories under the "*xi can*" tab, as the remaining tabs refer to "light salads" and "steaks." Therefore, there is no strict rule applied to the conceptual parallelism among the terms used.

More important for my cultural analysis, during the 2010s, the two labels corresponded to two broad categories of Italian-related eateries in China. While Italian restaurants that claimed to be genuine specialized in various traditional or modern Italian cooking, Italian-style restaurants such as Pizza Hut China often exclusively offered pizzas and pasta—not other types of Italian food—on their menus. The former category encompassed fine dining in restaurants operated by transnational Italian businesses and by star chefs, which most often offered modern Italian cuisine. In the case of Dianping.com, this category also included Italian restaurants managed by Italian migrants, by Chinese migrants who returned from Italy, or by Italians of Chinese heritage, some of which offered "rustic" or "family-style" food that is usually not considered fine dining in a strict sense. Typical examples of the latter category included chain restaurants that offered Italian American cuisine and Italian-inspired restaurants owned by people without an apparent social connection with Italy.[12] Indeed, pizza and pasta became two of the most widely recognizable and available non-Asian food in China thanks to Pizza Hut China, other American pizza franchises, and their Chinese imitations. A more comprehensive analysis of Italian foodscape in China, therefore, ought to consider both categories of "Italian" restaurants.

While both traditions of "Italian food" enabled culinary tourism by middle-class Chinese consumers, related food texts such as advertising and menus offered competing cultural narratives interpreting "Italian cuisine" in China. Two hegemonic Italian culinary repertoires have existed side by side in China since the 1990s, which middle-class consumers with considerable educational, economic, or cultural capital have used to appreciate Italian and Italian-style cuisines. In their narratives, some consumers deployed the Made in Italy food ethos, including the Slow Food discourse, which Italian food entrepreneurs enthusiastically promoted in the cultural domain between the 2000s and the 2010s. However, many more Chinese drew upon an American-influenced master narrative popularized by Pizza Hut China since the 1990s. This discourse stressed both pragmatic Italian food hybridity and conscious accommodation of Italian foodways to local Chinese palates. Particularly during the 2010s, these two main culinary repertoires provided cultural resources for middle-class Chinese to elaborate and make sense of their Italian culinary tourism. My interpretation draws from Ann Swidler's work on culture as a repertoire.[13] In more abstract terms, I inquire how a social actor draws cultural resources and tools from multiple repertoires, which they acquire and engage throughout their life, to orient their empirical actions and create meaningful narratives for themselves and others.

Furthermore, what have the two Italian culinary repertoires allowed the Chinese middle class to express about themselves against the backdrop of the rapidly evolving Chinese society since the 1990s? Italian culinary tourism was emblematic of what Lisa Rofel calls a "post-socialist technology of the self" through which the Chinese nation could begin to feel cosmopolitan.[14] To be sure, other Euro-American culinary tourism also offered opportunities for wealthy and accomplished Chinese consumers to articulate their food connoisseurship and a feeling of cosmopolitanism. French cuisine is a strong candidate in this regard. However, as this chapter shows, Pizza Hut and Italian fine dining restaurants have had unique features in their entrance into the Chinese market and even into the eating habits of ordinary middle-class Chinese, conjuring a complicated cultural picture of "Italian food." The story of French cuisine in China has not been so discursively complicated this way, nor has this gastronomy achieved such a widespread cultural understanding on Chinese soil. These circumstances made talking and writing about Italian culinary tourism a powerful cultural mechanism for a cosmopolitan, public self-presentation of middle-class Chinese people with significant economic or cultural capital. Indeed, the Chinese-Italian case here reflects what Claude Fischler writes with regard to incorporation in food consumption, "each act of incorporation implies not only a risk but also a chance and a hope—of becoming more what one is, or what one would like to be."[15]

Two disclaimers about my thesis should be mentioned here. First, my analysis mainly provides insights into diverse bodies of Italian food knowledge that Italian and American food entrepreneurs and chefs have made available to an elite group of middle-class gastronomy tourists living in Shanghai and Beijing. My analysis does not claim to represent the average middle-class Chinese citizen's experience with Italian(-style) food. My focus is also mainly on the cultural foodscape propagated by food entrepreneurs and not on the receiving end composed of consumers. Chapter 6 will analyze in more detail the reception of Chinese consumers of the various Italian food discourses.

What I provide in this chapter is a broad scan of the cultural field of resources about Italian cuisines made available to educated and wealthy Chinese consumers for their public cultural identity construction from the 1990s through the 2010s. Even within this carefully defined context, my chapter reveals a plurality of cultural experiences of identity formation thanks to the complex sociohistorical field of Italian and Italian-influenced food in China, which I reconstruct for the first time in critical literature. My analysis is premised on a discourse and textual analysis of a wide range of source materials, including product advertising, restaurant menus, customer reviews, previously published interviews with chefs, and an autobiography of a food entrepreneur. These cultural mediums have been some of the most popular forms of food writing worldwide, which communication food scholarship (Introduction) is particularly well-equipped to address.

Second, this chapter prioritizes digital primary texts from the 2000s and 2010s while relying on some print media for the period from the 1990s especially. This decision is made in line with larger trends in Chinese nationals' use of the Internet and mobile phones. Indeed, during the 2010s, when Chinese consumers' Italian culinary tourism truly took flight, their digital use also exponentially increased. In 2015, according to Internet World Statistics, a quarter of the world's Internet population was composed of Chinese speakers.[16] In 2014, 47 percent of Chinese people had Internet access (approximately 600 million users), as reported by the China Internet Network Information Center.[17] As the world's largest mobile market, in the mid-2010s, Chinese mobile Internet users accounted for 83 percent of Chinese Internet users.[18] Research on Chinese tourists in Italy shows that since the late 2000s, the Internet has been their primary tool for planning trips and making travel decisions.[19] Thus, for my analysis of food writings, we can safely assume that during the 2010s, most content was consumed on smartphones. For the 2010s, the digital domain is the premier place to source Chinese-language food-related texts for analysis.

More broadly, digital media also provides the latest site for communication food scholarship. By engaging the "digital production of amateur material media," such as food blogs, Isabelle de Solier's work predates more recent scholarship that explores food in relation to digital media.[20] Recent studies refer to food-related practices and representations in the digital sphere and the impact of digital technologies on the realm of food.[21] In an anthology that examines food-related interactions on social media, Alla Tovares and Cynthia Gordon identify a unifying theme of the volume's contributions: "Food serves as a fundamental resource for the process of meaning-making, ideological production, and identity construction; with their rich, multimodal, and collaborative environment, digital media provide an ideal site to enact and examine such processes."[22] Many works on (digital) media and food studies highlight multiple media technologies and their interactions with food studies. As Marshall McLuhan synthesizes the matter, the medium is the message.[23]

Indeed, the development of digital media and technologies in China and other parts of Asia reached a critical point during the 2010s, which has implications for media research and policy. Sun Sun Lim and Cheryll Ruth R. Soriano argue that scholarship ought to rethink the validity of existing analytical frames for digital media that originate from the Global North, as well as take into consideration "Asia's sophisticated intellectual heritage" and "the sociocultural practices of this dynamic region."[24] In the case of China, as Wenhong Chen and Stephen D. Reese observe, compared to situations in Western democracies, "digital media in China reflect many contradictions of the Chinese society: rapid diffusion but glaring digital divides, significant economic freedom but strict political control, new opportunities for civic engagement but with pervasive surveillance."[25]

To be sure, international food-related digital content can become a tool of civic or political engagement in China, as was the case with the previously mentioned Pizza Hut China advertising. However, in this chapter, I take the position that generally speaking, cultural digestion of foreign food has rarely been a top priority for digital surveillance by the state. In the

2010s, the Chinese digital culture surrounding Italian gastronomy tourism remained a space for articulating a *bon vivant* lifestyle perceived as befitting the aspirations and achievements of the wealthy Chinese bourgeoisie. I do not seek to show that these cultural symptoms necessarily reflected sociopolitical realities or people's real-world perceptions about Italian food from sociopolitical perspectives. This study is mainly concerned with the dimension of leisure during Chinese consumers' Italian culinary tourism on Chinese soil, as well as its implications in the narrators' public self-expression of their sociocultural identities.

Pizza Hut China's Italian-Style Cuisine

Between the end of the Cultural Revolution in the late 1970s and the early 1990s, market reforms in China were still not in full effect. Public dining options in China were thus limited. Hotel restaurants offering Chinese fine dining were typically reserved for foreigners and privileged Chinese. Formal restaurants were open to the public but were often only used for special occasions, such as family banquets. For ordinary people, dining services (called 食堂 *shitang*) were available at their workplaces throughout the day, and state-owned public eateries for small bites (called 小吃 *xiaochi*) were also widespread. However, in the late 1980s, the small private business sector (个体户 *getihu*) matured after a decade's experimentation following the Open Door Policy. The then inflation crisis demonstrated the need for the Chinese Central Government to allow private entrepreneurship. Consequently, the 1990s saw the flourishing of the small, private-owned restaurant sector as more people became used to the idea of eating out frequently.

During the 1990s, extensive economic restructuring, political attitudes more open to Western imports, and other changes in Chinese society helped nurture a new class of professionals, white-collar workers, and small business owners. They became the Communist country's first economic elites in the post-Mao period. As their spending power and their desire to distinguish themselves from other classes increased, they began seeking new culinary and social experiences. American fast-food franchises catered to this growing class, which for the most part consisted of young couples and their children. According to Yunxiang Yan, in 1990s China, the appearance and then popularity of American fast-food chains such as McDonald's not only reflected profound economic changes in the country but also helped redefine ordinary consumers' relationship with their social spaces.[26] For Yan, the first McDonald's restaurants in Beijing were social spaces that invited people to linger, a marked contrast with other eateries in the country that did not offer attractive eating environments or good service. Chinese consumers reportedly enjoyed the cleanliness, pleasurable ambiance, and friendly service in American fast-food places.

Against this backdrop, Pizza Hut entered the Chinese market and provided dining experiences similar to McDonald's with prices initially affordable only to wealthy Chinese. Pizza Hut's first Chinese location was opened in Beijing in 1990, closely following the first Chinese franchises of Kentucky Fried Chicken (KFC) in 1987 and McDonald's in 1990, which were also located in the capital city. The American press enthusiastically covered the September 10 opening of Pizza Hut China. The *Los Angeles Times* observed that 200 pizzas were served to "an invitation-only crowd of Chinese and foreigners before running out of dough."[27] "Most Chinese have never eaten pizza, and many do not like cheese, which is alien to the Chinese diet." But Henry Foo, then general manager of Beijing Pizza Corp., Ltd., which operated the outlet, said that "more guests turned up than expected." Jiang Tinzhi, the company's chairman, hoped to attract Chinese customers, as "pizzas have been accepted by other Asian communities." The *Baltimore Sun* referred to the political significance of Pizza Hut opening in Beijing after the 1989 Tiananmen Square crisis, quipping that it was opened "with so much diplomatic fanfare about stability, friendship, and progress that one would think a nuclear test ban treaty was being signed."[28] Drawing from Associated Press coverage, both newspapers mentioned how the 12-inch pizzas cost more than a week's pay for most Chinese workers, a fact that would prevent them from frequenting the place often or at all.[29] Indeed, according to the Chinese intellectual and calligrapher Hong Pimo's account written in Shanghai in 1997, compared to nearby and extremely crowded McDonald's and KFC locations, Pizza Hut appeared to be almost empty.[30] In his report, Hong attributes this phenomenon to Pizza Hut China's relatively high prices compared with similar American food chains.

Hong's account demonstrates the exploratory nature of his food adventure, thereby offering us a window into perceptions of Italian food offered at Pizza Hut China by a culinary tourist with elevated cultural capital at a time when the eateries were still relatively elitist. As Hong humorously relays, he dined there for the first time for two reasons. For one, his curiosity was whetted by rumors about the delicious taste of pizza. For another, his wife had recently done well in the stock market—which was reintroduced in China in 1990—and therefore wished to splurge, a fact that worked in his favor. In approaching Hong's account as a culinary tourist, we may consider the differentiation that Lucy Long makes in this regard: the food may turn out to be exotic, edible, and/or palatable.[31] According to this formulation, to borrow some examples from previous chapters, dogmeat was considered inedible and potentially dangerous. Italian food journalists and consumers perceived Chinese migrant cuisine as unfamiliar and exotic. Chinese imitations of Italian food were often viewed as unpalatable compared to the Italian originals.

Turning to Hong's account, he and his wife enjoyed the exotic flavors offered by the Pizza Hut pizza they ordered thanks to the combination of ingredients, which they perceived as far removed from the Chinese tradition. In Hong's words, this "impression of novelty" was created by the marriage of sausage, beef, and pork with onions, green peppers, mushrooms, and pineapple. As for the spaghetti with meat sauce that Hong and his wife also ate, both did not like the taste but considered their disappointment part of the culinary experience of tasting new food. Thus, the couple was particularly impressed by the exoticism that pizza offered, but not so much by the pasta dish. Both Hong's account and Dianping.com's "pizza" tab accentuate Chinese consumers' fascination with pizzas. The much less culturally influential and geographically distributed Domino's Pizza and Papa John's Pizza outlets in China further show this interest.

Though anecdotal—my research at the time of writing has yielded very few extended customers' accounts of Pizza Hut China during the 1990s and 2000s—Hong's essay confirms an important role played by Pizza Hut China during the 1990s. The American company helped cement the association of Italian or Italianate food with fashionable Western culinary tourism for middle-class Chinese with expendable economic or cultural capital. Even when compared to the culinary novelty offered by McDonald's and KFC in the same period, Pizza Hut China was still considered ranking higher and more elitist. Undoubtedly, a major reason can be attributed to the higher prices charged by Pizza Hut China among its American peers. Only consumers placed quite high within the class of professionals, white-collar workers, and small business owners could afford to eat there. Such culinary tourism thus expressed distinction in terms of higher economic capital in a mobile social system. Through this process, pasta and spaghetti were also viewed as more tasty and sophisticated foods than hamburgers and fried chicken.

After its initial decade, Pizza Hut China exercised influence over a significant portion of the middle-class Chinese consumer market during the 2000s, when its prices became increasingly affordable for consumers relative to their incomes. Culinary tourism also strengthened its status as a key leisure activity for the rising urban middle-class Chinese and ordinary Chinese with middle-class aspirations. In the early 2000s, the demarcation between Pizza Hut China as casual dining and McDonald's and KFC as fast food became solidified. Unlike its parent company in the United States, Pizza Hut China has always offered table service in a sit-down restaurant. It also has always fostered a comfortable dining ambience and welcomed families. Starting in the mid-2000s, with more "genuine" Italian fine dining appearing in major Chinese cities, Pizza Hut China lost its monopoly on interpreting "Italian" food for Chinese eaters. Particularly during the 2010s, the chain also lost considerable appeal to a wider customer base in China for reasons intrinsic to market fluctuations in the restaurant sector and because middle-class Chinese's gastronomy tourism became more multilayered overall. Nevertheless, in June 2020, on the occasion of Pizza Hut China's thirtieth anniversary, a statement from Yum China Holdings, Inc., which had exclusive rights in mainland China to Pizza Hut, claimed that the franchise was now the "leading casual dining restaurant brand in China" with "over 2,200 restaurants in more than 500 cities across the country."[32] The statement continues, Pizza Hut China "had more than 75 million digital members and digital orders accounted for over 60% of sales for the first half of 2020." By then, significant numbers of urban Chinese would have immediately recognized the apt connection between Wuhan noodles and Italian pasta depicted in the poster mentioned at the beginning of this chapter.[33]

Pizza Hut China's long history in influencing Chinese consumers' notion of Italian food means that its branding and advertising have also be multifaceted. According to an article published in *Global Brand Insight*, the leading Chinese magazine specialized in global advertising, Pizza Hut China helped the Chinese accept "pizza culture."[34] Written in collaboration with Yum China, the article details six phases of the company's branding from 1990 to 2018. From 1990 to 1998, the Chinese outlets replicated the ideal suburban American family lifestyle. The focus from 1998 through 2003 was to attract young professionals via the concept of, in the words of the company's promotional materials, "Western-style leisure meals and drinks." The period 2003–2010 initiated the so-called "Happiness Culture" campaign in China, which encompassed themes such as "happiness, leisure, comfort, fun, and classy taste" that were to remain the company's core branding identity ever since. The years between 2010 and 2015 deepened the "Happiness Culture" by strengthening the brand's customer service and culinary branding. From 2016 to 2018, the branding philosophy was articulated through promotions targeting a new generation of consumers and encouraging them to have a social experience of food with their friends and families. At the end of 2018, Pizza Hut China proposed to both further elevate the dining experience and stimulate culinary novelty. Sensitive to Chinese consumers' increasing penchant for Chinese flavors and their rising patriotism, beginning in 2018, Pizza Hut China began offering pizzas with Chinese toppings that evoked specific festivities or ceremonies, including a "state dinner pizza series." Similar to its Wuhan/Italian noodle poster, Pizza Hut China once again politicized its offerings by catering to what the article calls "the large backdrop of the reawakening of Chinese people's cultural self-confidence."

An interpretation of Pizza Hut China's advertising campaigns from the 1990s through the 2010s can be made with reference to Long's framework of culinary tourism. Long proposes five communication strategies when new foods are presented to customers: framing, naming (or translation), explication, menu selection, and recipe adaptation.[35] Framing designs a context for a food that renders it edible and exotic. Naming or translation identifies a food item in the consumer's language. Explication involves the description and explanation of ingredients, cooking methods, history, and other characteristics of a food. Menu selection consists of selecting specific dishes thought to best appeal to the consumer. Recipe adaptation refers to the manipulation of ingredients and preparation methods to accommodate consumers' foodways. We encountered examples of all of these negotiation strategies in Chapters 1 and 2, when both Chinese migrant food entrepreneurs and Italian food journalists presented Chinese-origin dishes to the wider Italian public. For example, the graphic novel *Chinamen* analyzed in Chapter 2 extensively uses the strategy of explication when promoting the legitimacy of the culinary profile and business operations of Milan's first formal Chinese restaurant.

According to Long's framework, which aspects of "Italian food" did Pizza Hut China convey to its Chinese consumers through its advertising? Naming was arguably the most widely adopted strategy. Given its specialty dishes and their novelty in China in the 1990s, Pizza Hut China was largely responsible for popularizing Chinese translations of pizza (比萨 *bisa*, a sound-based translation of "pizza") and pasta (意大利面 *Yidali mian*, or simply, 意面 *Yimian*, which literally means Italian noodles). Apart from popularizing the translations of the names of these and other dishes, the brand's Chinese name positioned itself at the forefront of Chinese consumers' exploration of non-Chinese food traditions. The roughly sound-based rendition, 必胜客 (*Bi sheng ke*), literally means a guest who is bound to win. One implication of this translation is that customers would gain a compelling victory over their peers by choosing to eat at Pizza Hut China. Moreover, the chain's menus were adapted to Chinese consumers' palates as well as their culinary curiosity. In the company's commercials and online menus posted to its Sina Weibo account during the 2010s, the "Pizza and More" slogan introduced eaters to a variety of food served in its restaurants, including pizzas with Chinese-inspired toppings, spaghetti and fried rice, steaks, deep-fried seafood, chicken wings with fries, and Western-style salads and desserts.[36] In this way, the company offered consumer-oriented product bundling, mixing Italian-style, Chinese, and American foods.

Explication and framing are strategies most suitable for discussing narratives about Italian food that Pizza Hut China has promoted among middle-class urban Chinese consumers throughout the decades. Despite the variety of food offered in its restaurants, pizza has remained the company's signature product. It was the only item on the menu that received a detailed explanation on the company's official Chinese website when I researched it in the early 2020s.[37] The text explains how the delicious taste of Pizza Hut China's pizzas is achieved through on-site baking, locally sourced fresh vegetables, choice ingredients, and a standardized cooking process to ensure uniform quality. Such explication points to a crucial framing in Pizza Hut China's advertising: it suggests a migration of the treasured Italian pasta and pizza from Italy to China, with the American brand acting as a much-appreciated intermediary.

This framing is tellingly illustrated by a 2006 Pizza Hut China commercial.[38] It begins with a scene set in an Italy of the past without signs of industrialization. A young mother feeds a teenage boy with such delicious home-made spaghetti that he spontaneously exclaims "Mamma mia" (here an expression of joy, such as "wow"). Next, the commercial introduces the brand's own spaghetti and rigatoni dishes, which the viewer does not see in the Italian segment. The advertisement ends with a scene set in a Pizza Hut China restaurant, where a Chinese man tastes a dish and cannot help but let out "Mamma mia." At this juncture, the Italian mother suddenly reappears onscreen and gives the customer a kiss on his forehead, in a gesture that recalls her kisses on her boy's cheeks in the Italian scene. This commercial conveys an endearing message about the nurturing Italian mother's culinary success with both her own Italian child and her adult Chinese customer. The happy ending is brought about by none other than the American company, which is represented by an insert placed in the middle of the commercial that presents the dishes.

This and other advertising campaigns supported a broader claim made by the *Global Brand Insight* article about the company's significance in shaping middle-class Chinese's Western food eating habits: "Beginning with Pizza Hut China, the Chinese attempted to use knives and forks, and to enjoy Western meals."[39] The emphasis on the use of knives and forks nudged McDonald's and KFC, which entered the Chinese market as proponents of Western food at the same time as Pizza Hut China did, for the absence of cutlery required for most of their signature foods such as hamburgers and chicken nuggets. To be sure, this statement exaggerated the influence of

Pizza Hut China among middle-class Chinese's rapport with Western cuisines. Consider how young generations of Chinese consumers encountering the restaurant chain during the 2010s could have more experience with Italian fine dining in China or with Italian cuisines consumed while traveling in Italy. The statement was truer for the generations living in the 1990s and 2000s. Nevertheless, the American mediation between Italian food and Chinese culinary tourism has taught an important lesson about food indigenization for middle-class Chinese consumers throughout the three decades.

To be sure, the indigenization of non-Chinese food is a strategic marketing ploy also adopted by other American-owned chain restaurants, such as McDonald's and KFC. But the persuasiveness of Pizza Hut China's story of food mobilities derives from a self-consciously transcultural and neoliberal frame involving three cultures. First, the promotional materials describe a movement from Italy to Italian America, insofar as the company's pizzas supposedly drew from a Neapolitan tradition but became famous in the United States. Further, the texts' emphasis on standardization—in this case, in pizza-making—reveals an important contribution for which American industries have been particularly globally known. Second, many items on Pizza Hut China's menus focus on Chinese renditions of Italian American pizzas, thereby consciously stressing various combinations of Italian, American, and Chinese ingredients as a signature of these pizzas. In this way, Pizza Hut China is proud of its double migration heritage and embraces food innovations in a highly transcultural manner befitting a neoliberal economy. It is a hallmark of the neoliberal gastronomy tourist to have the capacity to make their own culinary mix to satisfy their palates. Pizza Hut China's transcultural and neoliberal way of indigenizing Italian food has been a key cultural resource for middle-class Chinese culinary tourists to draw from when elaborating their encounters with Italian food in cultural accounts.

Transnational Italian Fine Dining

With their promotion of food indigenization and fusion, the ethos of Pizza Hut China stood in stark contrast to that of restaurants headed by European Italian chefs in China. High-end Italian dining, offering both modern and rustic Italian cuisines claiming to be authentic, became more widespread in major Chinese cities during the 2010s. The phenomenon can be divided into transnational Italian fine dining and migrant-managed Italian restaurants, which I address in this and the following sections. While the spread of Italian American pizza through Pizza Hut China did not overtly entail mobile humans as agents of culinary change, there would have been no Italian fine dining without migrant professionals from Italy. According to Ilaria Boncori, around the turn of the twenty-first century, Italian perceptions of China dramatically transitioned from a mainly cultural appreciation of the country's (ancient) traditions to a business-driven interest in visiting and working in China.[40] Boncori highlights the formulaic stories that Italian expatriates often provided in response to questions concerning their work and life experiences in China, including those regarding authenticity in food during Chinese consumers' Italian culinary tourism. What this authenticity actually consisted of on the ground and in cultural narratives drives my analysis here, which focuses on food knowledge created by white Italians.

In the 2010s, this knowledge originated from multiple centers and multiple sources. More than ten years after China entered the World Trade Organization in 2001, Chinese-language materials and events promoting Italian cuisines have become available in dizzyingly large numbers and varied formats. There were many lifestyle events promoting Italian cuisines and foods sponsored by the Italian Central Government, including Chinese editions of the "Settimana della Cucina Italiana nel Mondo" (Italian Cuisine Week in the World), which have taken place in various Chinese cities since 2016. Occasionally, the European Union also coordinated food-related programs. The 2019–2022 initiative "The European Art of Taste" highlighted "masterpieces of Italian fruits and vegetables" and toured in Asia. Individual Italian regions also frequently organized food fairs, tasting events, and special events in China. Italian wine and coffee firms often organized their own events.[41]

In 2010s China, cultural materials from which consumers might derive their knowledge about Made in Italy food culture were heterogeneous in nature. For example, brochures for specialized Italian culinary schools coexisted with online Italian language courses that focused on teaching food vocabulary and culture. Foodies could peruse cookbooks, many of which were translated from Italian and other non-Chinese (including, notably, Japanese) sources. Food and restaurant sections in travel guidebooks and online forums were readily accessible to the country's middle class. Documentary films about Italian cuisine and cooking techniques were available on popular video-sharing websites, including bilibili.com. Lifestyle magazines introduced Italian food and table etiquette. Food travel television journalism and reality shows were set in Italy. Specialized tourism websites and services focusing on destinations outside China allowed travelers to write food-related tips and recommendations for their online communities. Personal blogs presented the history and variety of Italian cuisine, some of which used American and Italian films as prompts to talk about regional Italian cuisines and dishes.[42]

While a thorough study of this vast literature is beyond the scope of the current section, we can nonetheless make some general observations about how this body of cultural texts may have influenced people's opinions by analyzing the main types of genuine Italian cuisine in China. Transnational Italian fine dining in China has had two noteworthy trends since the 2000s: hotel restaurants associated with transnational corporations and those opened by star chefs. Transnational Italian commercial groups and multinational corporations have invested in the restaurant business as an extension of their strategic deployment of the Made in Italy cachet in product advertising and sales. As an important example of this trend, the Niko Romito restaurants were housed in the Italian jewelry, fashion, and perfume company Bulgari's luxury hotels in Beijing (2017) and Shanghai (2018). The Beijing hotel's website describes the restaurant's menu as "optimally express[ing] the culture, elegance, and vitality of 'Made in Italy'."[43] As the menu indicates, Italian quality here refers to the chef's national origins; the cooking methods; such recognizable food as *tortellini*, *ravioli*, *lasagna*, and other pasta, said to be freshly made on-site; the presentation of the food and the service; and the furniture and interior decorations in the dining space, including the Murano (Venice) glass chandeliers.

In this menu, Italian identity is generally not demonstrated by the ingredients. The menu showcases premium ingredients, including Australian Wagyu sirloin steak, Canadian lobster, and Japanese bluefin tuna belly. Italian-made ingredients seem to be limited to imports such as olive oil, vinegar, cheese, risotto, pasta, herbs, and wines.[44] Given the appearance of Australian- and Canadian-origin foods, this selection does not reflect the restrictions of China's geography when sourcing meat and seafood from other parts of the world. Rather, the decision is tailored to foreign and Chinese consumers willing to pay high prices for non-Chinese meat, seafood, and occasionally vegetables, which are considered premium by contemporary international or Chinese standards. A complex global infrastructure has been operating behind this culinary cosmopolitanism in transporting perishable food whose integrity and legibility must be preserved.

Fittingly, the diverse geographical provenance of the ingredients on the menu reflected the global ambitions of the Bulgari-Marriott luxury brand. Before its Chinese hotels, Bulgari-Marriott had already established locations in Milan, London, Dubai, and Bali. Afterward, the company went on to open its Paris, Moscow, and Tokyo hotels. In the 2010s, similar ideas of elite transnational Italian fine dining were adopted by other high-end international hotel chains, including the Scena Italian Restaurant at the Ritz-Carlton and the Acqua Restaurant at Grand Kempinski Hotel in Shanghai. The Italian luxury car company Tonino Lamborghini's hotels in China also operated Italian fine dining restaurants.

Thus, the ethos of these restaurants was a far cry from the narrow geographical localism exhibited by the mozzarella makers analyzed in the previous chapter. The contrast points to the tension between transnational Italian corporations and small- and medium-sized enterprises regarding their Made in Italy reputations. The former tended to compromise on the provenance of ingredients and raw materials according to market demands and financial considerations while preserving Italian cooking expertise. In contrast, the latter insisted on the Italian origins of both the ingredients and the human, technological, and artistic expertise. There was thus a range of flexibility in emphasizing different dimensions of the Made in Italy cachet in relation to Italian food and cuisine. Food entrepreneurship intimately tied to Italian lands, climates, and workforce tended to be dogmatic in asserting and proving its Italian genuineness. In comparison, Italian food entrepreneurship, which was more liable to a neoliberal selection of authenticity in Italian food to present to their customers, remained more flexible about which aspects of the culinary trip—from the sourcing of primary ingredients through the cooking styles to the presentation of dishes and ambiences—to claim as authentic.

This point can be further appreciated by analyzing a previously published interview with a professional Italian chef who worked in a transnational Italian fine dining restaurant in China, Simonetta Garelli at Giovanni's located at Sheraton Shanghai Hongqiao Hotel (now Hongqiao Jin Jiang Hotel). The interview with Garelli from around 2010 is collected in Duccio Alabiso's useful volume of testimonies by Italians working in Shanghai, titled *Shanghai solo andata* (Shanghai One Way, 2011). Garelli distinguishes between her bona fide Italian cooking and her adaptation to what she considers to be local diners' eating habits and their concept of conviviality. As she opines, "Being an Italian cook abroad means maintaining one's integrity: the Bolognese sauce made here must be equal to that which found in Italy." (71)[45] As an analogy, Garelli mentions her dislike of how Chinese restaurants in Italy have changed cooking styles to suit local customers' palates. However, one must also "know the people that one relates to, and then try to adapt oneself to their style" (71). This ideology is a display of "humility" (71) in her approach to life, which has helped her succeed in China and elsewhere. What Garelli is proposing here is a dialectic between a purist approach to Italian culinary expertise, especially in cooking styles that particularly concern the profession of chefs and a pragmatic attitude toward customers' eating practices. She juxtaposes two ways of life along the axis of nation-states: the Italians ought to keep their food integrity by keeping their cooking techniques, and the Chinese may eat however they wish to.

Not surprisingly, Garelli's comments accentuate the Italian national identity of her cooking and herself to the exclusion of any contamination or hybridity, which so characterizes Pizza Hut's ethos in comparison. For one thing, her account clarifies that her contact with Chinese food, people, language, and culture was extremely limited. For example, she only visited Shanghai and moved around the metropolis by subway and taxi, even though she claimed to like traveling and viewed this job as an opportunity to do so. As she admits, she did not go to work in Shanghai because of her curiosity about China. Her narrative shows a rather stereotypical and outdated view of the country before her departure, which is reminiscent of grim Western accounts about the Cultural Revolution: "I did not know it [i.e., China] at all and it gave me the impression of being a grey country, composed of all similar persons, like toy soldiers." (67) Her website describes her Shanghai and subsequent Macau and Hong Kong experiences under the heading "The Silk Road: The East," and her Saudi Arabia period as "The Thousand and One Nights," thereby revealing an overtly and problematic Orientalist vision of these lands.[46] Garelli's high mobility through foreign countries throws into contrast her equally prominent static views and narratives about their cultures.

While it is complex to unpack the cultural origins of Garelli's conceptual stasis, we can nonetheless infer a crucial motivation by parsing her account. Bluntly stated, her career ambition was not to work in China, but to realize her dream of working for an American company—Starwood Hotels owned Sheraton. For Garelli, the work environment for a female chef was far more egalitarian in an American workplace than in an Italian one. Her claim argues that the professionalization of cooking in high-end Italian restaurants has been a predominantly male affair. Moreover, Garelli's narrative of Italianness, like many Italians abroad in China and elsewhere, basks in the cachet of Made in Italy and of Italy as a popular tourist destination. As she remarks, "The fact of being Italian is valorized abroad: the foreigners adore both Italian cuisine and Italy." (68) Thus, Garelli's self-reported performance of Italian identity in China in her account is intricately related to her professional affirmation, both as a woman and as an employee by the Americans.

It is instructive to consider Garelli's comments in relation to Simone Cinotto's insight on the rebranding of Italian food in the United States. For the critic, the elevated status of Italian cuisine in the United States and, by extension, that of Italian chefs, is the result of a popular series of cookbooks published there in the 1970s. These accounts shaped an extremely positive view of Italian food by distancing it from Italian American food and by responding to consumer desires for Italy.[47] By implicitly setting Italian fine dining apart from Pizza Hut China's Italian/American/Chinese food, and by reacting to the neoliberal era's thirst for a charming Italian lifestyle now sought after in China, Garelli's narrative exemplifies the Made in Italy food ethos in action. These conclusions likely have a broader resonance within this trend of Italian fine dining created and managed by the transnational Italian corporate world.

A second main trend of Italian fine dining in China has been transnational Italian star chefs who use their own names as branding. A paradigmatic example concerns Umberto Bombana and his group of restaurants with names that evoke cinema in general and Federico Fellini's films in specific.[48] Following a career in the United States, Japan, and South Korea, Bombana founded several restaurants named 8 ½ otto e mezzo BOMBANA in a reference to the title of a 1963 Fellini film.[49] He opened branches in Hong Kong (2010), Shanghai (2012), and Macau (2015). The Hong Kong outlet also became the first and, at the time of writing in the early 2020s, the only Michelin 3-star Italian restaurant outside of Italy. Using the word "opera," which in Italian can mean a masterpiece in any art, the chef opened Opera BOMBANA in Beijing in 2013. Finally, Bombana named two casual dining eateries in Hong Kong *Ciak*, which means clapperboard and which is also the name of a popular Italian film magazine: CIAK—In The Kitchen (2013) and CIAK—All Day Italian (2017). The branding of Bombana's restaurants, such as his distinctive cinematic references, was a marketing strategy similar to contemporary Western celebrity chefs and their television appearances. It was the Fellini connection that was presumably Bombana's signature culinary style, although the Fellinian imagination was mostly expressed through interior design in some locations. Nevertheless, compared to the Italian fine dining sponsored by transnational Italian companies, Bombana's restaurants aptly drew from an additional well-known Made in Italy cultural export: Italian cinema from the 1960s and 1970s. Its worldwide reputation was fashioned by masters including Fellini, Michelangelo Antonioni, Luchino Visconti, Lina Wertmüller, and others.

The consumer base for Bombana's higher-end Italian restaurants consisted of foreigners living in China and select upper-middle-class Chinese consumers. For analytical convenience, I will only examine reviews of Chinese culinary tourists of the Bombana Shanghai restaurant on Dianping.com to briefly consider the extent of the impact of the Made in Italy food ethos on such Chinese consumers in the late 2010s before the COVID-19 pandemic.[50] Many reviews compared the food served there to similar fine dining establishments in the metropolis. The reviewers' comparisons demonstrated their knowledge of the Hong Kong location of 8 ½ otto e mezzo BOMBANA, other reputable Italian and foreign restaurants in Shanghai, and

Italian food encountered in Italy. For some diners, the spaghetti cooked *al dente* was undercooked, even by Italian standards. For others, it was cooked to the perfect consistency as described in recipes. The risotto received similar comments. Some reviewers criticized guests at other tables for asking to eat the second course before the first course, thereby demonstrating their awareness of the typical Italian meal sequence from appetizers through the first and second courses to desserts. Others noted that some main dishes were excessively salty, and some lemon-based desserts were exceedingly sour, although the food quality was generally considered good. They believed that although such tastes—full-bodied saltiness and sourness—would contradict Chinese palates and sensibilities, they were "genuine" Italian flavors. But several reviewers also mentioned that they requested the salty dishes to be remade or taken away to varying degrees of success.

These Chinese diners' texts exhibited traits of foodie discourse on food's authenticity that Josée Johnston and Shyon Baumann summarize as geographic specificity, "simplicity," personal connection, history and tradition, and ethnic connection.[51] Deploying this "authenticity frame" in their restaurant reviews, Chinese customers helped both democratize knowledge of Italian fine dining and maintain a socialized hierarchy in taste during their Italian culinary tourism. Generally speaking, these reviews show that diners associated the Bombana Shanghai restaurant's truffle-based pasta and risotto, as well as tiramisu, with a distinctive Italian national identity. According to these online texts, wealthy and cosmopolitan Chinese consumers understood Italian haute cuisine by way of both specific ingredients (e.g., lemons and truffles)—although typically there was no discussion about the places of origin of these ingredients—and dishes long associated with Italy but beyond pizzas and pasta (e.g., tiramisu and risottos). Moreover, as the texts show, the diners learned to appreciate the Italian identity of pasta and risotto dishes by comparing staple Chinese noodles and rice dishes. Finally, this body of source materials also shows how these Chinese consumed Italian food and identity by drawing on both their past fine dining experiences in Shanghai and elsewhere and their knowledge of Italian cuisine gained during vacations there (more details in Chapter 6). During the 2010s, this culinary tourism was influenced by Italian food entrepreneurs and chefs' stress on genuine Italian cooking styles and tastes that resulted from the use of certain ingredients. In this process, while the Italian identity of ingredients was not always emphasized, the identity of chefs usually was. Even within the narrow sector of transnational Italian fine dining in China, the issue of authenticity in Italian food can be complicated.

Trattorie and Other Migrant-Managed Italian Restaurants

According to *Corriere della Sera*, in the mid-2000s, approximately fifteen Italian chefs were working in Shanghai in both luxury restaurants and more modest but still high-end establishments owned by Italian migrant entrepreneurs.[52] This section is concerned with the latter category of eateries owned by Italian food entrepreneurs who self-identify as migrants, unlike the chefs mentioned in the above section who would be hard-pressed to self-describe as labor migrants in Italy. Here we also need more substantial background information about Italian emigration to appreciate its iteration in China.

Contemporary Italian emigration and return migration have been widely covered in the Italian and international media.[53] Because of the news coverage, most informed readers associate this phenomenon with the so-called brain drain of college graduates and professionals, which often refers to European Italians. But naturalized Italian citizens of foreign ancestries, regardless of their educational and professional backgrounds, may also move to another country for permanent residence, often viewing Italian citizenship as a springboard for facilitating this process.[54] Against the backdrop of increasing neoliberalism that created unstable employment, a main driving force behind these migrations consisted of both the reality and the perception that there was a lack of adequate career prospects in Italy for young people.[55] Rigid hierarchy and unfair retribution within many professions were also often cited as reasons for leaving Italy. However, we should not disregard other factors for this migration, such as migrants' professional ambitions or their desire to explore other cultures.

The most comprehensive data collected on Italians residing abroad comes from reports issued by the AIRE (Anagrafe degli Italiani Residenti all'Estero, or Registry Office of Italians Residing Abroad) in collaboration with the

Fondazione Migrantes. The agency only tracks self-reporting by Italian citizens who relocate from their residence in Italy to other countries for a period longer than twelve months. This method makes the agency's statistics approximate, for the reports tend to underestimate the actual numbers of migrants, especially those who do not register with the AIRE and those whose temporary stays abroad are less than twelve months. The method is also not equipped to capture the high mobility of outcoming and incoming migrants. Despite these shortcomings, some useful conclusions can still be drawn.

According to the AIRE, in the late 2010s, Italian migrants' most popular destinations were other European countries, especially the United Kingdom, Germany, Switzerland, France, and Spain.[56] The United States, Brazil, and Argentina were secondary choices. To a lesser degree, Italians moved to Canada, Australia, Russia, South Africa, North Africa, and East Asia. In a country with a population of roughly 60 million throughout the 2010s, nearly five million Italians were officially registered as residing abroad in the late 2010s. The integrated European Union market facilitated and encouraged Italians' mobility for work and study opportunities. Immigration schemes in the United States, Canada, and Australia favored highly skilled workers and also attracted Italians.

Within this context, the scale of Italian migration to China was small, despite the country's status as the world's second largest economy. According to a 2014 AIRE study focused on Italians in China, the number increased from 1,989 in the 2000s to 6,746 in 2013, placing the country as the top destination in East Asia and one of the top twenty countries in the world for Italian expatriates.[57] This remains a miniscule figure among the more than four million Italians residing abroad captured in AIRE statistics that year. The report divides the Italian population in China into four geographic and consular areas: Hong Kong (37%); the Shanghai Municipality, Zhejiang, Jiangsu, and Anhui Provinces (34%); Guangdong, Guangxi, Fujian, and Hainan Provinces (13%); and Beijing and the remaining Chinese provinces (16%). Most Italians resided in China's economically prosperous cities and in areas along the coastline. Most of these Italians were between 25 and 54 years old (61%) and came from the northern regions of Italy.

According to information in this AIRE report, many Italians worked in trade, entrepreneurship, academia, restaurants, lifestyle businesses, the arts, and architecture.[58] The report found that Italian expatriates in China frequently struggled with complex local bureaucracies. They tended to lack a deep understanding of Chinese languages and cultures, which created difficulty in developing local and personal networks. Their job prospects were constrained by the Chinese market's demands for specific foreign expertise. Most often, Italian expatriates socialized with one another, with occasional ties to Chinese Italians. Most expatriates also had concerns about pollution and food safety in China.

My first example of Italian migrant-managed eatery concerns Da Marco, a historic establishment in Shanghai. The restaurant, which opened in 1999, was created by the Milanese chef Marco Barbieri, who first worked in an international hotel in the city in 1995 and then settled permanently in Shanghai after marrying a Chinese woman. With its main branch located at 103 East Zhu An Bang Road, the restaurant expanded into Da Marco Italian Restaurant Group, which owned two other locations in the city. The restaurant's website describes Da Marco as a trattoria, and indeed the dishes offered were hearty fare that did not resemble Romito, Garelli, or Bombana's modern Italian cooking.[59] What have been some of the core tenets in the identity construction of trattoria food in the evolving Italian foodscape in China? How can trattoria food be claimed to be even more "genuine" than Italian fine dining? How do Italian migrant food entrepreneurs and chefs narrate negotiations of culinary authenticity vis-à-vis their Chinese customers?

The basic features of the trattoria experience in China are recounted similar to what we already know about it on Italian soil, where trattorie and osterie (originally a bare-bones and cheap place for food and drinks) have saturated the foodscape of many cities for eaters seeking an authentic local culinary experience. In an interview with SHINE, a digital media outlet operated by *Shanghai Daily*, the city's largest English-language newspaper, Barbieri captures what he considers to be two most salient features of the best migrant-managed Italian eateries in Shanghai by highlighting trattoria-related qualities.[60] First, the establishment would be "a family style restaurant that makes you feel at home." Second, in catering to Chinese customers, many of whom had previous experience of traveling abroad and knew "the quality and taste of authentic Italian food," Da Marco stayed truthful to the Italian food ethos by not "adapting foreign cuisine to Chinese tastes." For Barbieri, a secret to his trattoria's longevity lies in not changing much of the menu since its establishment while "constantly improving our ingredients," although the details regarding ingredients are not elaborated. The result is what *Lonely Planet* calls a "homey spot" that has been around for two decades, "an eternity in Shanghai."[61]

Compared to fine dining analyzed in the previous section, the qualities of a trattoria that Barbieri mentions are squarely focused on the culinary experience itself, which is said to be genuinely Italian. Consider how, in authenticating Italian food offerings, transnational fine dining analyzed above call upon other Made in Italy industries to corroborate and mutually benefit in promoting Italian products and cultural ethos to the Chinese. These sectors range from Italian-designed and made luxury fashion, accessories, furniture, and cars, to highly recognizable Italian cultural production, such as films by influential Italian auteur cineastes. In China, transnational Italian fine dining has been a self-consciously strategic and concerted marketing move encompassing multiple Made in Italy sectors.[62] In comparison, the trattoria experience has been about more modest, individual migrants' led, family-size enterprises, which involve less stakes extrinsic to food itself. These migrant-managed trattorie may aspire to but lack the clout to effectively activate the country's other Made in Italy specializations to their advantage. Instead, trattorie owners evoke qualities more closely associated with Italian food traditions to brand themselves, such as the aura of classic Italian cuisine recalling a rural past.

Like Da Marco, Mercante in Beijing also adopted this Italian food rhetoric. "Trattoria" has been Mercante's business card in the capital city. According to Mercante's online introduction, in 2012, it was considered "unconventional to open a trattoria devoted to quality and authentic Italian flavors" in Beijing.[63] But over time, the narrative continues, the establishment became well-known among local and international diners. As the website proudly mentions, in 2018, Mercante was the only restaurant in the capital city that *Gambero Rosso* included in its "Top Italian Restaurants 2018" Guide with one red shrimp, a classification of honors by the Italian magazine. The publicity materials also mention the restaurant's inclusion in the "Hall of Fame" at Tripadvisor.com for five consecutive years of obtaining its Certificate of Excellence based on customer reviews.

In contrast to Da Marco's generic "Italian" food, Mercante's online introductory text consciously foregrounds the Emilia-Romagna regional cuisine in an extremely positive light to label its culinary specialty. In so doing, the text enhances the impression of *terroir* so prized in contemporary food discourse for its connotations of local benefits and traditions. Moreover, the original location of the trattoria strengthened the rhetorical force of its self-presentation as the guardian of this regional culinary tradition outside the territory. Mercante first opened in 2012 (and closed in 2022) in a *hutong* in Beijing. It is a type of traditional narrow alley that used to characterize large neighborhoods in the capital city, and which became trendy again among tourists in the 2010s after careless demolition that had occurred in previous decades. For many local people and in the broader Chinese cultural imagination, *hutong*s evoke intense nostalgia when the maze-like neighborhoods they created fostered closely-knit human relationships, which were thought to have diminished or even lost with the march of Chinese modernization. The preservation and valorization of *hutong*s would parallel those by Mercante for the Emilia-Romagna regional cuisine. The marriage between *hutong*s and the Emilia-Romagna cuisine in this publicity story would also be enhanced by the real-life romantic love between the two owners, Omar Maseroli from Italy and Yuan Yuan from China.[64] Mercante's land-based claims about its entrepreneurship heightened the aura of authenticity in food.

There were several other cultural mechanisms to authenticate Italian food, which Mercante's online promotion operationalized. The online introduction mentions how the restaurant offered "all handmade, home-style, traditional Emilia-Romagna food, focusing on high-quality imported Italian ingredients." Unlike Romito, Garelli, and Bombana, Mercante's marketing frequently referred to the use of Italian-imported ingredients to insist on its Italian identity. For example, the online introduction to Lievito, a gourmet pizzeria also operated by Mercante's owners beginning in 2017, lists the brands of its flour and olive oil as a way of communicating the authenticity of its ingredients.[65] However, like other Italian restaurants examined in this section, the Mercante presentations only mean transportable ingredients, not fresh produce, from Italy. But compared to Da Marco, Mercante's digital marketing claimed an even more extensive Italian authenticity, ranging from ingredients to recipes and cooking styles. Their kitchen motto—"Handmade, always. Shortcuts, never!"—further underscores the food's genuine quality. Common to all the examples I have examined so far, highlighting the chefs' Italian national identity was an essential guarantee of true Italian culinary experiences and cooking methods.

The last cultural technology of authentication of Italian food mentioned can be further elaborated by reference to Giovanni Messina's 2012 self-published memoir titled *Storia di un ristorante italiano in Cina* (Story of an Italian Restaurant in China). When setting up a small Italian restaurant in an unnamed city in China, Messina initially attempts to hire an Italian chef. He settles on a young Italian cook who, however, turns out to be utterly incompetent. The plot thus debunks the stereotype that any Italian person is a good cook. In desperation and by a stroke of luck, Messina finds a professional and hardworking chef, a French national. In Messina's kitchen, the Frenchman is the main cook and the Italian man is his assistant. In response to customers who repeatedly inquire about the Italian identity of the cook, Messina begins providing a formulaic answer: "We have two chefs. The one who takes care of the pizzeria is Italian. The other, who manages the various cooking [of other dishes], is French, but he is a great expert on Italian cuisine." (114)[66] Messina's remark seeks to both encourage and destabilize these customers' belief that in order to successfully achieve Italian culinary tourism, they must have an Italian national identity attached to every aspect of the restaurant, from its dishes to its chef and owner. What remains "Italian" in Messina's case are the recipes and the restaurant's branding, which prove insufficient for continued success. In explaining his decision to close the restaurant, Messina cites the Chinese consumers' reluctance to embrace the Italian lifestyle his food represents, as well as their wholehearted embrace of American fast food chains, including, unsurprisingly, Pizza Hut China.

How might issues of Italianness affect Chinese migrants returning from Italy and Chinese Italians, who were also among the entrepreneurs who began operating Italian restaurants in China in the 2010s? At the time of writing, evidence about this phenomenon, especially its conveyance in the media, was meager. While future research will provide a more complete picture of the dynamics in a fruitful area, I offer a possible interpretation here. I contend that these establishments tended to unsettle the restrictive view of food-related Italianness through some consideration of food or identity hybridity across Italy and China. I also use these examples to examine migrant-managed Italian restaurants not labeled as trattorie.

Consider Shanghai's deCanto Restaurant, which opened in 2013. The restaurant adopted the prevailing frame of aligning the chef's and the food's Italian national identity. Before its rebranding as Casanova Italian Dining & Lounge in 2016, deCanto featured Piedmontese regional cuisine prepared by a (female) Italian chef with imported ingredients. According to reviews on Dianping.com, the restaurant attracted wealthy locals through its minimalist, Italian-designed interiors.[67] Thus, deCanto's reputation seemed indistinguishable from other higher-end Italian restaurants in the city. However, the owner's Chinese-Italian background was also known by customers and the media as an added value to the restaurant's appeal. A positive review on *Time Out Shanghai*, the Shanghai edition of the global lifestyle, events, and tourism magazine, singles out the fact that the owner, Simone Zhang, was a "Wenzhou-born but Italy-raised restaurateur."[68] As Dianping.com's reviews tell us, some customers came to know and were impressed by the owner's Chinese-Italian identity and hospitality.[69]

As another example of Italian restaurants in China opened by Chinese nationals who spent substantial time in Italy, Primo1 in Shanghai, in operation in 2014 (no longer in business in the early 2020s), presented a more complicated story. According to media coverage, the restaurant's head chef, Jacky Xue (or Xue Zhejun), is a Chinese national who extensively studied culinary arts in Japan and Italy. The media profile nurtured by Primo1 and Xue himself highlighted his Italian-inspired fusion cuisine. *Gambero Rosso* quotes Xue as saying, "I make elegant food with a mix of superior Chinese products and excellent Italian specialties."[70] The online introduction to Primo1 by Italy's Accademia Italiana della Cucina (Italian Academy of Cuisine) praises it for being an "Italian restaurant with an innovative and fusion touch that is capable of bringing Italian cuisine close to Chinese tastes and culture."[71] A leading Chinese web portal, Sohu.com, enthusiastically covered Primo 1's mention in *Gambero Rosso*, lauding Xue's culinary expertise and entrepreneurship.[72] This article highlights Xue's use of Chinese-grown black truffles from Yunnan Province in his fusion dishes, thereby implicitly comparing it to the pervasive practice of using Italian truffles in China's Italian restaurants, and to cultural narratives of this practice as a crucial guarantee of Italianness.[73] As the endorsement of *Gambero Rosso* and the Accademia Italiana della Cucina indicates, by the 2010s, and in such a relatively late comer to Italian culinary tourism as China, some culinary experimentation had taken place, which paralleled the Milanese Italian-Chinese fusion food scene mentioned in Chapter 1. But this phenomenon remained minuscule compared to the hegemonic cultural adoption of the Made in Italy cachet by Italian migrant food entrepreneurs in China for publicity.

According to a news source, at the dawn of the COVID-19 pandemic, the names of 300 restaurants in Shanghai referenced Italy in some way. Fifty of these restaurants were "authentically Italian," by which the source probably meant they were owned by European Italians.[74] After China lifted its most stringent, initial pandemic lockdowns countrywide in early April 2020, many restaurants began reopening. We particularly understand the condition of migrant-managed fine dining in Shanghai thanks to media coverage.[75] Italian chefs and managers recounted the relatively brief period of government-enforced closures for approximately one or two months in January and February (depending on their districts in the metropolis), the slow reopening in March and April, and a roughly half-capacity operation in May, which satisfied physical distancing requirements. Many praised the quick response and strict measures taken by the district and local governments to combat the coronavirus; hardly anyone in the Italian media coverage I sample here—gleaned from *Corriere della Sera* and *Gambero Rosso*—complained about the regulations governing the reopening process. Nevertheless, revenue losses occurred because the number of international and domestic tourists in Shanghai declined sharply. Competition for food delivery and the demise of traditional buffet-style dining also contributed to a sense of unease about the future. Some restaurateurs and managers increased advertising targeting locals; many found it necessary to begin planning a long-term, post-COVID business strategy. At the time of writing in the early 2020s, while we do not yet fully know how Italian culinary tourism will change in China, 2020 was a watershed moment for food mobilities between Italy and China.

■

The Made in Italy cachet provided Italians working in China with a culinary repertoire to facilitate their narratives, which frequently marketed their national distinctiveness to their own advantage. As Mark I. Choate underscores, after the Second World War, "'Made in Italy' proved not just a powerful economic banner, but also the cornerstone of a non-Fascist Italian international identity."[76] Nowadays, this identity is associated with sleek design, high-quality fashion, healthy diet, well-preserved cultural patrimony, warm interpersonal relationships, and a relaxed approach to life. This is also the global identity of a desirable country, a leader in comfort, glamor, and style that the world is encouraged to admire and experience in person. During the 2000s and 2010s, Made in Italy represented the go-to culinary repertoire for Italian food entrepreneurs and chefs when describing and deriving meanings from their lives in China. The cultural mechanisms and technologies I have discussed illustrate the deployment of the repertoire's many cultural resources.

It bears repeating that for my analysis, Made in Italy only provides cultural solutions in narratives about Italian migrants' behaviors in China; it does not impact behaviors directly in the empirical world in an unmediated way. Studies find that many Italian migrants have adapted to local Chinese contexts to varying degrees or at least valued the opportunities for accommodation that the migration to China has offered them. According to Boncori, during the 2000s, Italian expatriates in China highly valued, in the order of importance, "flexibility, abandonment of their Western mentality, openness to different culture, desire to understand and integrate with the Chinese environment, loss of any feeling of Western superiority and arrogance, linguistic competence," and so on.[77]

Made in Italy food discourses distinguished "genuine" Italian food from Pizza Hut China's Italian/American/Chinese food and refined Chinese, French, and other European food, which all competed for middle-class Chinese consumers. Pizza Hut China's advertising, in particular, presented a formidable alternative to the Made in Italy food ethos, especially for most middle-class Chinese citizens, thanks to more accessible prices. Not only did Pizza Hut China champion a pragmatic approach to catering to Chinese palates and cultural sensibilities, but it also promoted a highly self-conscious and proud discourse about Italian-origin culinary hybridity. Since the 1990s, public communications about Pizza Hut China have nurtured a culinary repertoire that provided cultural solutions to appreciate Italian food hybridization and a highly customer-oriented, neoliberal business attitude. In so doing, Pizza Hut China showed Chinese culinary tourists that when interpreting "Italian" food, different (here, American) food and business cultures can be mobilized in discursive contention with the self-referential Made in Italy food culture. As my next chapter shows, Chinese culinary tourists in 2010s Italy learned this lesson about transcultural food mobilities well.

SIX

Slow and Fast, Sweet and Sour: Chinese Foodie Travelers in Italy

Between 2011 and 2012, the well-known Chinese food critic and writer 殳俏 Shu Qiao penned a series of essays about her culinary tourism in Italy published in a Chinese lifestyle magazine. She praised the Italian combination of savory and sweet ingredients in certain appetizers.[1] Comparisons between Italian *ravioli* and Chinese dumplings were made.[2] When participating in a Slow Food cooking class in the Italian south, Shu wondered whether the Italian appreciation for lemons had more to do with the fruit's wide availability there than with the slow lifestyle that the citrus purportedly embodied.[3] In these accounts, Shu described her culinary enjoyment, demonstrated fluency in appreciating specific dishes and foodways, and shared her interpretations of Italian gastronomy as a foodie traveler. She also linked these descriptions to her childhood memories and other culinary tourism, exhibiting a wide range of ways of food appreciation. Shu's case illustrates the emphasis that Josée Johnston and Shyon Baumann put on the role played by food in "narratives of self-identity" when discussing what unites foodies despite the differences in the "details and intensity of the foodie lifestyle."[4]

Shu's food journalism partook in the larger phenomenon of slower and faster modes of Chinese culinary tourism in popular tourist destinations in 2010s Italy. My chapter addresses this subject by examining Chinese knowledge and cultural negotiation with both Slow Food and Made in Italy food ethos and practices more generally. I ask two questions in this regard. Accustomed to a fast-paced lifestyle in China and lacking time to travel slowly in Italy, how did Chinese gastronomy tourists in Italy prepare their trips, experience various Italian culinary offerings, and view Slow Food? What dimensions of cosmopolitanism did the consumption of Italian food in Italy compel Chinese culinary tourists to articulate vis-à-vis their existing Italian culinary repertoires acquired in China?

In the 2010s, middle-class Chinese consumers' Italian food-assisted cosmopolitanism analyzed in Chapter 5 both conditioned and was enhanced by their culinary tourism in Italy. This cosmopolitanism has had an ambivalent relationship with Slow Food and with Italian gastronomy encountered in Italy more generally. In cultural narratives, sweet appreciation for a fulfilling and socially conscious lifestyle co-exists with skepticism soured by Slow Food's apparent resistance to speed, industrialization, and globalization. Consider how the Pizza Hut China-nurtured culinary repertoire emphasizes hybrid foods and has been deeply ingrained in the Chinese encounter with Italian cuisine. This repertoire runs against Slow Food-influenced Italian gastronationalism, a type of nationalism expressed through frequent, dogmatic interpretations of local food traditions that are often romanticized or invented. Not surprisingly, some Chinese foodie travelers perceived Slow Food as expressing food parochialism, which risked devolving into food fundamentalism. However, others have also enthusiastically adopted Slow Food to appreciate the specific Italian lifestyle promoted and to enhance Chinese culinary nationalism. Thus, during the 2010s, while Italian cuisine allowed Chinese culinary tourists to gain sophistication in taste, it also showed them the importance of exhibiting broad-mindedness about world cuisines. Indeed, as Johnston and Baumann write, foodie culture both champions "democratic openness to exploring new food cultures" and reinforces "exclusion, inequality, and exploitation in the gourmet foodscape."⁵ In this chapter, I view these processes as illustrating transculturation in China-Italy food mobilities (more in Introduction). I discuss the cultural assumptions underlying these narratives of delight and frustration that Chinese foodies said they experienced vis-à-vis Italian cuisine and its makers and promoters.

Chinese Tourism in Italy

An explanation of Chinese tourism in Italy is needed to better contextualize my analysis of Chinese culinary tourism there. According to Wolfgang Arlt, during the first wave of outbound Chinese tourism from 1983 to 1997, Chinese citizens went to other parts of Asia for family reunions, and Chinese delegations visited Western countries for business and diplomacy.[6] In 1997, China officially approved overseas leisure tourism. From 1997 to 2005, many more Chinese tourists traveled abroad. Some paid for packaged group tours to countries that were permitted by the Chinese government as part of its "Approved Destination Status" policy. In 2009, approved countries included many European countries and the United States. A steady increase in outbound tourists since 2005 made China the world's largest tourist-sending country in 2012. According to tourism literature, in 2001, there were 12 million Chinese tourists worldwide, a number which increased to 34 million in 2006 and to 41 million in 2007.[7] The World Tourism Organization (UNWTO), the United Nations agency responsible for tourism-related data collection, reports that the number of Chinese tourists in international destinations grew from 57.4 million in 2010 to 154.6 million at the dawn of the COVID-19 pandemic in 2019.[8]

Writing in the early 2010s, Magda Antonioli Corigliano claims that Europe attracted about 9 percent of international tourists from China. Among European countries, Italy was the fourth most common destination for Chinese tourists, behind Germany, France, and the United Kingdom.[9] According to Silvia Gravili and Pierfelice Rosato, Italy briefly became the most popular European destination for Chinese tourists during 2011–2012. In subsequent years, the country remained popular.[10] Indeed, Italy's respected daily *La Stampa* covered that in 2017, Italy was the most popular European destination country for arrivals and overnight stays of Chinese tourists.

The newspaper cited a report by the Ufficio Studi Enit, an entity within Italy's National Agency for Tourism, that there were 3 million arrivals and 5 million stays in Italy that year, with Milan, Rome, Florence, and Venice as the top destinations.[11]

For Antonioli Corigliano, during the 2000s–2010s, Chinese nationals' main reasons for visiting Italy were leisure, business, and connecting with friends and relatives.[12] In terms of leisure tourism from this period, which my chapter focuses on, Chinese tourists had four broad areas of interest in Italy: famous destinations associated with historical and cultural interest; nature; social customs, local life, and traditions; and leisure and sports.[13] Gravili and Rosato propose a typology of Chinese leisure tourists during the 2010s.[14] "Dry-foot fishermen" were tourists in their fifties and sixties who purchased organized packages from tour operators and visited several European countries on one trip. "Vase connoisseurs" typically had previous experience in Italy for study or work. Therefore, for their vacations in the country, they valued quality service and viewed their travel as a way of expressing China's soft power. "Long-tailed kites" were independent travelers particularly interested in thematic itineraries and luxury tourism. "Snowflakes on bamboo" were not overtly invested in visiting famous places; rather, they valued hospitality. "Freshwater crocodiles" refer to China's younger generations who embarked on a "Grand Tour" across Europe for shopping and fun and who deeply engaged with digital culture from travel planning to sharing travel tips. Indeed, as Han Shen, Ligang Peng, and Antonio Usai show, the predominant source of tourism information about Italy has been the Internet.[15] Recommendations from friends and family, advertising, news, entertainment, and social media also played a vital role in providing travel ideas and tips to leisure tourists.

"A Beautiful Relationship Between People and Food": Slow Food Journalism

三联生活周刊 (*Sanlian shenghuo zhoukan*)/*Sanlian Lifeweek* is a leading Chinese news, culture, and lifestyle magazine that dedicates considerable space to food appreciation. Writing in the early 2010s for this magazine in a sophisticated but personable language, the abovementioned food writer Shu examines the sourcing, preparation, and consumption of Italian food. These first-person essays, taken as a whole, cover elements of a typical Italian meal sequence, explain northern, central, and southern Italian food traditions, and pay special attention to summer and fall seasonal cuisines. Shu's textual culinary journey through various Italian regional cuisines provides a window into the agency of a cosmopolitan Chinese national vis-à-vis the Made in Italy food ethos. This is slow food journalism written by a professional meant for educated readers who are interested in broadening their knowledge of global lifestyles.

Based on her stay in Florence one September, Shu vividly conjures a breakfast scene when she had seasonal fruits with cured meats to express her appreciation for what she perceived as typical Italian flavors. Quickly overcoming her initial surprise at the pairing, Shu took a liking to the "classic combination" of the juice of a melon "flowing with gold-like honey" and thin, delicate slices of prosciutto rolled up "like a rose."[16] She was also eager to try similar combinations of ingredients that are often served as appetizers, including the specialty cured meats *finocchiona* and *soppressata* paired with fresh figs. When the figs were opened, their red flesh "would burn your eyes." Shu experienced immense tactile and visual pleasure. Much of the two descriptions is devoted to expressing the experience of seemingly contradictory tastes. Indeed, what Shu describes is a sensorial complexity that originates from pairing the salty with the sweet, the fatty with the fibrous, the dry with the juicy, and the spicy with the refreshing. Shu educates the Chinese reader about an eating custom that is far removed from their own. Her narrative intimates that as cured meats and fresh fruits interact to reveal their individual qualities, they are good companions that produce pleasure. Shu the journalist does this without explaining detailed information about the philosophical and historical reasons behind the combinations. Instead, by relaying her own sensorial delight, she invites readers to experience these combinations for themselves when in Italy. Through these depictions, Shu also conveys a basic Italian food practice: consuming seasonal fruits and *terroir*-specific food.

Shu discusses typical Italian first courses of pasta by referring to her Chinese reader's culinary traditions. An analogy is made between the wonton-dumpling relationship and that of *tortellini* and *ravioli*.[17] In her musings, the former (i.e., wontons and *tortellini*) display a feminine disposition, while the latter (i.e., dumpling and *ravioli*) exude a masculine appearance. The free association is based on their sizes and the varying degrees of thickness of their dough. Furthermore, Shu juxtaposes the shapes of Lanzhou hand-pulled noodles and those of pasta, taking delight in listing and discussing the many names for both.[18] In both comparisons, the author does not explain pasta's pairing with specific sauces or fillings in contemporary Italian meals, which would help determine the shapes used. Shu's strategic conveyance of Italian food culture points to her agenda to make an unfamiliar food item appetizing to the Chinese reader by drawing analogies from within their cultural milieu.

Despite the affinities that Shu believes exist between Italian pasta and Chinese dumplings, the author highlights a particular episode of struggle and resistance in her final essay, which is a lively account of a full meal that she helped prepare and then ate in Positano, on the Amalfi coast in southern Italy.[19] Unlike on other occasions when she only consumed Italian food, the culinary tourist participated in cooking the meal this time. Under the lemon trees at the instructor's house, while drinking homemade limoncello, members of Shu's cooking class made a risotto, a breaded and fried veal dish (unnamed but possibly a *cotoletta*, or veal cutlet), a cake, tiramisu, and fried donuts, all of which used lemon as a key ingredient. At the outset of the class, the instructor, a neighborhood housewife, announced that the first thing for participants to learn was "to slow down." Through simple ingredients and attention to the preparation and cooking processes, the class was taught to embody the ethos of Italy's Slow Food Movement.

However, Shu's take on slowness in her account can be skeptical, circumspect, and ironic, which gently countered Slow Food's cultural politics of resistance to modern speed and industrialization.[20] To be sure, Shu expresses appreciation for the careful selection of the most fragrant lemons from the cook's trees, an act praised as ecologically sustainable. However, Shu equally stresses the economic conditions that make this practice sensible; she notes that lemons are among the region's cheapest and most widely available fruits. While she says she took delight in slowly preparing and cooking the meal, she implies that part of the reason for the slowness was the cook's halting English instruction of her students. According to Shu, after a long day of preparing and cooking, just when she and others were beginning to enjoy the food, the instructor admonished the city dwellers: you are eating too fast. As Carlnita P. Greene observes, the art of dining in Slow Food should be viewed as a performance that helps mold the movement as a social style.[21] Eating is the final step of this social stylizing. At this point, Shu the journalist cannot help but quip about the instructor's gendered labor in preparing food for her class and presumably also for her family: "Learning to slow down is in fact very easy. It means going with Aunt Maria [i.e., the instructor] to pick lemons in her garden in the morning." As Shu's tone seems to imply, not all working women teach cooking to tourists for a living; some may not be able to slow down because of forces out of their control after a working day.

Shu views this cooking class and the Slow Food Movement it embodies as rituals of a somewhat dogmatic way of life, which, according to her, is but one plausible truth in a multicentered, globalized society that can entertain many culinary practices and philosophies. This contestation intensifies when the food critic refers to Chinese and other global culinary contexts to make sense of food that Italians use for similar purposes. As Shu explains, Italian figs and Middle Eastern or North African cactus flesh are seasonal fruits with cooling effects that pair well with cured meats.[22] In her experience, French cuisine displays a similar disposition toward combining contrasting ingredients to achieve complex tastes, implying that the Italians are not unique among Europeans in practicing this culinary custom.[23] While describing her experience eating the gelatin-based Italian cream panna cotta in 2010s Italy, Shu cherishes the memory of her generation's enjoyment of agar-based fruit jellies in early 1980s China. For her, both the panna cotta and gelatin snacks are easy-to-make summer desserts.[24] These insights into food comparisons align with Shu's culinary repertoire, inculcated by her adoption of Chinese, European, and Japanese cuisines in her diet as the offspring of a well-connected and highly educated family in Shanghai.[25]

Through making these comparisons, Shu illustrates similar traits of the "cosmopolitan mobilities of culinary tourism" by white and middle-class Euro-Americans that Jennie Germann Molz analyzes.[26]

As my analysis of Shu's 2010s essays indicates, in narratives about Chinese foodie travelers' culinary tourism in Italy, a mindless total assimilation of Italian culinary philosophy and foodways is rare. A Chinese indigenization of these food-related ideas and practices is stressed. As I have argued in Chapter 5, this process was championed by Pizza Hut China in the evolution of Chinese consumers' post-socialist encounters with Italian food starting in the 1990s. To be sure, unlike Pizza Hut China, Shu does not mention hybridized Italian food. Instead, her preferred discursive strategy concerns cross-cultural comparisons of food items and practices. Nonetheless, this strategy can be viewed as food writings that deploy differing cultural mobilities to unsettle the semantic circularity and stability within the Made in Italy food communications. Since the 1990s, Pizza Hut China culture has been the first and foremost cultural contender in China with the Made in Italy ethos on issues relating to "Italian" food creation, consumption, and business. From the perspective of cultural resistance, Shu's food journalism can be viewed as an heir to Pizza Hut China's public narratives. The quality of food at Pizza Hut China restaurants is not what Shu would endorse. But her outlook on Italian Slow Food uncannily meshes well with the American company's public identity. The Chinese edition of *Harper's Bazaar* magazine quotes Shu as viewing eating according to fixed criteria as a humorous and inopportune suggestion. Instead, "The most important thing is that people who adopt different ways of eating are all able to find their own joys."[27] In Shu's interpretation, then, the Italian cooking instructor in Positano did not read the room well enough to understand the joys that she brought to her students when they wasted no time devouring the food they prepared for long hours.

Shu's enjoyment of and resistance to Slow Food in Italy reflected the larger 2000s and 2010s cultural landscape of Italian food appreciation in China. In particular, her notion of Slow Food is symptomatic of how the movement initially founded by Carlo Petrini was only slowly gaining recognition in China during this period, even among the country's cultural elites. According to Nanxi Yan, the first Slow Food chapter in China was established in

2002 in Shanghai. Subsequently, Beijing, Macau, Hong Kong, and Yunnan built their own local chapters.[28] These chapters organized tasting and educational events that were not well-attended. Nevertheless, as examined in Yan's study, in Beijing in the mid-2010s, the attendees' acceptance level of Slow Food was high, and most of them were highly educated young people.[29] In 2015, Slow Food Great China was created as a national-level, officially registered association. It adheres to policies and guidelines from Slow Food International, the headquarters that are located in the Piedmontese town Bra.[30] In 2017, the Seventh International Slow Food Congress took place in Chengdu in central-western China. With slow growth, Slow Food in China has not yet acquired a sharply defined core identity either in line with or deviating from the original Italian ideal. In 2010s China, Slow Food's influence was mostly limited to food enthusiasts participating in local chapters and cultural workers on gastronomy topics.

However, one major case study shows how Chinese cultural elites and food enthusiasts incorporated elements of Slow Food into the creative process of a major food documentary serial widely viewed and appreciated in China. The first season of 舌尖上的中国 (*Shejian shang de Zhongguo*, literally, China on the tip of tongue)/*A Bite of China* (Xiaoqing Chen 2012) was aired at 10:30 p.m. during May 14–22, 2012, on CCTV 1, the main channel of the state-run television company. *A Bite of China* was wildly popular among Chinese viewers with high figures obtained from all the publicly available audience measurements. The series also garnered 9.6 out of 10 audience ratings on douban.com, China's foremost online database of films, books, music, and other mediums, which also functions as online community building and networking.[31] Individual businesses and specialty dishes examined in the series became instant successes following the airing, underscoring the power of food media in shaping the economic circumstances of food vendors in contemporary China.[32] Subsequently, *A Bite of China* enjoyed two other seasons in 2014 and 2018. The phenomenon was responsible for launching a new era in Chinese-produced high-quality food documentary films about various Chinese regional and local cuisines.

According to the serial's creative team, the technical dimension of the project involved several Chinese and Western sources of inspiration, including Chinese encyclopedias on culinary varieties in the country, on-location shooting of food ethnography according to the model first popularized by BBC (British Broadcasting Corporation), visual storytelling exemplified by the American magazine *National Geographic*, and the genre of Western food documentaries. In particular, Slow Food provided the main conceptual framework for this complex project.[33] Changzhen Ren, the executive head director of the series' first season, cited Petrini's book, *Buono, pulito e giusto. Principi di nuova gastronomia* (Good, Clean, and Just: Principles of New Gastronomy, 2005), as her major influence.[34] The English translation of Petrini's book appeared in 2007, and a Chinese translation based on this English edition was published in 2010.[35] According to Ren, Petrini's *Buono, pulito e giusto* helped her frame the series' seven 50-minute episodes. She explains that the first episode, "Nature's Gift," draws from Petrini's first principle in the book, which mentions "botany, which then concerns species, nature, and soil." Moreover, "Principle Number Eleven concerns arts, industry, human knowledge, and search for methods to treat, protect, and preserve food at a high cost. In fact, this [principle] gives birth to 'Secrets in the Kitchen' [i.e., the title of fifth episode]." But the most important idea from *Buono, pulito e giusto*, Ren continues, is reflected as "tastes preserved in memory" in *A Bite of China*: "Using a slower pace to eat food and to live life. Food here is the most original, clean, simple, and natural one."[36]

Ren did not, however, slavishly adhere to Petrini's principles when structuring and fleshing out details for the documentary project. While Slow Food does not highlight staple foods, Ren calls the second episode "Story of Staple Foods" because "the most fundamental goal of human food consumption is satiety."[37] Here, she invokes the frequently cited Chinese saying, 民以食为天 (*Min yi shi wei tian*), or "Food is the first necessity of the people." Thus, to be sure, the success of *A Bite of China* can be attributed to the series' appealing visuals in line with the current Western genre of food films and documentaries. The success is also related to its role in helping raise Chinese consumers' consciousness of preserving food traditions and appreciating naturally sourced quality foods, which Slow Food eloquently articulates and promotes. Nevertheless, the spirit of *A Bite of China* lies in, to borrow the words of a Chinese critic of the series, "industry, cult for nature, and search for harmony and balance," which Chinese viewers can viscerally relate to thanks to their own culinary cultural conditioning.[38] Most stories also highlight the intimate relations between food and family, another perennial connection made in cultural products about Chinese people. Moreover, referring to the massive numbers of Chinese eaters, some details contradict the slow pace and small-scale food production championed by Slow Food. A scene shows how many workers in a factory worked extremely rapidly to wrap rice-based fillings in bamboo leaves to make *zongzi*, a type of beloved Chinese rice dumplings. Another episode underscores the necessity for young cooks in a culinary school to quickly learn and master the most demanded current dishes served in local restaurants. These approaches to Chinese sensibilities and foodways are manifest in Shu's culinary tourism in Italy and are evident in the tales told by Chinese culinary tourists with less cultural capital than Shu in the next section's analysis. In appropriating Slow Food and other Western visual and journalistic input for telling Chinese culinary stories, *A Bite of China* becomes a transcultural product subtly transmitting Slow Food philosophy, which is adjusted for the Chinese audience's sensibilities for nature, family, and the sheer size of the country's population.

Transcultural Chinese-Italian Slow Food depictions in *A Bite of China* exhibit certain traits of gastronationalism. This may also explain why the creative team found Slow Food to be adaptable to their Chinese case. According to Michaela DeSourcey, gastronationalism "signals the use of food production, distribution, and consumption to demarcate and sustain the emotive power of national attachment, as well as the use of nationalist sentiments to produce and market food."[39] Slow Food, in DeSourcey's analysis, provides "institutional support and recognition for foods and food producers they consider 'authentic'," thereby potentially romanticizing a past enjoyed largely only by social elites while ignoring the "travails of peasants, farmers, and the poor."[40] Turning to *A Bite of China*, the financing and broadcast of the serial by CCTV 1 means that the project has received enormous institutional endorsement for showcasing "authentic" Chinese foods. The audiovisual power that the series wields stokes the viewers' national pride in achieving emotional resonance with the food stories told, according to news coverage that quotes interviewees.[41] Lanlan Kuang also asks us to consider the CCTV's political agenda behind the aestheticization of certain foods in the series.[42]

Targeting non-Chinese speaking viewers, *A Bite of China* was also translated into English, French, and Spanish.[43] This state media-backed decision helped the series to represent the highest level of quality food documentary made in China to international audiences. Indeed, the Chinese news media enthusiastically covered how non-Chinese audiences and Chinese migrants praised the serial, believing it represented a delightfully digestible and relatable experience for outsiders.[44] This global aspiration speaks to the ambition of the publicity machine behind the series to have middle-class Chinese viewers inscribed into the global foodie culture. Indeed, *A Bite of China* accentuates the laboriousness with which agricultural workers and ordinary cooks approach their foods, often bordering on romanticizing it vis-à-vis viewers presumed to be city dwellers out of touch with "authentic" foods. This practice in *A Bite of China* may be viewed as close in spirit to the roots of the Slow Food Movement with the Italian Communist Party, who hoped to increase economic opportunities for working-class food producers and restaurateurs in the 1970s against the backdrop of the advancement of globalized corporate food companies.[45] More broadly, the representational dichotomy between middle-class culinary tourists/viewers and "genuine" agricultural and food workers is a traditional trope in Western food documentaries. Gastronationalism in *A Bite of China* is a peculiar mix of nationalist, transcultural, cosmopolitan, and localist cultural and socioeconomic aspirations, all prompted by engaging Slow Food through the media.

Based on the foregoing analysis, I suggest that, through viewing *A Bite of China*, significant numbers of Chinese consumers have learned about the Italian Slow Food ethos in a largely unconscious and highly transcultural way. Granted, the mediated influence has not been directly relevant to Chinese consumers' sensibility for Italian cuisine, as the serial's purpose is to cultivate their appreciation for regional varieties of Chinese cuisines. Nevertheless, a vast number of Chinese food consumers have been provided with an opportunity to gain considerable competency in culinary appreciation overall. When this competency comes into interaction with their existing Italian culinary repertoires, the experience of Chinese culinary tourists in Italy would be conceivably enhanced. Future reception studies would be needed to test this hypothesis thoroughly.

What is more certain is Slow Food's major influence on shaping Chinese cultural elites' notions of Chinese and international cuisines. In 2013, Ren, the head director of *A Bite of China*, was also the filmmaker of a six-episode food documentary titled 悦食中国 (*Yueshi Zhongguo*, literally, Pleasant Eating in China)/*Yueshi China* (2013) about handmade Chinese food. The series producer was Shu, who, in 2012, began creating and organizing a food and culture initiative using the same name as the television program.[46] The associated food and lifestyle magazine, titled 悦食*Epicure*, maintains an active Sina Weibo account, displaying posts and photographs that explore the "beautiful relationship between people and food," befitting Shu's main message about her initiative. This expression is also the title of Shu's 2017 talk for 一席/YiXi, a Chinese platform for live general-audience lectures held on-site in select Chinese cities and broadcast online.[47] In this talk, Shu relays that the idea behind this expression originated from her experience in the early 2000s as a writer responsible for a newspaper's column on the history of medicine. Drawing from her university specialization in this subject, she treated topics such as bloodletting, cancers, abortion, and assisted dying from historical perspectives. Not long after, the director of the newspaper asked Shu to consider writing more about "happy" topics by integrating food into the history of medicine. Having acted upon the suggestion, Shu found her readers to be more interested in her food writings than in her writings about the history of medicine in this column. More important, she found herself drawn to her food writings for another newspaper as a respite from writing for the column on the history of medicine. She draws a lesson from this episode: "Probably food is really the thing that boosts people's morale."

Shu's story echoes what Janet Chrzan considers the "uber-principle of Slow Food": "the right to pleasure—a belief which reifies the consumer-rights motif."[48] But Chrzan's assessment of Slow Food is cautiously positive. This former member of Slow Food United States openly acknowledges her "ambivalent feelings about Slow Food."[49] For example, despite lauding the achievements of Slow Food in creating sustainable markets and taste education, among others, Chrzan believes "the first discontinuity is between the right to pleasure and the preservation of a sustainable system."[50] Likewise, Shu's stance on food and Italian culinary tourism evidences a "sweet and sour" attitude—an ambivalence—toward Slow Food. In Shu's account of the lemon-based cooking class, she critiques the aspect of Slow Food that borders on food-facilitated fundamentalism, pitting the good slow life against the bad fast life, which Slow Food's official Manifesto indeed promotes.[51] However, the unappetizing prospect of losing traditional Chinese foods and foodways would be powerful enough to deter Shu from embracing a total rejection of Slow Food. After all, the preservation and exaltation of such local food traditions are what Slow Food staunchly stands for and has become an effective rallying point in the international arena. In principle, a cosmopolitan Chinese foodie traveler and gastronomy worker like Shu would happily take sides with this food-related stance. In navigating this food-articulated complexity, Shu's remedy has been to create a "beautiful relationship between people and food" that is both sensitive to Chinese culture and open to Slow Food and other international culinary practices.

Fast Gastronomy Tourism, Digitally Enhanced

By the end of the 2010s, middle-class Chinese tourists in Italy had produced a sizeable body of travel tips, restaurant reviews, and personal blogs on tourism websites. Whereas Shu nurtured an ambivalent attitude toward Italian Slow Food practices marketed to foreign foodie travelers, the majority of tourism websites embraced the explicit agenda of catering to fast-paced travel plans, which would maximize the extent of Italian gastronomic appreciation. Shu's food journalism could be perused for the literary enjoyment of armchair travelers. Instead, tourism websites supplied prospective travelers with practical information. As opposed to Shu's advice couched in metaphorical language targeting higher-waged professionals and intellectuals, written and visual texts on popular tourism websites can be viewed as informal peer education provided to middle-class Chinese tourists with enough economic capital to travel to Italy for leisure tourism. During the 2010s, such peer-to-peer digital communications played a vital role in channeling ideas of Italian culinary tourism for prospective Chinese travelers. These digital materials also revealed much about the transcultural negotiation of Chinese foodies with their two Italian culinary repertoires.

Food was highlighted in major Chinese tourism websites as a key area of leisure activity abroad. As Han Shen, Ligang Peng, and Antonio Usai's empirical study relays, in the 2010s, outbound Chinese tourists mostly used, in descending order, WeChat, Ctrip.com, Qyer.com, Sina Weibo, and Tripadvisor.com to make travel decisions.[52] Because social media, including WeChat and Sina Weibo, does not present a product with a single master approach to promoting tourism in Italy, and because Tripadvisor.com is not designed by the Chinese, I focus on Ctrip.com and Qyer.com. To be sure, the mobile apps of both of these websites have additional features that are more user-friendly and resemble social media. According to the statistics regarding China's Internet access and use of mobile phones, which was cited in Chapter 5, conceivably more people used mobile apps than websites during the 2010s. For analytical convenience, however, I only examine the websites to provide an overview of how they present Italian culinary tourism.

This analysis allows me to identify key cultural characteristics of Chinese consumers' digital culinary tourism in interaction with their fast-paced culinary tourism through Italian eateries in person. I analyze how 2010s Chinese digital ecology helped lead Chinese culinary tourists away from core tenets of the Slow Food culture, such as respect for a slow rhythm of food appreciation and food's nutritional and historical backgrounds, and instead toward a culinarily hybridized, pragmatic, fast-paced business culture that Pizza Hut China first promoted in Chinese consumers' contacts with Italian-origin food. The current analysis shows that contemporary China's digitally armed culinary tourists in Italy were more inclined to deploy the Pizza Hut China–influenced culinary repertoire than the Slow Food culinary repertoire. This cultural practice was different from Shu's and Ren's analyzed in the previous section, for whom the point of reference of their ambivalent engagement remained Slow Food.

The main purpose of Ctrip.com was to help travelers book accommodations and tickets for public transportation, functions stressed on its home page. Tourism information, however, was a featured section on the home page at the time of my research in the late 2010s. The Italian National Tourist Board hosted a web page on Ctrip.com, which the search engine highlighted when searching for keywords related to Italy.[53] While this page was well-structured, presenting thematically driven highlights of major sights and travel diaries, it had no mention of culinary tourism. Ctrip.com's pages dedicated to major Italian cities, however, featured regional cuisines that did not always match the regions being introduced. For example, for Venice, the web page recommended both squid ink spaghetti and Margherita pizza, the latter of which is famously a Neapolitan specialty.[54] What ctrip.com occasionally lacked in accurate and elaborate informational web pages, it made up for with individual travel diaries. For example, the section of individual travelers' self-posted diaries on Milan allowed the visitor to filter by trip length (from 1 to 2 days to 15 days), months in which the trip would occur, types of travel companions (e.g., single travelers or couples), and tourist interests (e.g., shopping, photography, and culture), where culinary tourism was mentioned as the first type listed under this category.[55] These brief travel diaries or photo essays functioned similarly to social media, where travelers posted personal perspectives on their travel and tasting experiences.

In comparison, tourism information on Qyer.com, which was reputedly the premier website for Chinese overseas tourism, tended to be more thorough and precise. In the June 2020 edition of the website, gastronomy was a freestanding section included on the main menu on the home page dedicated to Italy.[56] Other sections of the main menu were as follows: popular destinations, practical information about the country, sights, travel services and assistance, travel strategies, itineraries, forums, maps, and reviews. On this platform, visitors could find restaurants by searching several categories, including national cuisine and types of eateries (e.g., trattoria, osterie, restaurants, etc.). Although the categories encompassed much more than Italian food (for example, the list of Chinese restaurants in Italy was comprehensive), "Italian specialty food" was featured.

Tips on Italian food on Qyer.com also took the form of country-specific guides. The website captured essential Italian table etiquette on a separate and detailed web page.[57] This guide uses a direct style with short and rapid sentences instructing tourists on how to quickly orient themselves in a new country and meet their nutritional needs. At times, the tone of this text can be cautionary but sincere. For example, the guide asks the visitor to be careful about buying bottled sparkling water because "the taste is very strange and normally Chinese people would not be able to accept it." The guidelines also admonish prospective travelers against speaking extremely loudly, which would invite unwanted attention and raise eyebrows. Both occurrences mentioned here are said to be common behavior of Chinese tourists, many of whom traveled on organized group tours in Europe. Even more detailed practical culinary suggestions are collected in a downloadable document titled "Taste of Italy," written by two Chinese students who studied in Italy.[58] This document was stored in a section of Qyer.com that hosted a significant number of downloadable guides on specialized topics sorted by country. At the time of writing, apart from Italy, only France and Barcelona, among all European countries and cities, had guides exclusively dedicated to their culinary scenes.[59]

Compared to such guides, reviews and tips left by fellow travelers likely received more attention from visitors to Qyer.com. This was a body of interactive practical knowledge constantly being updated and enriched. It can be viewed as an entry-level pedagogical tool for visitors to quickly grasp what each eatery offers. On Qyer.com, for one of the most reviewed and highly ranked restaurants in Florence, Trattoria Osteria dall'Oste, nearly all the visitors remarked on the *bistecca alla fiorentina* (Florentine-style steak), especially on how to be the savvy foodies who ordered the steak medium rare.[60] Eating alongside other Chinese and Korean tourists was often mentioned as an unavoidable side effect of publicity about the restaurant. Apart from reviews of individual restaurants, the website also hosted tips written by fellow travelers in mini-guides, travel notes, and forum articles about travel planning, all of which occasionally contained tips on food.[61] Such materials tended to be brief but lively accounts with photographs and personal perspectives on food quality and dining experiences. These posts gave prospective visitors almost real-time updates on individual restaurants' service and food. Through peer comparison, the posts also helped shape other culinary tourists' restaurant choices and their attitudes toward the dining experience.

Similarly, the emerging genre of Chinese reality television food shows added to the collective, community-based, and immersion-focused creation of knowledge about Italian cuisine by and for the Chinese public with the means to travel to Italy for culinary and leisure tourism. The genre is part of the digital ecology typical of contemporary Chinese life, where materials are delivered digitally and simultaneously on multiple platforms, but with the Internet functioning as the infrastructure. More broadly, this phenomenon is part of twenty-first-century, globally widespread "media convergence": "the merging of previously distinct media technologies and platforms through digitization and computer networking."[62] An important example is 2018XFun吃货俱乐部 (*Chihuo jülebu*, 2018XFun Foodie Club, Iqiyi, 2018), an eight-episode serial created and hosted by a leading Chinese entertainment company, 爱奇艺 (*Aiqiyi*)/iQIYI (2010-Present) at *Iqiyi.com*. The serial features television hosts and others traveling through Rome, Positano, Sorrento, Capri, and Naples on two-week trips sampling local gastronomical delicacies.[63] The show illustrates Isabelle de Solier's thesis about the foodie's production of food knowledge in leisure and through the media.[64] Following this line of inquiry, I take food knowledge to mean the show's foodie travelers' appreciation and negotiation with Italian food and foodways. I also discuss the conventions of reality television in shaping this knowledge. Overall, *2018XFun Foodie Club* provides an example of culinary tourism facilitated by deployment of diverse digital technologies in China's digital domain, which conditioned these tourists' identity performance.

The spirit of a food pilgrimage can be immediately felt through the show's coverage of several types of eateries that Italy offered to culinary tourists in the late 2010s. The protagonists dined at sit-down and higher-end restaurants and appreciated expensive dishes made with ingredients such as lobster, beef, veal, and truffles. Meanwhile, they visited osterie that served large portions of roast meats at affordable prices. Street foods, including panini (sandwiches), *supplì* (Roman-style fried rice balls), and lemon shaved ice are also featured in the program as an integral part of the wealthy traveler's culinary tourism, which drew on the philosophy of "staying like a local." This broad spectrum of eateries speaks to the show's desire to match mainstream Western understandings of Italian foodscapes conveyed in popular culture. As Greene and Janet M. Cramer remark, "We use food as a means of identifying with others," which is one way for us to view food as communication.[65] Italian food is one of the few world cuisines that can be easily understood by the public as signaling good taste and social distinction. As the program intimates, by consuming Italian cuisines and lifestyle, middle-class Chinese have also become part of the worldwide middle class.

Showing the process from the foodie travelers' research on specific restaurants and specialty dishes to their remarks on the dining experience,

2018XFun Foodie Club also demonstrates the steps of preparation, consumption, and reflection during culinary tourism. The hosts went to places they had researched beforehand and often claimed were recommended by the online community. During the first meal in the first episode, which was set in Rome, the hosts did not exhibit any awareness of the typical Italian meal sequence, eating both pasta and meat dishes simultaneously. They also shared dishes, a common practice in China. They quickly identified the ingredient that they liked, namely, truffles, which they associated with Italy and this particular Roman restaurant. Although the conventions of reality television require the hosts to perform in front of the camera, we may still appreciate their subjective and comparative judgments of specific Italian dishes. At strategic moments, the voice-over identifies ingredients and other specialty items (such as varieties of coffee) in more detail, enhancing the show's dual pedagogical and entertainment agendas. The technique also simulates what an actual diner may do upon encountering unfamiliar dishes: a quick search on their cell phone. The culinary knowledge viewers of *2018XFun Foodie Club* received was oriented toward practices, be they a better discernment of authentic food or a greater enjoyment of specialty dishes. The brief detour into Italian foodways was not meant to be an in-depth philosophical, intellectual, technical, ethical, or poetic analysis.

Further, we can analyze food tourism in *2018XFun Foodie Club* by considering how the show encouraged viewers to treat Italian culinary tourism as a quasi-carnivalesque moment for eating an abundant amount of rich food. Conceivably, in these travelers' middle-class lives in China, they would dedicate a significant amount of time to personal care and their bodies, including a careful diet. Ironically, however, the intense eating shown in the show was scheduled in order to include all the eateries that its hosts thought were noteworthy. To understand this dynamic, one may find it useful to recall that time was of the essence for Chinese foodie travelers in the 2010s. They must maximize the limited vacation time available to them, which was typically one or two weeks during extended national holidays, such as the October 1 National Day and Chinese New Year. This is a plausible explanation, although it cannot be applied to the condition of any middle-class Chinese foodie travelers without qualification, given the heterogeneity internal to this category of leisure tourists.

2018XFun Foodie Club also provides cautionary information about Italian food and the country itself that were relevant to prospective Chinese tourists' dietary needs. To start, Italian seafood dishes are said to have portions too small to satiate a typical Chinese traveler. This and similar remarks about eating to satiate hunger recur across the food texts I analyze in this section.[66] This enunciation reveals that occasionally Chinese food tourists did not embody, or did not wish to adopt, in Pierre Bourdieu's words, "a habitus of order, restraint, and propriety," which was typical of the middle class in the critic's modeling of French society in the 1960s.[67] While this travel tip is not specific to the tourists' exploration of the Italian diet, it stands in peculiar contrast to other narratives about cosmopolitan consumers with a wide generalist knowledge of various national cuisines, who clearly treated eating not as a primal desire to satisfy hunger, but as an art.[68] Moreover, the show's hosts prepared a Chinese dinner every few days, positing the occasion as a necessary break from Italian food. While the foodie travelers' Italian food pilgrimage was important in maximizing their overall enjoyment of the trips, their culinary home remained in China. Finally, the program provides ample examples of Italian criminality, unreliability, dishonesty, and racism, which Chinese tourists are said to likely encounter on their quest to taste delicious food. Indeed, Italy is to "be loved and hated at the same time," as the show's concluding remarks proclaim.

The Italian Recipe, or "Roman Holiday in Chinese Sauce"

Following Cristiano Bortone's film *Caffè* analyzed in Chapter 4, in 2022, the second Chinese-Italian film co-production, also with German contributions, was premiered at the Far East Film Festival held in Udine in northeastern Italy and was subsequently released in theaters in China. Directed by Zuxin Hou and written by Hou, Alberto Simone, and Bortone, the film was already in development in 2016. The filming began in Rome in early 2020 when COVID-19 was not yet widespread in Italy. Its Chinese title, 遇见你之后 (*Yujian ni zhi hou*), literally "After I meet you," is silent on any food connection. However, the film's Italian title directly recalls Italian food: *La ricetta italiana* (The Italian Recipe). Thus, like *Caffè*, *La ricetta italiana* capitalizes on the Chinese and Italian appreciation for Italian cuisine and culinary ingredients as a springboard to fictionalizing China-Italy friendship. The narrative is also premised on Chinese leisure tourism in Italy. *La ricetta italiana* tells the story of a Chinese pop star, Peng (Xun Liu), who travels to Rome to work on a reality show about lifestyle and romance. There, he meets a Chinese migrant woman named Mandy (Yao Huang) by chance. They fall in love after overcoming a misunderstanding. Through this brief romantic encounter, each affirms their determination to realize their career dreams. Peng will quit his job as a pop star to focus on writing independent music. Mandy will abandon her plans to take the national law examination and become a chef in an Italian restaurant. The two protagonists' personal growth takes place against the backdrop of Rome's beguiling monuments. Alluring depictions of Italian and Chinese food enhance the making of their romance.

Similar to *Caffè*, the conceptualization of China-Italy dynamics in *La ricetta italiana* is triangulated through another culture—here, American popular culture about Italy. By working on this second Chinese-Italian film co-production, Bortone expressed a strong desire to create "a remake of *Roman Holiday* with food as an additional element." As he continued in the same interview by referring to Made in Italy, *La ricetta italiana* would be a film that "manages to transport ideas and culture, and it is a very important mechanism for exporting our know-how."[69] Quoting Bortone, Italy's largest news agency, ANSA, called the Italian film a "*Roman Holiday* in Chinese sauce."[70] The invocation of the 1953 American film directed by William Wyler implies that Bortone and some mainstream media would be inclined to view the 2000s–2010s Chinese leisure tourism as equal in importance to 1950s American leisure tourism in Italy. Through this lens, Italy became a conduit for articulating the two nations' wealth and their citizens' search for an elegant, simple, and cultured lifestyle. In both cases, leisure tourism was intimately connected with the film industry and the commercial trade between Italy and the United States or China. During the 1950s, the American film industry heavily invested in Italy for the first time. In the 2000s, Italy and China signed the first treaty for film co-productions, which took effect in the following decade. In the 1950s, Americans were the most powerful customer base for Made in Italy exports and shaped the country's ready-to-wear sector. During the 2000s–2010s, the Chinese middle class became avid consumers of Made in Italy products, with stores of high-end Italian fashion on Chinese streets as a visible sign.

How does *La ricetta italiana* emulate the American classic about Italy? What role does Italy play in the narrative that negotiates certain aspects of China–United States dynamics as currently rivaling world powers? How do cinematic depictions of food, particularly those about Italian food, articulate these geopolitical complexities or fantasies? How does the film address Chinese tourists and migrants' relationship with Italian and Chinese cuisines made in Italy? Considering these questions helps me deepen the subject of the current chapter and rehearse important conclusions from this book's previous chapters.

The main dramatic tension in *La ricetta italiana* emulates that in *Roman Holiday*, although the gender roles of the protagonists are reversed. While news reporter Joe (Gregory Peck) introduces visiting European crown princess Ann (Audrey Hepburn) to Rome, Mandy is Peng's guide. Mandy has been living in Rome since when she was twelve years old. She knows how to handle Italian customs and culture rather well as a non-white person in the country. Though a newbie to Rome's sights, Peng is a veteran in performing the conventions expected of a contemporary Chinese pop star, including maintaining a pervasive social media presence in connecting with followers and fans. Despite the gender reversals, *La ricetta italiana* compares its male and female leads, respectively, with their counterparts in *Roman Holiday*. Both Peng and Joe juggle work and love. Joe is unable to bring his initial scheme to interview and cover Ann to an end because of their budding love. At the end of the movie, he meets Ann on a formal occasion in front of the press without revealing their story together. In parallel, Peng could have used his night spent with Mandy to better sell the reality show he is filming and sustain the online fandom's interest in him. But he renounces this opportunity and indeed his career as a pop star because of his love for her and the self-awareness that grows with it. *La ricetta italiana* also reinvents Mandy's story by referring to Ann's destiny. Initially, Ann is unsure about her royal duty. She accepts it after spending time in Rome with Joe. She refrains from revealing their relationship to the press, just as Joe does. Ann and Joe's story ends in disappointment and separation. In contrast, Mandy gives up the opportunity to take the national law examination to participate in an important culinary contest happening on the same day. Mandy is successful in the contest and eventually becomes the chef of a new Italian restaurant in Beijing. In the Chinese capital, she goes to meet Peng at a music bar where he is performing to rekindle their love born in the Italian capital. By now, the former pop star has been making his own music and exhibiting it on social media for some time. They embrace passionately. *La ricetta italiana* conjures a happy ending, highlighting sentimental fulfillment.

These examples of emulation through characterization and plots illustrate how highly conscious the Chinese-directed movie is in recreating the American classic by adapting to Chinese cultural sensibilities and proposing Chinese heroes and antiheroes. This cinematic transaction is not surprising when considering 2010s Chinese cinematic culture. To refer to the most glaring example, the top-grossing film 战狼2 (*Zhanlang 2*, or Wolf Warrior 2, Wu Jing, 2017) is, in Stephen Teo's words, "considered a crucial model for Chinese cinema's integration of its own form of heroic genre cinema with the more established conventions of Hollywood cinema."[71] Influential Chinese films imagined and narrated such a rivalry with powerful American cinematic precedents. Beginning in the 2000s, cinema played a key role in culturally channeling China's symbolic competition with the United States. Such a cinematically facilitated competition may involve the mediation of a third geopolitical region. In *Zhanlang 2*, it is Africa that provides such a terrain on which to provide alternative narrative solutions to conventional Hollywood endings. Italy as the consumerist and lifestyle paradise par excellence is exploited in *La ricetta italiana* to emulate *Roman Holiday*. Following the steps of past Grand Tour writings, to which *Roman Holiday* is an heir, *La ricetta italiana* also perceives Italy as a prime location for foreign travelers' self-discovery and self-growth. Indeed, in this regard, *La ricetta italiana* recalls more recent American romantic films in the tradition of *Roman Holiday*, which, however, feature food, including *Under the Tuscan Sun* (Audrey Wells, 2003) and *Eat Pray Love* (Ryan Murphy, 2010).

Consider the role played by Rome in *Roman Holiday* and *La ricetta italiana*. While both films share similar representational aesthetics in depicting Rome, the latter further elevates Italy's status as a destination for a desirable lifestyle and self-exploration of identities. Rome is the setting in which the two couples, none of whom are Italians by birth, fall in love. This premise posits Italy as having the potential to give birth to romantic love for foreign visitors, be they temporary tourists or long-term migrants. Many postcards and dolly shots showcase easily recognizable urban sights and monuments in the Italian capital, with specific lighting and camera angles that conjure a romantic feeling. *Roman Holiday* follows the itinerary of a typical Grand Tourist, covering all the significant sights in Rome. *La ricetta italiana* does similar things but on a smaller scale, as it reserves significant narrative space for non-touristy sights in which to advance its main plot.

The Mouth of Truth is the set for an important scene in *Roman Holiday*, where the two protagonists test each other's honesty about their identities and budding love interest for the first time in the narrative. *La ricetta italiana* stages a similarly revealing scene about Peng and Mandy in an auditorium in Rome's famed music conservatory, Santa Cecilia, at night. The scene in *Roman Holiday* is the conclusion of Joe and Ann's tour through Roman sights together, whereas the scene from *La ricetta italiana* leads to shots of Mandy and Peng's time spent together as romantic lovers walking the streets of Rome. Indeed, the two memorable scenes occur at similar points of the films' duration—approximately 73 percent, signaling their importance in driving the narratives to their climaxes. However, the two scenes differ significantly in their narrative agendas. The Mouth of Truth scene does not advance the identity-making process in the larger scheme of the film's narrative. Instead, it is a lighthearted and cleverly staged episode that enhances the viewer's enjoyment of a romantic comedy. In contrast, in the auditorium scene, Peng's musical composition and Mandy's cooking are compared both cinematically and narratively to underscore their mutual recognition and emotional resonance with one another.

Indeed, Italian music and food have a much more prominent presence in *La ricetta italiana* than in *Roman Holiday*. In both films, apart from functioning as the setting for romantic love, Rome is the window through which to exhibit Made in Italy products. Italian men's fashion, women's hairstyles, gelati ice creams, and scooters (i.e., Vespa) are showcased in *Roman Holiday*. In *La ricetta italiana*, apart from scooters, luxury fashion, pianos, and drinks (i.e., Aperol spritz, a popular Italian aperitif), the most cherished product is

Italian food. The food narratives involving Mandy are multilayered and can be explained with reference to details analyzed in Chapters 1–5. To continue with the metaphor by ANSA referred to earlier in the section, the "Chinese sauce" added to *Roman Holiday* regards precisely the many food narratives in *La ricetta italiana*.

At the outset of the movie, Mandy is introduced as a part-time assistant in an Italian restaurant, whose main task is to peel potatoes and wash dishes and pots. The camera steals glances from her at food preparation and cooking done by the kitchen's white Italian cooks. She is there not just to make a wage by working a menial job; she has the ambition to learn the trade of Italian cooking. When Mandy successfully puts condiments on an artichoke following the instructions of a cook, the main chef—a woman—curtly reminds her that she is not a cook and ought to take out the garbage immediately. Halfway through the film, the first major food scene involving Mandy takes place. A group of Chinese tourists arrive at the Italian restaurant where she works at midnight because of their flight's delay. While the chief chef explains to them that the kitchen is closed, the Chinese insist that they have a reservation at 8 P.M. that evening and that the delay is out of their control. When Mandy arrives on the scene, she sees an opportunity to cook for the tourists and temporarily become the chef of that Italian kitchen. The head chef consents, and Mandy comes up with three simple Chinese dishes: congee, fried rice with various chopped vegetables, and freshly smashed cucumbers with oil, salt, and spices. The protein of this improvised meal consists of Italian cured meats and cheeses. The camerawork is fast-paced, crisp, and cheerful, simulating Mandy's emotional state.

Mandy's first time cooking onscreen is noticeably associated with her Chinese identity, and her customers are her co-nationals. This scene illustrates a detail relayed in the previous section about the Chinese food reality show. Despite delicious Italian food and a desire to experience culinary novelty, Chinese leisure tourists in Italy are represented as having the occasional craving to feel at their culinary home. The scene is also premised on the dictum performed by *Cenci in Cina* analyzed in Chapter 4: Chinese cooks ought to cook their own ethnic food and not try their hand at Italian cooking. Echoing information about widespread low-quality Chinese food relayed in Chapter 1, Chinese dishes here are represented as simple and not as artistically complicated as Italian dishes seen in the scene where Mandy works as an assistant. There is a narrative justification for this setup. The Chinese tourists urgently want to eat, and simple dishes are made because there is no preparation of ingredients in advance.

Later on, when Mandy is sad about her romantic involvement with Peng, her uncle and aunt treat her to home cooking served at a small table. She is seen eating plain white-rice congee and a white-flour bun. Her aunt repeats a formula that Mandy's mother, now deceased, used to tell her: "There is no obstacle that cannot be overcome with a hot meal." The easily digestible, unadorned Chinese food that both Mandy and the Chinese tourists consume, therefore, becomes a vehicle for expressing their need to feel at home and find comfort in stressful moments. Mandy is emotionally upset and confused about her prospects with Peng and her culinary aspirations, and the Chinese tourists are hungry and frustrated because of the delay after a long flight from China. Ultimately, from the perspective of the movie, Mandy's uncomplicated Chinese cooking expresses her Chinese sensibility that associates home with food and family members who prepare this food that nurtures her.

Mandy as a promising chef is also depicted in another major scene, which establishes her competency in elaborate Italian cooking. Mandy goes to the Italian restaurant at midnight because she has decided to make a new cake for her friend's wedding, which is happening the day after. Several shots then showcase Mandy's skills in preparing different layers of the cake using flour mixes in various colors. She carefully mounts multiple layers to form a three-tier tall cake. She also makes dough from scratch to wrap the exterior of the tiered cake, thereby making it stable as a structure. Finally, various small colorful patches are made using inventive patterns and are attached to the cake for decoration. We witness Mandy's attentiveness through the eyes of Peng, who helps as her assistant. The cake concept is Mandy's, which is retrieved from a description in a notebook that she keeps. The inventiveness of the concept consists in melding Western-style cake-making with decorations that recall Chinese silk embroidery.

A similarly creative process occurs when Mandy makes a first-course meal for Peng by using existing ingredients in the fridge. She comes up with a spaghetti dish, which the camera highlights by using a close-up that displays the content at the center of the frame. Judging from the garnish, which is composed of tomato in thin slices, green puree (possibly of peas), pomegranate seeds, dill, and chives, it is a modern interpretation of spaghetti that is meant to express the chef's creativity. Indeed, Mandy starts preparing the spaghetti dish by announcing that she will "follow her feelings." In both cases, the substance or foundation of the cake and the spaghetti is Italian, while the inspiration for the decorations or garnish may be Chinese or Western, depending on Mandy's creative mind. In Chapter 2, I have given examples of Milan's hybrid Chinese-Italian cuisine, which lends empirical support to the film's depiction of Mandy's Italian culinary knowledge. Mandy's creativity would also be a rebuttal to some Italian cultural workers' perception of Chinese cooks of Italian cuisine as imitative creatures, as analyzed in Chapter 4.

Mandy's Italian culinary competency as a highly skilled cook would unsettle the debate on authenticity in Italian food analyzed in Chapter 4. She passes on the chance to take the annual national law examination that she has prepared for a long time to participate in a contest organized by the Italian star chef Antonino Cannavacciuolo on the same day. She wins a place as his assistant, as the end of the movie intimates. This detail may be based on a real-world occurrence. *Antonino Chef Academy* was an Italian talent show that chose a winner each season to work at the chef's high-end Villa Crespi restaurant. In its first edition, aired in 2019, an Italian Chinese cook named Federico Liu was featured and won third place.[72] Near the end of *La ricetta italiana*, we learn that Mandy's (unnamed) master teacher has opened an Italian restaurant in Beijing, echoing the Bombana examples analyzed in Chapter 5. We are also led to understand that Mandy is the principal chef there, joining the exclusive group of female Italian chefs and Italian Chinese chefs mentioned in Chapter 5.

Unlike gendered professionalization within Italy's Chinese restaurants examined in Chapter 1, which casts Chinese women as waitresses, home cooks, and entrepreneurs, Mandy is a female chef heading a new Italian restaurant in Beijing. It is no wonder that she is highly conscious of the difficulty she faces in the profession, commenting at one point that only 7 percent of professional chefs worldwide are women. This detail echoes a remark by Simonetta Garelli analyzed in Chapter 5 and possibly is also a reflection of the film's female director, Hou, with regard to her own profession. To be sure, in the realm of professional cooking, Mandy's journey is helped by winning the contest and working with Cannavacciuolo, assuming that is what happens, although the film is not entirely clear on the details. However, her journey is made possible by a network of professional female cooks in her life. In the film's first scene, in which Mandy tries to put oil on an artichoke, she is taught by a female cook. Initially, the main female chef of the Italian restaurant only views Mandy as a kitchen assistant charged with taking care of chores. But during the crisis involving the Chinese tourists, the chef lets Mandy cook for them. After witnessing Mandy's success, the chef also permits her to use the kitchen to make the wedding cake. Most important, Mandy's mother was a restaurateur of a small eatery who nurtured the daughter's passion for food and cooking. The notebook that Mandy keeps contains not only inventive recipes and personal notes but also photographs of the mother and daughter holding cooking utensils and laughing together. Mandy's identity as a female chef in the movie is equally constructed by showing her competency in both Chinese and Italian cuisines and by staking her positionality as a woman.

By positively depicting Chinese and Italian culinary practices by Italy's migrants for themselves and for Chinese leisure tourists, *La ricetta italiana* intends to surpass *Roman Holiday* in interpreting the meanings of love as nurtured by Italy. In the Italian-Chinese-German film, love is posited as more than romantic or profession-related, as is the case with the American classic. Through food, *La ricetta italiana* adds family to the definition of love and in interaction with romantic love—a perennial theme articulating a deep-seated Chinese sensibility as demonstrated in countless fiction. In the film's view, this aligns with the Italian tradition; in the film's only explicitly verbalized Italian-Chinese mutual recognition, Mandy justifies her speedy Vespa ride to the Italian cops as resulting from rushing to take care of family members.

Through this food-love focus, *La ricetta italiana* also dampens the cinematic need to differentiate between Chinese consumers' Pizza Hut and Slow Food Italian culinary repertoires. No character encounters any resistance to their food needs and preferences. A Chinese tourist in Italy like Peng can claim that Mandy's spaghetti is the best he has ever tasted because of his growing love for her. The Chinese tourists on an organized tour can be treated to a simple but comforting Chinese meal in an Italian restaurant at midnight. Italian chefs are happy to teach Mandy, the Chinese migrant cook, and have a young woman lead in an Italian restaurant in China. The feel-good movie has a culinary repertoire all to its own insofar as China-Italy food mobilities are concerned: love trumps everything. This cinematic imagination alerts us to how all of this can be accomplished very rarely in reality. *La ricetta italiana* is a testimony of cinematic gratification for a 2010s Chinese cosmopolitan self-identity construction via Italian food and vis-à-vis American popular culture.

In Chapters 5 and 6, I have operationalized Long's model of culinary tourism as a "framework for seeing the varieties of interfaces in which adventurous eating occurs as instances of negotiating individual and social perceptions of the exotic."[73] Only by interrogating a broad range of sources, such as Chinese tourism websites and Italian migrant self-reports, can we better examine the complexity of what "Italian cuisine" could mean for middle-class Chinese, who ate and narrated Italian food both in China and in Italy starting in the 1990s. I have also analyzed several "interfaces" concerning Chinese culinary tourism in Italian cuisines, whether Pizza Hut China's mediation of Italian/American/Chinese pizzas and pastas or Chinese culinary tourists' manipulation of discourses on Slow food. The Slow Food ethos transmitted by Italian-origin food entrepreneurs and chefs and American food and business cultures taught by Pizza Hut China remained two conspicuous cultural repertoires available for the culinary tourists' elaboration of their sociocultural identities within China's digital ecology. Ultimately, I have addressed how Italian culinary tourism allowed (upper-)middle-class Chinese consumers and food enthusiasts to express cosmopolitanism and connoisseurship for themselves and their nation-state.

CONCLUSION

Italian-Chinese commercial and sociopolitical exchanges have been rife with food-based metaphors, images, narratives, biases, collaborations, and frictions. My book is the first study about contemporary China-Italy food mobilities in popular culture. Specifically, I have examined transcultural China-Italy food mobilities from the 1980s through the 2010s. As I claim, recent China-Italy food mobilities have been integral to public conversations in each country about sociocultural identity-making. Broadly speaking, my analysis in this book demonstrates how food discourses can be used to interpret the most recent decades of long-standing cultural communications and dynamics between China and Italy. In reaching these conclusions, I have operationalized an analytical framework about transcultural China-Italy food mobilities that foregrounds three discursive and cultural interfaces: two-way labor migrations between China and Italy, labor migration and culinary tourism, and contacts with American business and popular cultures. The analytical framework's functioning in my analysis draws from several methodological and theoretical considerations. Most important, I have examined the persuasive mechanisms of discourses, adopted a cultural-studies lens on questions about power and politics in these meaning-making scenarios, and interpreted narratives as containing cultural resources that are capable of meaning-making.

Through the discussions in Chapters 1–4, I argue that the cultural conveyance of the Chinese migrant restaurant sector in Italy had a different logic than its historical evolution and empirical conditions. While the migration-restaurant-crime frame prevalent in cultural works drew on Chinese restaurants' supposed business practices, it can be better explained by considering how Italians have grappled with immigration into the country since the 1980s. Another key factor was how Italy has viewed its place in globalization since the 2000s in relation to China. For example, specific Lavazza advertising depicts Chinese imitations of its products or attempts to purchase a controlling interest in the company. These representations point to authenticity issues in food and Italians' food-related expertise. During the 2000s and 2010s, such concerns articulated Italians' intention to safeguard the integrity of Lavazza's company, community, and national identity. Apart from Chinese imitations of Italian food, other influential Italian alimentary stereotypes were often articulated through gendered and outdated American archetypes about Chinese restaurants. The highly racialized dogmeat cliché circulated widely in American popular culture before it appeared in *Fantozzi*. The American context was also crucial in understanding how *Corriere della Sera* compared Milan and Rome's Chinese cuisines with that of New York City. By doing so, the journalists rhetorically elevated the status of the two Italian cities as cosmopolitan cities and destinations for culinary tourism.

Turning to Italian culinary tourism in China in Chapters 5–6, I reveal how it allowed middle-class Chinese consumers to express themselves in relation to both the diverse communities to which they belonged, such as the foodie culture and rapidly changing Chinese society, thanks in no small part to pervasive digital cultures. Chinese culinary tourists' first contact with Italian food occurred during the early 1990s, a decade after the Open Door

Policy that welcomed Western investment. This experience was mediated through Italian American food, with Pizza Hut's pizzas and spaghetti dishes as prime examples. Since the 2000s, transnational Italian fine-dining and migrant-managed Italian restaurants have also impacted the Chinese public's narratives about Italian cuisine, particularly through their emphasis on the Made in Italy cachet. The Slow Food discourse and Pizza Hut China's American food and business cultures constituted two major cultural repertoires for Chinese culinary tourists to narratively elaborate their cosmopolitan sociocultural identities. This dynamic can be appreciated through the phenomenon of Chinese leisure tourists who made food tourism a central activity during their trips to Italy in the 2010s. For instance, the popular Chinese food critic and author Shu Qiao viewed some Slow Food practices skeptically because they represented what she considered to be a slightly dogmatic way of life. But gastronationalism championed by Slow Food was also adopted by some Chinese cultural practitioners to advance the values of Chinese cuisine. A reason for these occurrences lies in Slow Food's association with the Made in Italy cachet, which Italian food entrepreneurs frequently highlighted in their marketing narratives but which elicited differing reactions from Chinese consumers.

Overall, I have shown how food-assisted cultural narratives fundamentally influenced Chinese and Italian culinary tourism in each other's cuisine. These food discourses also played a key role in negotiating the socioeconomic identities of food consumers, workers, and entrepreneurs. In both countries, this culinary tourism developed a symbiotic relationship with labor migration in the food and restaurant sector. This relationship made Chinese food widely known in Italy and vice versa. I have examined this relationship through the lens of popular culture and claimed that food has become a quintessential cultural tool through which to ethnicize and gender Chinese in Italy and Italians in China. The interaction between food-related migration and tourism in these multifaceted contexts also helped culturally mediate other recent China-Italy relations. Notably, Chinese migrants' foodscape has been a crucible where advocates and critics debated Italy's management of Chinese migrants' entrepreneurship and its other foreign populations. In China, consumption of Made in Italy food and other goods has provided the Chinese middle class with a concrete conduit to feel cosmopolitan and contemplate what they believe to be the limits of Slow Food and the Made in Italy discourse more broadly.

Much work remains to be done on transcultural China-Italy food mobilities and their larger impact on China-Italy exchanges in popular culture. Three gaps can be mentioned here. First, we still do not know much about the early cultural histories of Chinese food in Italy, such as during the 1980s–1990s, the period immediately preceding the timeframe under scrutiny in this book. How did the role of Chinese food shape the evolving Italian views of Chinese culinary culture? How did such a food culture influence larger Italian-Chinese cultural contacts and scripts? The two decades represent the beginning of Italians' Chinese culinary tourism and the emergence of other "ethnic" cuisines in Italy. Knowing more about this dimension can enhance our historical understanding of the intersection of Chinese labor migration and Italian culinary tourism within a culinary landscape that was becoming more complicated than ever in Italian history.

Second, there may be archival sources and period newspapers where Chinese consumption of Italian food from the First Opium War (1840) through the end of the Republic of China (1912–1949) are described. Italians traveled to China in numbers never seen in history. This was a period when Italy and China first forged official diplomatic relations and Italian political, business, military, and colonial interests in China intensified. How might narratives about Italian food made or consumed in China have played a role in articulating this new historical moment in China-Italy relations? Moreover, in the scholarship that examines Italian travel writings about China and the Chinese, where culinary descriptions are frequent, a critical analysis of food is almost categorically ignored. There is a critical need to reread such primary texts from the angle of food studies to capture the fundamental experience of Italian travelers while journeying through Chinese culture, customs, and politics.

Finally, future detailed studies about Japanese food in Italy and French food in China can become fruitful comparisons for the China-Italy case, further enriching scholarship on transcultural food mobilities. As analyzed in Chapter 3, while the dogmeat is its centerpiece, *Fantozzi*'s culinary premise is also built upon Italians' judgment of Japanese food. In Chapter 1, I relay how Chinese restaurateurs opened many Japanese eateries after the

SARS crisis, thereby complicating what "Chinese migrant-managed restaurants" mean. The Japanese-Chinese food dynamics in Italian popular culture and empirical reality may be more complicated than we currently understand. Turning to the French-Chinese case, as mentioned in Chapter 5, French cuisine is highly regarded in China and is a quintessential competitor to Italian cuisine on many levels, such as culinary connoisseurship and social status. What cultural inroad has French cuisine made into middle-class Chinese consumers' culinary narratives? How may such cultural accounts interact with ones about Italian food in China? Both the Japanese-Italian and French-Chinese cases are promising avenues for exploring transcultural food mobilities more broadly.

In March 2020, approximately a month after Laika's poster of Sonia Zhou—discussed in the Introduction—was publicly released, Italy became the European ground zero of the pandemic, forcing most businesses around the country to close temporarily. The virus was no longer associated exclusively with ethnic Chinese; it became the virus from Milan, as Lombardy became the epicenter of the country's outbreak, owing to poor management of its early stages.[1] Zhou's restaurant was closed because her staff returned to China in haste, which by now was perceived as a safer place than Italy, where more stringent sanitary, quarantine, and monitoring measures were implemented.[2]

With *la dolce vita* (the sweet life) gone, how will Zhou's restaurant and Italy's Chinese restaurant sector weather this pandemic? How will Italian cultural narratives about Chinese food change after the pandemic? What similar and differing processes and mechanisms have been at play regarding Italian food in China? Prompted by these questions about an uncertain future, I have provided an interpretive framework in this book to help readers navigate the sophisticated landscape of transcultural China-Italy food mobilities. I also hope that along the way, readers have found important clues about current China-Italy socioeconomic and political-historical relations in a world context where American culture remains palpable.

ACKNOWLEDGMENTS

The idea of a book on transcultural China-Italy food mobilities first came into focus when I was co-organizing a conference on Italy and East Asia at Stony Brook University in October 2018. At the time, when I talked about media depictions of Chinese migrants in Italy—the topic of my previous monograph—I often found my interlocutors expressing keen interest in migrant cuisine and foodways. Meanwhile, upon learning that I am an Italian professor working in North America, people invariably tried to scope what my favorite Italian restaurants were in Vancouver, Los Angeles, Toronto, and New York City. Therefore, it was natural for me to think of food as the most fitting topic for the Stony Brook conference, especially when my co-organizer and host, Mario Mignone, aimed to reach a broader spectrum of audiences than their previous Italian-themed conferences. However, there was, and still is, very little critical literature on food dynamics between China and Italy. In consultation with Donna Gabaccia, whom I knew from the University of Toronto when I worked there, I determined that hosting two specialists in Chinese and Italian migrant cuisines in the American context was my next best choice. A seed was planted in me to write a monograph about China-Italy food cultures.

Three more events prompted me to start writing the manuscript that would eventually become part of the current book. In the fall of 2019, on Deanna Shemek and Yong Chen's kind invitation, I delivered a lecture and taught a class at the University of California, Irvine. For Chen's class on cuisines in America, I was given the task of speaking about Chinese migrant cuisine in Italy. This was the first time I focused on this topic and made a series of notes and slides with undergraduate students in mind. The UC Irvine experience gave me the impetus to create a new undergraduate course about Italian food cultures in the spring semester of 2020 at my institution, the University of British Columbia. After a two-year trial, a new course code was created for this content, and the number of students grew noticeably from year to year. In designing and teaching Italian food cultures from both national and global perspectives, I systematically thought about and strategically selected a significant body of primary texts about Italy's local and hybrid foods. My students also provided insights when studying the teaching materials, which furthered my thinking of the book. Therefore, when the COVID-19 lockdowns and travel restrictions began in Canada, and worldwide, I had ample time to draft my chapters throughout 2020–2022. In the following year, I was a research fellow at the European University Institute in Florence for another project, but I revised the manuscript.

During the research and drafting phase, I received tremendous help from two research assistants, Han Fei and Claire Ping, who compiled, updated, and analyzed food literature for me. I exchanged ideas about the book with Fei, and Ping also helped me draft the literature review in the current book's Introduction. Valentina Pedone of the University of Florence has been a trustworthy interlocutor with me on this manuscript, providing me with constructive critiques of my arguments and chapters. Gabaccia also exchanged ideas with me regarding the book's structure and main intellectual project, particularly its concept of food and mobility. Kristina Varade of the City University of New York read chapters from a previous version of the manuscript and gave me useful feedback. Ruth Ben-Ghiat, my former New York University advisor, coached me on how to approach peer reviews and a previous publisher when disagreements arose. When revising my manuscript, I have also benefited from conversations with Valerie McGuire of the University of Texas at Austin. Colleagues and students at the University of British Columbia have offered their feedback to me over meals and in seminars. My University of Southern California postdoctoral mentor, Tita Rosenthal, helped me strengthen the book's structure and chapter titles in its final form. Elizabeth Venditto copyedited a significant portion of the manuscript and vastly improved my expression. I also wish to thank Laura Ruberto and Nancy C. Carnevale for embracing my project from the moment I contacted them for inclusion in the series "Critical Studies in Italian Migrations." Fredric Nachbaur, Director of Fordham University Press, was a pleasure to work with.

Several universities have invited me to deliver stand-alone lectures or to teach classes on food topics relevant to the book: The College of William & Mary (Monica Seger), Purdue University (Tatjana Babic Williams, Manabu Taketani, and Kristina Pamela Sari), Yale University (Lydia Tuan), Pennsylvania State University (Xin Liu and Eleonora Sartoni), and Italian Canadians for Black Lives (Paolo Frascà and Leah Bernardo-Ciddio). I am grateful to the hosts who invited me, as the experiences allowed me to further observe the audience's variegated responses to my topics and integrate them into the manuscript. I also wish to thank two organizations whose financial support allowed me to complete the manuscript. SSHRC (Social Sciences and Humanities Research Council) of Canada offered me an Insight Development Grant in 2018, part of which was used to fund my research on food. I also benefited from using resources at the European University Institute, where I was a Jean Monnet Fellow on sabbatical during 2022–2023.

My passion for eating and for food has been nurtured by my mother and father, Yuan Shuijuan and Zhang Erjun, and their home cooking. My mother has always emphasized the importance of diet, and my father is a fantastic cook. This was the case when our family's economic conditions were not optimal during the 1980s–1990s, and it remains so today when my parents are aging, and their diet has to be modified accordingly. I want to dedicate this book to them, first and foremost. I am also grateful to David Prelini and his family, who have treated me to Milanese home cooking and who have been with me on many occasions of culinary tourism in Italy and beyond. Finally, I want to dedicate this book to friends who have eaten with me or cooked for me and, in the meantime, taught me something more about food that I was ignorant about. These conversations over meals have immensely enhanced my culinary pleasure and given this book a reason to exist.

NOTES

INTRODUCTION: TRANSCULTURAL CHINA-ITALY FOOD MOBILITIES

1. For examples of Italian coverage of anti-Chinese racism, see Maurizio Crosetti, "Coronavirus, in Italia è psicosi Cina. Clienti in fuga dai negozi e record di mascherine," *La Repubblica*, January 29, 2020; Federica Cavadini, "Coronavirus Italia, la prof cinese derisa in treno e il tweet virale," *Corriere della Sera*, February 18, 2020; and Fabio Giuffrida, "L'incubo di essere cinesi in Italia con il coronavirus," *Open*, February 26, 2020, https://www.open.online/2020/02/26/lincubo-di-essere-cinesi-in-italia-con-il-coronavirus-un-ragazzo-preso-a-bottigliate-in-veneto/, accessed June 12, 2020.

2. For example, Lanbo Hu, ed., *Noi restiamo qui: come la comunità cinese ha vissuto l'epidemia* (Roma: Cina in Italia, 2020); and Lala Hu, *Semi di tè* (Busto Arsizio: People, 2020).

3. For examples of communications about the COVID-19 epidemic from the Chinese embassy in Rome as reported in Italian newspapers, see news from early 2020 posted on the following webpage, http://it.chineseembassy.org/chn/sbyw/, accessed June 12, 2020.

4. For examples of coverage of battling racism, see Sina Editorial, "'没有一个中国人被感染,'" www.sina.cn, March 26, 2020, https://tech.sina.cn/2020-03-26/detail-iimxyqwa3206451.d.html, accessed June 12, 2020; and Chen 陈雅儒, "米兰华侨华人互助抗疫: 餐厅闭店, 向当地医院捐资捐物," 澎湃新闻, March 5, 2020, https://www.thepaper.cn/newsDetail_forward_6346652, accessed June 12, 2020.

5. The number of such news articles is significant. For relevant examples, see the articles quoted in the following notes.

6. Redazione Online, "Coronavirus Italia, Sala a Chinatown," *Corriere della Sera*, February 8, 2020, https://milano.corriere.it/notizie/cronaca/20_febbraio_08/coronavirus-italia-sala-chinatown-dobbiamo-sentirci-parte-una-comunita-bb896aac-4a6d-11ea-b474-2022aed4301a.shtml, accessed October 16,

2022; and Editorial, "Roma, il pranzo della sindaca in un ristorante cinese dell'Esquilino," *La Repubblica*, February 8, 2020.

7. Fabio Giuffrida, "Milano, la notte delle bacchette: è arrivato il momento di aiutare (davvero) la comunità cinese," *Open*, February 17, 2020, https://www.open.online/2020/02/17/milano-la-notte-delle-bacchette-e-arrivato-il-momento-di-aiutare-davvero-la-comunita-cinese/, accessed November 23, 2022.

8. To view images of the poster, see Editorial, "Coronavirus, a Roma spunta il murale con la ristoratrice cinese Sonia in tuta bianca: 'Dobbiamo proteggerci,'" *Il Messaggero*, February 4, 2020, https://www.ilmessaggero.it/roma/news/coronavirus_murale_ristoratrice_cinese_sonia_tuta_bianca_ultime_notizie-5028444.html, accessed June 1, 2021.

9. I follow the transliteration of 杭州 as "Hang Zhou" used by the restaurant itself and in the media. According to *pinyin*, the official romanization system of Mandarin Chinese in China, the transliteration is "Hangzhou."

10. The translation is mine.

11. For another celebrity restaurateur who managed a much larger enterprise, see Alessandra Spalletta, "Storia di Cristian Lin, il cinese che in Italia ha creato un impero di cibo giapponese," *AGI* (Agenzia Giornalistica Italiana), June 25, 2018. Chefs offering Chinese cuisine also appeared on Italian television, such as in the show *Menù di Benedetta* (Benedetta's Menu), La7, https://www.la7.it/i-men%C3%B9-di-benedetta/rivedila7/menu-cinese-07-07-2015-134151, accessed May 29, 2020; and in *La cucina straniera con Anna Moroni* (Foreign Cuisine with Anna Moroni), Rai, https://www.raiplay.it/video/2017/10/La-Cina-b8b6fb0b-8399-4acd-af39-d3efc5adc24e.html, accessed May 29, 2020.

12. Editorial, "Coronavirus, Racism, and Solidarity Before and After Italy's Lockdown," *Guardian*, March 16, 2020, https://www.youtube.com/watch?v=O_3Nol8Fq6A, accessed May 29, 2020. Zhou is also featured in Elisa Amoruso's documentary film titled *Strane Straniere* (Strange Foreign Women, 2016).

13. Lorenzo Rossi Doria, "Sonia Zhou, un'italianissima cinese," *L'Espresso*, September 23, 2017; and Annarita Curcio, "Sonia racconta Hang Zhou," *Gambero Rosso*, January 20, 2014.

14. Rossi Doria, "Sonia Zhou, un'italianissima cinese."

15. Giancarlo Buonomo, "How Rome Fell in Love with Chinese Food," *Vice*, January 24, 2018.

16. Tim Cresswell, *On the Move: Mobility in the Modern Western World* (New York: Routledge, 2006), 2–3 and 21; and Stephen Greenblatt, ed. *Cultural Mobility* (Cambridge: Cambridge University Press, 2010), 1–23 and 250–253.

17. Daniel E. Bender and Simone Cinotto, "Introduction: Mobility and the Making of World Cuisines," in *Food Mobilities: Making World Cuisines*, ed. Daniel E. Bender and Simone Cinotto (Toronto: University of Toronto Press, 2024), 3.

18. Laila Abu-Er-Rub, Christiane Brosius, Sebastian Meurer, Diamantis Panagiotopoulos, and Susan Richter, "Introduction: Engaging Transculturality," in *Engaging Transculturality: Concepts, Key Terms, Case Studies*, ed. Laila Abu-Er-Rub, Christiane Brosius, Sebastian Meurer, Diamiantis Panagiotopoulos, and Susan Richter (London: Routledge, 2019), xxiv–xxvii.

19. Charles Burdett, Loredana Polezzi, and Barbara Spadaro, ed. *Transcultural Italies: Mobility, Memory and Translation* (Liverpool: Liverpool University Press, 2020).

20. Valentina Pedone and Gaoheng Zhang, "Introduction," in *Cultural Mobilities Between China and Italy*, ed. Valentina Pedone and Gaoheng Zhang (Cham, Switzerland: Springer; Palgrave Macmillan, 2024), 6–8.

21. For a definition of "foodscape," see Josée Johnston and Shyon Baumann, *Foodies: Democracy and Distinction in the Gourmet Foodscape* (New York: Routledge, 2014), 2–3.

22. Kathleen LeBesco and Peter Naccarato, ed. *The Bloomsbury Handbook of Food and Popular Culture* (London: Bloomsbury Academic, 2018), 1.

23. Fabio Parasecoli, *Bite Me: Food in Popular Culture* (Oxford: Berg Publishers, 2008), 4.

24. LeBesco and Naccarato, *Bloomsbury Handbook*, 3.

25. Ibid., 2. On the difficulty of defining popular culture, see John Storey, *From Popular Culture to Everyday Life* (New York: Routledge, 2014), 1–13.

26. Fabio Parasecoli, "Food, Cultural Studies, and Popular Culture," in *Routledge International Handbook of Food Studies*, ed. Ken Albala (London: Routledge, 2013), 276–277. During the 1960s and 1970s, cultural studies was socially driven by the postcolonial, civil rights, feminist, and gay and lesbian liberation movements, as well as their critics. Continuing this legacy, throughout the book, I focus on issues of class, gender, sexuality, race, ethnicity, ethics, representation, and social justice, as well as how these categories help us navigate politics of identity construction, structures of power, and agency. To be sure, with regard to diverse cultural-studies approaches, Cary Nelson, Paula A. Treichler, and Lawrence Grossberg claim that "no methodology can be privileged or even temporarily employed with total security and confidence, yet none can be eliminated out of hand" (Cary, Nelson, Paula A. Treichler, and Lawrence Grossberg, "Cultural Studies: An Introduction," in *Cultural Studies*, ed. Lawrence Grossberg, Cary Nelson, and Paula A. Treichler [New York: Routledge, 1992], 2 and 6). Nevertheless, many

practitioners hope that the discipline's overall theoretical practice has the potential to engender social change. For example, according to Rey Chow, in the late 1990s, cultural studies in North America revolved around four areas of study, all of which had progressive social agendas: postcolonial critique, subaltern analyses of gender, race, and otherness; cultural expressions by minorities and the subordinated; and hybridity and multiculturalism (Rey Chow, *Ethics after Idealism: Theory, Culture, Ethnicity, Reading*. [Bloomington: Indiana University Press, 1998], 2–4). Indeed, for Simon During, despite its close ties with neoliberal entrepreneurialism via the university, cultural studies is rooted in social engagement with "a sensitivity to the ways in which culture is (in part) a field of power-relations involving centers and peripheries, status hierarchies, connections to norms that impose repressions or marginalizations" (Simon During, *Cultural Studies: A Critical Introduction* [London: Routledge, 2005], 9, see also 14–17 and 214). Many such power-relations originate from diverse intellectual traditions and lead to uneven knowledge distribution. But Ackbar Abbas and John Nguyet Erni view this situation positively for cultural studies because it would help further "internationalize" the discipline (Ackbar Abbas and John Nguyet Erni, "General Introduction," in *Internationalizing Cultural Studies: An Anthology*, ed. Ackbar Abbas and John Nguyet Erni [Malden, MA: Blackwell, 2005], 2).

27. Bob Ashley, Joanne Hollows, Steve Jones, and Ben Taylor, *Food and Cultural Studies* (New York: Routledge, 2004).

28. Eva Illouz, *Oprah Winfrey and the Glamour of Misery: An Essay on Popular Culture* (New York: Columbia University Press, 2003), 120–122.

29. Donna R. Gabaccia, "Food, Mobility, and World History," in *The Oxford Handbook of Food History*, ed. Jeffery M. Pilcher (Oxford: Oxford University Press, 2012). For Paulette K. Schuster, "Food is a daily reminder of the past and a foundation for the future," see Paulette K. Schuster, "Interconnectivities: Mobility, Food and Place," in *Handbook of Culture and Migration*, ed. Jeffrey H. Cohen and Ibrahim Sirkeci (Cheltenham, UK: Edward Elgar, 2021), 388.

30. Tiana B. Hayden and Dhan Zunino Singh, "Food and Mobility," *Journal of Transport History* 41, no. 2 (2020): 286.

31. Sarah Gibson, "Food Mobilities," *Space and Culture* 10, no. 1 (2007): 16.

32. Kevin Hannam, Mimi Sheller, and John Urry, "Editorial: Mobilities, Immobilities and Moorings," *Mobilities* 1, no. 1 (2006): 10–12 and 14–15. See also Mimi Sheller and John Urry, "The New Mobilities Paradigm," *Environment and Planning* 38 (2006): 212–214.

33. Bender and Cinotto, "Introduction," 13.

34. For representative works on Italian cuisine, see Alberto Capatti and Massimo Montanari, *Italian Cuisine: A Cultural History* (New York: Columbia

University Press, 2003); Carol Helstosky, *Garlic and Oil: Politics and Food in Italy* (Oxford: Berg, 2004); Emanuela Scarpellini, *Food and Foodways in Italy from 1861 to the Present* (New York: Palgrave Macmillan, 2016); David Gentilcore, *Pomodoro!: A History of the Tomato in Italy* (New York: Columbia University Press, 2010); David Gentilcore, *Italy and the Potato: A History, 1550–2000* (London: A & C Black, 2012); Peter Naccarato, Zachary Nowak, and Elgin K. Eckert, eds., *Representing Italy Through Food* (London: Bloomsbury, 2017); and Roberta Sassatelli, ed., *Italians and Food* (Cham, Switzerland: Palgrave Macmillan, 2019). For representative works on Chinese cuisine, see E. N. Anderson, *The Food of China* (New Haven, CT: Yale University Press, 1988); K. C. Chang, ed., *Food in Chinese Culture: Anthropological and Historical Perspectives* (New Haven, CT: Yale University Press, 1977); Frederick J. Simoons, *Food in China: A Cultural and Historical Inquiry* (Boca Raton: CRC Press, 1990); Brian R. Dott, *The Chile Pepper in China: A Cultural Biography* (New York: Columbia University Press, 2020); and Jin Feng, *Tasting Paradise on Earth: Jiangnan Foodways* (Seattle: University of Washington Press, 2019).

35. Jeffrey M. Pilcher, *Food in World History* (New York: Routledge, 2006), 90–98.

36. Haiming Liu, *From Canton Restaurant to Panda Express: A History of Chinese Food in the United States* (New Brunswick, NJ: Rutgers University Press, 2015), 1–2. Anne Mendelson provides a culinary and political history of Chinese American migrants, along with in-depth studies of English-language Chinese cookbooks and Chinese restaurants in the United States (Anne Mendelson, *Chow Chop Suey: Food and the Chinese American Journey* [New York: Columbia University Press, 2016]). Taking a cue from the history of an iconic Chinese American dish, *chop suey*, in studying the rise of Chinese food in the United States, Yong Chen underscores the role of food as "a marker of identity" for Chinese Americans (Yong Chen, *Chop Suey, USA: The Story of Chinses Food in America* [New York: Columbia University Press], 29).

37. Simone Cinotto, *The Italian American Table: Food, Family, and Community in New York City* (Urbana: University of Illinois Press, 2013), 7. Cinotto argues that food held a central place in Italian American culture, which was key to understanding migration, racialization, Americanization, and nationalism (16). Donna Gabaccia and Hasia R. Diner discuss Italian immigrants and their culinary culture, recognizing food as a crucial part of the Italian American experience (Donna Gabaccia, *We Are What We Eat: Ethnic Food and the Making of Americans* [Cambridge, MA: Harvard University Press, 1998]; and Hasia R. Diner, *Hungering for America: Italian, Irish and Jewish Foodways in the Age of Migration* [Cambridge, MA: Harvard University Press, 2001]).

38. The critic suggests that food served not merely as an opportunity for employment and entrepreneurship but "also as cultural mediators who produced new spaces and meanings about gender, ethnicity, race, and nationhood in their host countries." Elizabeth Zanoni, *Migrant Marketplaces: Food and Italians in North and South America* (Urbana: University of Illinois Press, 2018), 9.

39. Robert Ji-Song Ku, *Dubious Gastronomy: The Cultural Politics of Eating Asian in the USA* (Honolulu: University of Hawai'i Press, 2014), 4.

40. Scarpellini, *Food and Foodways*, 167.

41. J. A. G. Roberts, *China to Chinatown: Chinese Food in the West* (London: Reaktion, 2002), 11–12 and 135–228.

42. Zanoni, *Migrant Marketplaces*.

43. For the mobility forms of migration and tourism, which are part of the corporeal travel of people, see John Urry, *Mobilities* (Cambridge: Polity, 2007), 10–11 and 47.

44. Gabaccia, "Food, Mobility, and World History"; Scarpellini, *Food and Foodways*; and David Y. H. Wu and Sidney C. H. Cheung, eds., *The Globalization of Chinese Food* (Honolulu: University of Hawai'i Press, 2002).

45. Chiara Rabbiosi, "Locating Italianicity Through Food and Tourism: Playing with Geographical Associations," in *Italians and Food*, ed. Roberta Sassatelli (Cham, Switzerland: Palgrave Macmillan, 2019), 71.

46. Cited in Naccarato, Nowak, and Eckert, *Representing Italy*, 4.

47. Sassatelli, *Italians and Food*, 2. In Italian food cultural studies, scholars also highlight the significant role of food in nation-building and identity formation, in which tourism occupies a central place. Capatti and Montanari, *Italian Cuisine*; and Naccarato, Nowak, and Eckert, *Representing Italy*.

48. Lucy M. Long, *Culinary Tourism* (Lexington: University Press of Kentucky, 2013), 390.

49. Roberts, *China to Chinatown*, 216–217.

50. Scarpellini, *Food and Foodways*, 167.

51. Michael Volgger and Harald Pechlaner, "Responses to Chinese Tourists' Interest in Wine and Food: An Italian Perspective," in *Food, Wine and China: A Tourism Perspective*, ed. Christof Pforr and Ian Phau (New York: Routledge, 2018), 219–237.

52. "Hang Zhou da Sonia—Sede Unica," https://www.facebook.com/photo/?fbid=10159541453247472&set=pb.100063474372842.-2207520000, Facebook, June 1, 2021, accessed January 5, 2023.

53. For examples of important, recent monographs, see Graziella Parati, *Migrant Writers and Urban Space in Italy: Proximities and Affect in Literature and Film* (Cham, Switzerland: Palgrave Macmillan, 2017); Emma Bond,

Writing Migration through the Body (Cham, Switzerland: Palgrave Macmillan, 2018); Vetri Nathan, *Marvelous Bodies: Italy's New Migrant Cinema* (West Lafayette, Indiana: Purdue University Press, 2017); Áine O'Healy, *Migrant Anxieties: Italian Cinema in a Transnational Frame* (Bloomington: Indiana University Press, 2019); Teresa Fiore, *Pre-Occupied Spaces: Remapping Italy's Transnational Migrations and Colonial Legacies* (New York: Fordham University Press, 2017); and Stephanie Malia Hom, *Empire's Mobius Strip: Historical Echoes in Italy's Crisis of Migration and Detention* (Ithaca, NY: Cornell University Press, 2019).

54. For an example of these critical concerns expressed with regard to Asia and the Pacific, as well as research into migrant-migrant and migrant-Indigenous relationships and communication, see Jacqueline Leckie, Angela McCarthy, and Angela Wanhalla, "Introduction: Migrant Cross-cultural Encounters in Asia and the Pacific," in *Migrant Cross-cultural Encounters in Asia and the Pacific*, ed. Jacqueline Leckie, Angela McCarthy, and Angela Wanhalla (London: Routledge, 2016), 1–8.

55. A recent exception is Simone Cinotto, *Gastrofascism and Empire: Food in Italian East Africa, 1935–1941* (London: Bloomsbury, 2024).

56. Gitanjali G. Shahani, "Introduction," in *Food and Literature*, ed. Gitanjali G. Shahani (Cambridge: Cambridge University Press, 2018), 17.

57. See Amy L. Tigner and Allison Carruth, *Literature and Food Studies* (New York: Routledge, 2018), 3; Shahani, *Food and Literature*, 6; and J. Michelle Coghlan, ed., *The Cambridge Companion to Literature and Food* (Cambridge: Cambridge University Press, 2020), 2; Lorna Piatti-Farnell and Donna Lee Brien, *The Routledge Companion to Literature and Food* (New York: Routledge, 2018), 4; and Nicola Humble, *The Literature of Food: An Introduction from 1830 to Present* (London: Bloomsbury Academic, 2020), 2.

58. The well-established scholarship at the interaction of food and literature is vast and varied. For general works, see Coghlan, *The Cambridge Companion to Literature and Food*; Piatti-Farnell and Brien, *The Routledge Companion to Literature and Food*; Shahani, *Food and Literature*; and Tigner and Carruth, *Literature and Food Studies*. For food and Asian American literature, see Ann Anlin Cheng, "Digesting Asian America," in *The Cambridge Companion to Literature and Food*, ed. J. Michelle Coghlan (Cambridge: Cambridge University Press, 2020), 215–227; and Wenying Xu, *Eating Identities: Reading Food in Asian American Literature* (Honolulu: University of Hawai'i Press, 2008). For transnational Italian case studies, see Gian-Paolo Biasin, *The Flavors of Modernity: Food and the Novel* (Princeton, NJ: Princeton University Press, 1993); Elgin K. Eckert, "Inspector Montalbano *a tavola*: Food in Andrea Camilleri's Police Fiction," in *Representing Italy Through Food*, ed.

Peter Naccarato, Zachary Nowak, and Elgin K. Eckert (London: Bloomsbury, 2017), 95–110; Fabio Parasecoli, "The Invention of Authentic Italian Food: Narratives, Rhetoric, and Media," in *Italians and Food*, ed. Roberta Sassatelli (Cham, Switzerland: Palgrave Macmillan, 2019), 36–37; Rohit Chopra, "Comic Books and the Culinary Logic of Late Capitalism," in *Food and Literature*, ed. Gitanjali G. Shahani (Cambridge: Cambridge University Press, 2018), 237–249; Paul Mountfort, "*Tintin* and the Secrets of Food: The Body Fantastic, Cultural Others, and Limits of Language," in *The Routledge Companion to Literature and Food*, ed. Lorna Piatti-Farnell and Donna Lee Brien (New York: Routledge, 2018), 101–110; Fabio Parasecoli, "Gluttonous Crimes: *Chew*, Comic Books, and the Ingestion of Masculinity," *Women's Studies International Forum* 44 (May–June 2014): 236–246; Mihaela Precup, "Food, Memory, and Ethics in Graphic Narratives," in *The Routledge Companion to Literature and Food*, ed. Lorna Piatti-Farnell and Donna Lee Brien (New York: Routledge, 2018), 470–480; Donna Lee Brien, "Food in the Singaporean Graphic Memoir," in *The Routledge Companion to Literature and Food*, ed. Lorna Piatti-Farnell and Donna Lee Brien (New York: Routledge, 2018), 219–231; Amanda Eaton McMenamin, "Eating to Live, Living to Tell: Foundational Food in the Latina Testimonial Text," in *The Routledge Companion to Literature and Food*, ed. Lorna Piatti-Farnell and Donna Lee Brien (New York: Routledge, 2018), 450–459; and Barbara Spadaro, "Transnational Italian Comics: Graphic Journalism across Memories and Cultures," in *Transcultural Italies: Mobility, Memory and Translation*, ed. Charles Burdett, Loredana Polezzi, and Barbara Spadaro (Liverpool: Liverpool University Press, 2020), 287–308.

59. Roger Dickinson, "Food and the Media: Production, Representation, and Consumption," in *The Handbook of Food Research*, ed. Anne Murcott, Warren Belasco, and Peter Jackson (London: Bloomsbury Academic, 2013), 439–454; LeBesco and Naccarato, *The Bloomsbury Handbook of Food and Popular Culture*; Parasecoli, *Bite Me*; Gabaccia, "Food, Mobility, and World History"; Jonatan Leer and Karen Klitgaard Povlsen, eds., *Food and Media: Practices, Distinctions and Heterotopias* (New York: Routledge, 2016); Lanlan Kuang, "China's Emerging Food Media," *Gastronomica* 17, no. 3 (Fall 2017): 68–81; and Feng, *Tasting Paradise on Earth*.

60. Laura Lindenfeld and Fabio Parasecoli, "Food and Cinema: An Evolving Relationship," in *The Bloomsbury Handbook of Food and Popular Culture*, ed. Kathleen LeBesco and Peter Naccarato (London: Bloomsbury Academic, 2018), 27–39; Gaye Poole, *Reel Meals, Set Meals: Food in Film and Theatre* (Sydney: Currency Press, 1999); Jane Ferry, *Food in Film: A Culinary Performance of Communication* (London: Routledge, 2015); Anne L. Bower, ed.,

Reel Food: Essays on Food and Film (New York: Routledge, 2004); Peter Naccarato, "There's a Mobster in the Kitchen: Cooking, Eating, and Complications of Gender in *The Godfather* and *Goodfellas*," in *Representing Italy Through Food*, ed. Peter Naccarato, Zachary Nowak, and Elgin K. Eckert (London: Bloomsbury, 2017), 111–124; and Elgin K. Eckert and Zachary Nowak, "*In cibo veritas*: Food Preparation and Consumption in Özpetek's 'Queer' Films," in *Representing Italy Through Food*, ed. Peter Naccarato, Zachary Nowak, and Elgin K. Eckert (London: Bloomsbury, 2017), 125–137.

61. Classic studies in semiotics, linguistics, and anthropology have examined food as a quasi-linguistic system endowed with its own communicative capacities. Based on an analysis of its semiotic power, Roland Barthes asserts that food is "a system of communication" (Roland Barthes, "Toward a Psychosociology of Contemporary Food Consumption," in *Food and Culture: A Reader*, ed. Carole Counihan and Penny Van Esterik [New York: Routledge, 2012], 23). Working from a structuralist point of view, Claude Lévi-Strauss and Mary Douglas both suggest that we can view food as a code that articulates social relationships in ways similar to language. Although such notions of food, language, and semiotics have had their fair share of criticism, their basic understanding of food's close connection to communication is valuable for more recent work, which showcases the multidirectional practices of this research stream (Carlnita P. Greene and Janet M. Cramer, "Beyond Mere Sustenance: Food as Communication/Communication as Food," in *Food as Communication: Communication as Food*, ed. Janet M. Cramer, Carlnita Greene, and Lynn Walters [New York: Peter Lang, 2011], x). According to Carole Counihan and Penny Van Esterik, who focus on the materiality of food, thanks to "food's multi-sensorial properties of taste, touch, sight, sound, and smell, it has the ability to communicate in a variety of registers" (Carole Counihan and Penny Van Esterik, eds., *Food and Culture: A Reader* [New York: Routledge, 2012], 10). Understanding food as a means for identification, Carlnita P. Greene and Janet M. Cramer state that food "functions symbolically as a communicative practice by which we create, manage, and share meanings with others" (Greene and Cramer, "Beyond Mere Sustenance," xi). The critics also believe that scholarship on food as communication has the potential to both inform food studies and reconsider the definition of communication.

62. Ann Swidler, *Talk of Love: How Culture Matters* (Chicago: University of Chicago Press, 2001), 1 and 24.

63. Arthur Lizie, "Food and Communication," in *Routledge International Handbook of Food Studies*, ed. Ken Albala (London: Routledge, 2012), 27. Lizie's article also identifies four major intellectual fields in communication food

210 *Notes to pages 19–20*

scholarship which are instructive for my book's methodology: rhetoric, public relations, media effects and advertising, and cultural studies. Cultural studies is the most relevant direction for my book. When explaining this field, Lizie recognizes Roland Barthes's semiotic analysis of food in everyday life—especially his 1961 semiotics essay titled "Toward a Psychosociology of Contemporary Food Consumption"—as a major influence on the cultural-studies approach in food communication scholarship, which explores "how industries, texts, and audiences share symbols to create meanings" (Lizie, "Food and Communication," 31). Lizie also acknowledges other broad influences in making this connection, including Michel Foucault and Jean Baudrillard's theories of power and culture, Pierre Bourdieu's studies of class and distinction, Marxist criticism, and the Frankfurt and Birmingham Schools' critical cultural analysis. Such studies revolve around the analysis of two areas of social discourse: lifestyle construction and identity construction. Lizie further divides the former into two branches that focus on corporate identity construction and consumer lifestyle construction, respectively. For example, on corporate identity construction, Davide Girardelli adopts methods of semiotic analysis to explore the "mythical" construction of Italian food by the Fazoli restaurant chain. Some scholars investigate "how concepts about food translate from one culture to another [. . .] often focusing on the analysis of the use (often revulsion, then incorporation) of co-cultural and subcultural foodways by dominant national cultures." Others examine the social construction of gender roles and, more recently, the "mediated construction of masculinity/ies" (Lizie, "Food and Communication," 32). Finally, Lizie observes that cultural-studies scholarship on food and communication often focuses on the analysis of texts as well as their reception by audiences, although the number of reception studies is limited.

64. Wendy Griswold, *Cultures and Societies in a Changing World* (Thousand Oaks, CA: Sage, 2013), 15. For another model for comprehensively analyzing cultural objects, which is a tool from the tradition of cultural studies, see "the circuit of culture" as explained in Paul Du Gay, Stuart Hall, Linda Janes, Anders Koed Madsen, Hugh Mackay, and Keith Negus, *Doing Cultural Studies: The Story of the Sony Walkman* (London: Sage, 1997).

65. Wendy Griswold, "A Methodological Framework for the Sociology of Culture," *Sociological Methodology* 17 (1987): 26.

66. Griswold, *Cultures and Societies in a Changing World*, 19–45.

67. Dickinson, "Food and the Media," 442–444.

68. Nonetheless, recognizing that cultural studies work often does not address the media's role in shaping actual food or eating choices, Dickinson advocates for an approach which combines "sociological concerns" and "tools

of cultural analysis" in studies of food and the media. See Dickinson, "Food and the Media," 444 and 446.

69. In so doing, I consciously adopt critical standpoints and methods of both sociology of culture and cultural studies, which have overlapping concerns, but which have followed different intellectual paths. According to David Inglis, Andrew Blaikie, and Robin Wagner-Pacifici, a focus more fundamental in cultural sociology than in cultural studies is the signifier "social" (David Inglis, Andrew Blaikie, and Robin Wagner-Pacifici, "Editorial: Sociology, Culture and the Twenty-First Century," *Cultural Sociology* 1, no. 1 [2007]: 8–9). For Eva Illouz, the focus on the dynamics between ideology and resistance in cultural studies has contributed immensely to the study of culture. However, such an intellectual project "produces a sociological narrative devoid of tensions, inner contradictions, and a sense of 'poignancy' of the social, a poignancy that could derive, for example, from the tension between the coercive power of institutions and their ability to procure security and stability" (Illouz, *Oprah Winfrey and the Glamour of Misery*, 122). Nick Couldry remarks that the issue of symbolic meanings of human action in society concerns both Jeffrey C. Alexander, a prominent cultural sociology proponent, and a leading cultural-studies figure like Raymond Williams (Nick Couldry, "Sociology and Cultural Studies: An Interrupted Dialogue," in *Handbook of Cultural Sociology*, ed. John R. Hall, Laura Grindstaff and Minng-Cheng Lo [London: Routledge, 2010], 77–86). But both share one major blind spot in their work: they generally implicate culture as a unified system. Thus, Couldry identifies three strands of research within early cultural studies which can be useful to intersect with contemporary cultural sociology and potentially deflect a totalizing view of systemized cultures: contemporary popular culture, semiotic and poststructuralist reading cultures, and democratic culture. While keeping these debates in mind, in the present study, I am eclectic in using theoretical insights from these literatures to address concrete cases. I analyze the role of cultural resources in meaning-making and assess the power relations of such meaning-making. Simon During discusses the differing methodologies of both disciplines in *Cultural Studies*, 30.

1. CHINESE MIGRANTS' FOOD ENTREPRENEURSHIP AND ITALIANS' CULINARY TOURISM, 1962–2020

1. Dino Buzzati, "Ti piace la marosta?" *Corriere d'informazione*, October 2–3, 1962.

2. Stefano Bonilli, "Dietro i nomi esotici, sapori 'de noantri,'" *Corriere della Sera*, February 25, 1996.

3. Allan Bay, "Gong," https://allanbay.it/, April 12, 2019, https://allanbay.it/ristoranti-a-milano/gong/, accessed November 14, 2023.

4. Lucy M. Long, *Culinary Tourism* (Lexington: University Press of Kentucky, 2013), 21.

5. Ibid., 23.

6. Ibid., 23–32.

7. Krishnendu Ray, *The Ethnic Restaurateur* (London: Bloomsbury, 2016), 1 and 191–192.

8. This section's account is based on the introduction and chapter 1 of my previous book. See Gaoheng Zhang, *Migration and the Media: Debating Chinese Migration to Italy, 1992–2012* (Toronto: University of Toronto Press, 2019), 3–44. For the body of social scientific work on the subject, see references quoted in Zhang, *Migration and the Media*, 17–24 and 205–206. New information about the Chinese migration from the 2010s is also added to the current account.

9. Ministero del Lavoro e delle Politiche Sociali, "La comunità cinese in Italia: Rapporto annuale sulla presenza dei migranti" (Rome: Ministero del Lavoro e delle Politiche Sociali, 2021), 6.

10. Fabrizio Gatti, "Se il padrone è cinese. L'Italia dei padroni cinesi," *L'Espresso*, June 20, 2013.

11. Grazia Ting Deng, *Chinese Espresso: Contested Race and Convivial Space in Contemporary Italy* (Princeton, NJ: Princeton University Press, 2024).

12. Pino Pignatta, "Barge e Bagnolo, il dragone all'ombra del Monviso," *Famiglia Cristiana*, December 13, 2013.

13. Cristina Da Rold, "Cinesi in Italia, è davvero integrazione?," *L'Espresso*, February 18, 2016; Yang Shi Shi, *Cuore di seta* (Milano: Mondadori, 2017); and Lala Hu, *Semi di tè* (Busto Arsizio: People, 2020).

14. Daniele Brigadoi Cologna, "Il quartiere cinese di Milano: territorio conteso o laboratorio di ridefinizione dell'identità sociale degli immigrati cinesi in Italia?," *Mondo cinese*, no. 134 (2008).

15. https://www.cecn.it/, accessed October 31, 2022.

16. Fabio Berti and Valentina Pedone, "A Bridge between the Spiritual and the Worldly," in *Chinese Religions Going Global*, ed. Nanlai Cao, Giuseppe Giordan, and Fenggang Yang (Leiden: Brill, 2020), 43.

17. Ministero del Lavoro e delle Politiche Sociali, "La comunità cinese in Italia," 11.

18. For a recent overview of Chinese migrations in Europe, see Frank N. Pieke and Tabitha Speelman, "Chinese Investment Strategies and Migration—Does Diaspora Matter?," in *Chinese Migration and Economic Relations with Europe*, ed. Marco Sanfilippo and Agnieszka Weinar (New York: Routledge, 2016), 12–32.

19. Jason Horowitz, "A Forgotten Italian Port Could Become a Chinese Gateway to Europe," *New York Times*, March 18, 2019; and Francesca Ghiretti, "Demystifying China's Role in Italy's Port of Trieste," *Diplomat*, October 15, 2020.

20. Giselda Vagnoni and Laurie Chen, "Meloni Vows to 'Relaunch' Italy's Cooperation with China," *Reuters*, July 28, 2024.

21. Federica Redi, "Bacchette e forchette: la diffusione della cucina cinese in Italia," *Mondo cinese* 95 (1997): 41–67. In the following pages, I capture key research findings from previous scholarship on Chinese restaurants and catering in Italy. For the sake of a fluid narrative, I omit references to specific page numbers in the studies from which my information is derived. But the context of any individual paragraph makes clear which specific source it derives from.

22. Pierpaolo Mudu, "The People's Food: The Ingredients of 'Ethnic' Hierarchies and the Development of Chinese Restaurants in Rome," *GeoJournal* 68, no. 2/3 (2007): 195–210.

23. Dino Martirano, "E i cinesi festeggiano Capodanno," *Corriere della Sera*, February 10, 1994; and Massimo Alberini, "A tavola con le bacchette," *Corriere della Sera*, March 18, 1988. Another source indicates that four Chinese restaurants existed in Rome in 1970. See Enrico Altavilla, "Babele sulle rive del Tevere," *Corriere della Sera*, September 22, 1970.

24. Nicoletta Bressan, "L'imprenditoria cinese in Italia: due casi studio. La ristorazione cinese a Milano e il distretto del porfido a Trento" (Thesis, University of Trento, 2013), 197–266. This paragraph draws on this source. For additional information about the sector in the mid-2000s, see also Fabio Parasecoli, "Chinese Food Ways in Italy," *Chinese Food in Europe* 12, no. 2 (2005): 5, 8, and 16.

25. Simone Cinotto, *The Italian American Table: Food, Family, and Community in New York City* (Urbana: University of Illinois Press, 2013), 8.

26. Emanuela Scarpellini attributes the emergence of ethnic cuisines in Italy in this period to both Italians' increased travel abroad and growing migrant communities. Like previous scholars, Scarpellini counts curiosity, low prices, and the Italians' increased demand for eating out among the main reasons that led to the success of ethnic restaurants in Italy. Emanuela Scarpellini, *Food and Foodways in Italy from 1861 to the Present* (New York: Palgrave Macmillan, 2016), 167.

27. Massimo Alberini, "Quei cinesi così gentili," *Corriere della Sera*, August 1, 1989.

28. Laura Montanari, "I cinesi scoprono la campagna: boom di orti e serre in Toscana," *La Repubblica*, April 30, 2015.

29. For a sociological and anthropological study of Chinese-managed coffee bars in Italy, see Deng, *Chinese Espresso*.

30. Daniele Cologna, "Intervista/Walter Sirtori e Hujian Zhou (Angiè)," *Mondo cinese*, No. 163 (2017): 113–114.

31. Livio Zanini, "Non solo involtini primavera: Dinamiche dell'imprenditoria cinese nel settore della ristorazione in Veneto," in *Cinesi tra le maglie del lavoro*, ed. Maurizio Rasera and Devi Sacchetto (Milano: Franco Angeli, 2018), 145–178.

32. The abbreviations in the parentheses are used in Italy to indicate the corresponding types of company.

33. Bressan, "L'imprenditoria cinese in Italia," 197–266.

34. In Daniele Cologna's account of Chinese restaurants in Milan's Via Sarpi, the main thoroughfare of the city's Chinese neighborhood, the eatery Ravioleria hired female workers who made northeastern Chinese dumplings and crepes facing a transparent window. But this would still be viewed as manual labor and not as the work of a chef. See Cologna, "Intervista," 105–106.

35. For a list of notable Chinese restaurants in Italy, see "Sezione: Ristoranti Cinesi," *Cina in Italia*, https://cinainitalia.com/category/ristoranti-cinesi/, accessed May 29, 2020. For two useful lists of notable Chinese restaurants in Milan, see Annalisa Zordan, "I migliori ristoranti cinesi di Milano," *Gambero Rosso*, February 4, 2020, https://www.gamberorosso.it/notizie/i-migliori-ristoranti-cinesi-di-milano/, accessed June 15, 2020; and Edoardo Abate, "Elenco dei ristoranti cinesi di Milano," *Cina in Italia*, November 22, 2018, https://cinainitalia.com/2018/11/22/ristoranti-cinesi-milano/, accessed June 15, 2020. For an example of Chinese-Italian fusion cuisine, see "Mi-Cucina di confine" in Milan, http://www.mi-cucinadiconfine.it/, accessed June 15, 2020.

36. https://www.bon-wei.it/about-us/?lang=en, accessed May 26, 2022. English originals.

37. https://www.bon-wei.it/wp-content/uploads/2018/10/2018_CARTA_BONWEI_OK.pdf, accessed May 26, 2022.

38. For a contemporary explanation of the name of this dish from an English-language Chinese newspaper, see Li Anlan, "The legend of a beggar's chicken," *SHINE*, July 14, 2019, https://www.shine.cn/feature/taste/1907148368/, accessed January 25, 2023.

39. Tripadvisor.it, https://www.tripadvisor.it/Restaurant_Review-g187849-d2019316-Reviews-Bon_Wei-Milan_Lombardy.html, accessed May 28, 2020.

40. https://www.facebook.com/ristorantemao/about/?ref=page_internal, accessed May 28, 2020.

41. Tripadvisor.it, https://www.tripadvisor.it/Restaurant_Review-g187849-d8677564-Reviews-or40-Mao_Hunan-Milan_Lombardy.html, accessed May 28, 2020. For an analysis of Chinese students in Italy and their relationship with Chinese food, see Daniele Cologna, "L'importanza crescente degli studenti universitari cinesi per la società italiana," *Orizzonte Cina* 7, no. 6 (2016): 16–17.

42. Editorial, "Ristorazione cinese, settore con 1.300 locali," *Avvenire*, January 26, 2020.

43. For coverage of this phenomenon, see Maria Pranzo, "E a Milano è boom dei delivery Made in Asia," *La Repubblica*, May 5, 2020. For information on Guua Now, see http://now.guua.com/page/about, accessed January 25, 2023.

44. Fabio Parasecoli, *Bite Me: Food in Popular Culture* (Oxford: Berg, 2008), 128.

45. Roberto Della Rovere, "Una serata diversa? Provare con l'Asia," *Corriere della Sera*, July 19, 1985.

46. Carlo Petrini, *Slow Food: The Case for Taste* (New York: Columbia University Press, 2003), 26–34.

47. Jack Goody, *Food and Love: A Cultural History of East and West* (London: Verso, 2010), 166.

48. Ibid., 170. See also J. A. G. Roberts, *China to Chinatown: Chinese Food in the West* (London: Reaktion, 2002), 225–226.

49. Buzzati, "Ti piace la marosta?"

50. On the figure of cinesina in literature, see Gaoheng Zhang, "The *Chinaman* and the *Cinesina*: Gendering Chinese Migrants in Italian Novels," *Journal of Romance Studies* 19, no. 1 (2019): 72–74 and 85–92.

51. Dino Buzzati, "Ti piace la marosta?" *Corriere della Sera*, August 14, 2014. For the legacy of La Pagoda that the Chinese restaurant in Milan Oren continues, see http://www.oren.it/2020/04/18/history/, accessed June 15, 2020.

52. Stefano Bonilli, "Dietro i nomi esotici, sapori 'de noantri,'" *Corriere della Sera*, February 25, 1996.

53. Alessandra Dal Monte, "Soup dumplings, ecco 6 indirizzi in cui mangiarli a Milano," *Corriere della Sera*, December 8, 2017.

54. For a discussion on meal sequences in Italy and in China, see Parasecoli, "Chinese Food Ways in Italy."

55. Monica Paternesi, "E la cena cinese arrivò in tavola," *Corriere della Sera*, July 21, 1986.

56. Massimo Alberini, "Cina, oltre il 'vecchio' menu," *Corriere della Sera*, June 9, 1988.

57. Bruno Vergottini, "Gusto d'oriente per l'ultimo imperatore," *Corriere della Sera*, March 20, 1992.

58. "Gampiero" is a typo from the text. The first name of the chef Giampiero Tung is mentioned earlier in the news account.

59. For a brief context of this detail, see Roberts, *China to Chinatown*, 227–228.

60. Parasecoli, "Chinese Food Ways in Italy."

61. Scarpellini, *Food and Foodways*, 167.

62. For a list of dishes that the author discusses, see Bamboo Hirst, *Il riso non cresce sugli alberi* (Milano: La Tartaruga Edizioni, 1988), 163–165.

63. Allan Bay, "In trent'anni un boom di ristoranti," *Corriere della Sera*, July 1, 1997.

64. On the history of chop suey, see Yong Chen, *Chop Suey, USA: The Story of Chinses Food in America* (New York: Columbia University Press), 139–147; Haiming Liu, *From Canton Restaurant to Panda Express: A History of Chinese Food in the United States* (New Brunswick, NJ: Rutgers University Press, 2015), 49–70; and Anne Mendelson, *Chow Chop Suey: Food and the Chinese American Journey* (New York: Columbia University Press, 2016), 99–137.

65. Liu, *From Canton Restaurant to Panda Express*, 3 and 49.

2. ROMANTIC WAITRESSES VS. "KUNG FOOD" WORKERS: GENDERING THE CHINESE RESTAURANT

1. For examples of these perceptions, see Enzo d'Errico, "Il Dragone sul racket dei botti," *Corriere della Sera*, December 29, 1988; and Massimo Alberini, "Cina, oltre il 'vecchio' menu," *Corriere della Sera*, June 9, 1988.

2. David Beriss, "Haute, Fast, and Historic: Restaurants and the Rise of Popular Culture," in *The Bloomsbury Handbook of Food and Popular Culture*, ed. Kathleen LeBesco and Peter Naccarato (London: Bloomsbury Academic, 2018), 124. For another example of a recent study of restaurant culture and communication issues, see Vincent (Tzu-Wen) Cheng, "'A Four-legged Duck?': Chinese Restaurant Culture in the United States from a Crosscultural/Inter-cultural Communication Perspective," in *Food as Communication: Communication as Food*, ed. Janet M. Cramer, Carlnita Greene, and Lynn Walters (New York: Peter Lang, 2011), 195–216.

3. See references in the Introduction on Chinese and Italian migrant identity-making in the United States. See also Isabelle de Solier, *Food and the Self: Consumption, Production and Material Culture* (London: Bloomsbury Academic, 2013).

4. Peter Bondanella, *A History of Italian Cinema* (New York: Continuum, 2009), 453–456.

5. Roberto Curti, *Italia odia: il cinema poliziesco italiano* (Torino: Lindau, 2007), 338.

6. Ibid., 457–458.

7. John Urry and Jonas Larsen, *The Tourist Gaze 3.0* (London: Sage, 2011), 119.

8. Giraldi's background, which is recounted in other films involving this character, includes a prolonged involvement in Roman organized crime. On Giraldi's past, see Curti, *Italia odia*, 187.

9. Laura Lindenfeld and Fabio Parasecoli, "Food and Cinema: An Evolving Relationship," in *The Bloomsbury Handbook of Food and Popular Culture*, ed. Kathleen LeBesco and Peter Naccarato (London: Bloomsbury Academic, 2018), 35.

10. Bondanella lists more examples of American cinematic influences on polizieschi films, including the car chase. Bondanella, *A History of Italian Cinema*, 459.

11. Gina Marchetti, *Romance and the "Yellow Peril": Race, Sex, and Discursive Strategies in Hollywood Fiction* (Berkeley: University of California Press, 1993), 2–4.

12. Krystyn R. Moon, *Yellowface: Creating the Chinese in American Popular Music and Performance, 1850s–1920s* (New Brunswick, NJ: Rutgers University Press, 2004), 6 and 8.

13. Dino Martirano, "Trucidati due cinesi," *Corriere Roma*, March 27, 1994.

14. Gaoheng Zhang, *Migration and the Media: Debating Chinese Migration to Italy, 1992–2012* (Toronto: University of Toronto Press, 2019), 49–50.

15. Ibid., 48–56. For television representations of the Chinese mafia, see Gaoheng Zhang, "Chinese Migrants and the 'Chinese Mafia' in Contemporary Italian Culture," in *Transcending Borders: Selected Papers in East Asian Studies*, ed. Valentina Pedone and Sagiyama Ikuko (Firenze: Firenze University Press, 2016), 67–86.

16. For examples, see Cesare De Simone, "Roma, la mafia cinese sequestra ristoratore," *Corriere della Sera*, December 5, 1992; and Ranieri Orlandi, "Rapito dalla mafia gialla," *Corriere della Sera*, June 27, 1993.

17. Dino Martirano, "Allarme 'sole rosso,' racket cinese," *Corriere della Sera*, May 16, 1992.

18. Gianfranco Ambrosini, "Il racket degli 'schiavi' reclutati in Cina," *Corriere della Sera*, February 15, 1992.

19. For examples, see Lavinia Di Gianvito, "Mafia dagli occhi a mandorla," *Corriere della Sera*, February 1, 1995; Maurizio Donelli, "La rete del dragone," *Corriere della Sera*, February 27, 1995; Ranieri Orlandi, "Colpo alla mafia

cinese," *Corriere della Sera*, June 25, 1995; and Paolo Brogi, "Zan Xian, il cinese dei misteri," *Corriere della Sera*, September 16, 1998.

20. Zhang, *Migration and the Media*, 10–12 and 37–44.

21. For an overview of key fiction and documentary films and their frames and agendas, see Gaoheng Zhang, "Frames and Agendas in Italian Films about Chinese Migrants," *LEA—Lingue e letterature d'Oriente e d'Occidente* 8 (2019): 123–137. For an analysis of film ethics in this body of films, see Gaoheng Zhang, "Chinese migrants, morality and film ethics in Italian cinema," *Journal of Modern Italian Studies* 22, no. 3 (2017): 385–405. For an overview of Italian films about the Chinese, see Mary Ann McDonald Carolan, *Orienting Italy: China through the Lens of Italian Filmmakers* (Buffalo: State University of New York, 2022).

22. While *Gorbaciof* was released in 2010, its script was developed beginning in the early 2000s. See Gabriele Barcaro, "Stefano Incerti, Regista. Un apologo Lirico su misura per Toni Servillo," https://cineuropa.org/it/interview/151528/ (accessed April 23, 2022). This is the primary reason I grouped the filmed among films produced at the end of the 2000s, as the section title indicates. Similarly, I view *Io sono Li* as part of a wave of films designed and conceived in the 2000s rather than in the 2010s. According to Francesco Bonsembiante, production of the film began in 2008. See Francesco Bonsembiante, "Production notes," http://www.iosonoli.com/en/note-di-produzione/, accessed April 23, 2022.

23. Marchetti, *Romance and the "Yellow Peril,"* 8.

24. Renee Tajima-Peña, "Lotus Blossoms Don't Bleed: Images of Asian Women," in *Making Waves: An Anthology of Writings By and About Asian American Women*, ed. Asian Women United (Boston: Beacon Press, 1989), 309 and 314.

25. Gaoheng Zhang, "The Three Riddles in Puccini's *Turandot*: Masculinity, Empire, and Orientalism," in *Der musikalisch modellierte Mann: Interkulturelle und interdisziplinäre Männlichkeitsstudien zur Oper und Literatur des 19. und frühen 20. Jahrhunderts*, ed. Ester Saletta and Barbara Hindinger (Vienna: Praesens, 2012), 397–416.

26. Zhang, *Migration and the Media*, 61–68.

27. Marchetti, *Romance and the "Yellow Peril,"* 8.

28. See Zhang, "Chinese Migrants, Morality and Film Ethics in Italian Cinema," 395–401. For other studies of this film, see Hillary Chung and Bernadette Luciano, "The Dis/locat/ing Migrant as an Agent of Transposition: Borensztein's *Un cuento chino* and Segre's *Io sono Li*," *Studies in European Cinema* 11, no. 3 (2014): 191–211; Eddie Bertozzi, "The Possibility of Chineseness: Negotiating Chinese Identity in *Shun Li and the Poet* and *The Arrival of*

Wang," *Journal of Italian Cinema and Media Studies* 2, no. 1 (2014): 59–73; and Áine O'Healy, *Migrant Anxieties: Italian Cinema in a Transnational Frame* (Bloomington: Indiana University Press, 2019), 186–192.

29. For examples, see Celestino Deleyto, "Looking from the Border: A Cosmopolitan Approach to Contemporary Cinema," *Transnational Cinemas* 8, no. 2 (2017): 95–112; Ron Kubati, "Comunità chiuse: *Io sono Li, La giusta distanza* e *Cose dell'altro mondo*," *NEMLA Italian Studies, Special Issue: New Perspectives on Veneto Literary and Cultural Itineraries* xxxv (2013): 221–244; and Lisa Dolasinski, "Media-ting 'Sterile Masculinity': On Male Aging, Migration, and Biopolitics in a (Post)Berlusconi Italy," *Gender/Sexuality/Italy* 5 (2018): 80–106.

30. Jane Ferry, *Food in Film: A Culinary Performance of Communication* (London: Routledge, 2015), 29.

31. The concept is expressed as *utramque partem* in Latin-language rhetorical treatises. Aristotle contends that developing the skill of arguing both sides of an unsettled controversy helps to better understand the more just arguments. See Stephen Leighton, "Passions and Persuasion," in *A Companion to Aristotle*, ed. Georgios Anagnostopoulos (Malden, MA: Wiley-Blackwell, 2009), 606.

32. See Zhang, *Migration and the Media*; Zhang, "Frames and Agendas in Italian Films about Chinese Migrants"; Zhang, "Chinese migrants, morality and film ethics in Italian cinema"; Zhang, "Chinese Migrants and the 'Chinese Mafia' in Contemporary Italian Culture"; Gaoheng Zhang, "Contemporary Italian Novels on Chinese Immigration to Italy," *California Italian Studies* 4, no. 2 (2013): 1–38; and Zhang, "The Chinaman and the *Cinesina*."

33. Jachinson Chan, *Chinese American Masculinities: From Fu Manchu to Bruce Lee* (New York: Routledge: 2001), 73–78; and Kam Louie, *Theorising Chinese Masculinity: Society and Gender in China* (Cambridge: Cambridge University Press, 2002), 145–149.

34. On patricide, see Chan, *Chinese American Masculinities*, 97–102.

35. The comics refer to Segre's film in episode 2 through two details. First, the name "Shun Li" appears as a store's name. Second, a female barista in a Chinese-managed Italian coffee bar is bullied by Italians.

36. Elspeth Probyn, *Carnal Appetites: FoodSexIdentities* (London: Routledge, 2000), 7.

37. Chan, *Chinese American Masculinities*, 51–72. On the model minority discourse in Asian America, see Viet Thanh Nguyen, *Race and Resistance: Literature and Politics in Asian America* (Oxford: Oxford University Press, 2002), 146–149.

38. Chan, *Chinese American Masculinities*, 53.

39. Louie, *Theorising Chinese Masculinity*, 14–15, 19, and 146–147.

40. Allan Bay, "Con lo sguardo oltre la Cina," *Corriere della Sera*, February 8, 2012.

41. Allan Bay, "Tutto il buono della Manciuria," *Corriere della Sera*, May 9, 2012 and Roberta Schira, "L'evoluzione del raviolo," *Corriere della Sera*, June 30, 2018.

42. Laura Vincenti, "Hai detto panino?" *Corriere della Sera*, February 8, 2019; and Alessandra Dal Monte, "Hotpotmania," *Corriere della Sera*, February 16, 2018.

43. *Corriere della Sera* covered La Pagoda and mentioned a chef there, possibly Chou Zirong mentioned in *Chinamen*. See G. L. P., "Ha voluto far sapere che non è più cinese," *Corriere della Sera*, July 16, 1973.

44. For an example focused on Chinese restaurants, see Cecilia Zecchinelli, "Il più ricco dei tanti cinesi," *Corrier Economia*, June 19, 2000.

45. On these issues in the Chinese American context, see Shun Lu and Gary Alan Fine, "The Presentation of Ethnic Authenticity: Chinese Food as a Social Accomplishment," *Sociological Quarterly* 36, no. 3 (1995): 535–553.

46. As Andrea Scibetta argues, the graphic novel also restores a "polycentric image of Chinese people in Italy" in its overall design. See Andrea Scibetta, "Chinese Migration(s) to Italy Beyond Stereotypes and Simplistic Views: The Case of the Graphic Novels *Primavere e Autunni* and *Chinamen*," in *Tracing Pathways: Interdisciplinary Studies on Modern and Contemporary East Asia*, ed. Diego Cucinelli and Andrea Scibetta (Firenze: Firenze University Press, 2020), 96 and 102–106.

47. Térésa Faucon, "*Kung food*: chorégraphier les gestes culinaires," *Anthropology of Food*, no. 15 (2021).

3. THE CHINESE WHO EAT DOGMEAT: RACIALIZATION OF CHINESE FOOD CONSUMPTION

1. https://www.actionprojectanimal.org/, accessed July 10, 2020; and Mauro Giordano, "La missione di Elisabetta Franchi per salvare i cani di Yulin," *Corriere di Bologna*, April 2, 2018.

2. Jiaqi Luo, "The Taboo Topics Brands Need to Avoid in China," *Jing Daily*, May 13, 2020.

3. According to another related stereotype about domestic pets, the Chinese eat cat meat. But this stereotype is much less common. For an example, see Editorial, "'I cinesi hanno rapito molti gatti,'" *Corriere della Sera*, April 14, 2010.

4. David Beriss, "Haute, Fast, and Historic: Restaurants and the Rise of Popular Culture," in *The Bloomsbury Handbook of Food and Popular Culture*, ed. Kathleen LeBesco and Peter Naccarato (London: Bloomsbury Academic,

2018); and Aliza S. Wong, "Authenticity *all'italiana*: Food Discourses, Diasporas, and the Limits of Cuisine in Contemporary Italy," in *Representing Italy Through Food*, ed. Peter Naccarato, Zachary Nowak, and Elgin K. Eckert (London: Bloomsbury, 2017), 33–54.

5. For examples of such coverage in *Corriere della Sera*, see Vittorio Alessi, "Il mondo stravagante con cui si nutre il popolo cinese," *Corriere della Sera*, February 17, 1940; Piero Ostellino, "E alle nove di sera i cinesi vanno a dormire," *Corriere della Sera*, February 2, 1979; Renato Ferraro, "Per i cinesi il capodanno va bene una strage di animali," *Corriere della Sera*, February 6, 1988; Marina Martorana, "I popoli a tavola," *Corriere della Sera*, July 26, 1993; and Paolo Salom, "Olimpiadi, carne di cane vietata. 'Agli stranieri non piace,'" *Corriere della Sera*, July 12, 2008.

6. Flavio Haver, "Cani e gatti uccisi, controlli nei ristoranti," *Corriere Roma*, June 2, 1994.

7. Roberto Della Rovere, "'Chiudete quei ristoranti cinesi,'" *Corriere Roma*, February 24, 1996.

8. Gianni Santucci, "'Carne di cane offerta nei ristoranti cinesi,'" *Corriere della Sera*, August 6, 2006; and Michele Focarete, "Gli animalisti: cani macellati in casa per mangiarli," *Corriere della Sera*, September 27, 2009.

9. Mary Douglas, *Purity and Danger: An Analysis of Concept of Pollution and Taboo* (London: Routledge, 2003), 51.

10. For a critique of structuralism in cultural interpretations of food, see Bob Ashley, Joanne Hollows, Steve Jones, and Ben Taylor, *Food and Cultural Studies* (New York: Routledge, 2004), 3–8.

11. Douglas, *Purity and Danger*, 60–62.

12. Sidney W. Mintz, "Foreword: Food for Thought," in *The Globalization of Chinese Food*, ed. David Y. H. Wu and Sidney C. H. Cheung (Honolulu: University of Hawai'i Press, 2002), xvii.

13. On the film's influence in Italian popular culture and the environment in which it was created, see Rory McKenzie, "Italy's *ragioniere*? The National and International Relevance of Ugo Fantozzi," *Journal of Italian Cinema and Media Studies* 9, no. 2 (2021): 245–248 and 253.

14. Japanese restaurants emerged in Rome in the mid-1970s and in Milan in the late 1980s, including Roma Hamasei, http://www.roma-hamasei.com/it_storia.html; and Poporoya, https://www.poporoyamilano.com/chi-siamo/, accessed July 10, 2020.

15. Massimo Alberini, "I ristorante? Un giallo telefonico," *Corriere della Sera*, February 24, 1988; and Pierpaolo Mudu, "The People's Food: The Ingredients of 'Ethnic' Hierarchies and the Development of Chinese Restaurants in Rome," *GeoJournal* 68, no. 2/3 (2007), 207.

16. Gaoheng Zhang, "Chinese Migrants and the 'Chinese Mafia' in Contemporary Italian Culture," in *Transcending Borders: Selected Papers in East Asian Studies*, ed. Valentina Pedone and Sagiyama Ikuko (Firenze: Firenze University Press, 2016), 77–83.

17. Francesco Ricatti, "Humiliation and Love: Villaggio, Benigni, and the Cultural Politics of Emotions," *Incontri: Rivista europea di studi italiani* 29, no. 2 (2014): 11–13.

18. For primary texts in western languages that describe this habit, beginning with Marco Polo's diaries, see J. A. G. Roberts, *China to Chinatown: Chinese Food in the West* (London: Reaktion, 2002), 13–131.

19. Gaoheng Zhang, *Migration and the Media: Debating Chinese Migration to Italy, 1992–2012* (Toronto: University of Toronto Press, 2019), 48–57.

20. Yong Chen, "Food, Race, and Ethnicity," in *The Oxford Handbook of Food History*, ed. Jefferey M. Pilcher (Oxford: Oxford University Press, 2012), 434; and Robert Ji-Song Ku, *Dubious Gastronomy: The Cultural Politics of Eating Asian in the USA* (Honolulu: University of Hawai'i Press, 2014), 146–147. The trope distantly draws on Marco Polo's travel diaries, which contain many descriptions of Asian eating habits that were unusual and unappetizing for the European traveler.

21. The circumstances of the Reuters story are recounted in Ku, *Dubious Gastronomy*, 134–135.

22. During the 1970s, two well-known Chinese American authors, Maxine Hong Kingston and Frank Chin, reinforced the dogmeat stereotype by highlighting it in their writings.

23. On *Mondo Cane*'s influence, see Gino J. Moliterno, "*Mondo Cane* and the Invention of the Shockumentary," in *The Italian Cinema Book*, ed. Peter Bondanella (Cham, Switzerland: Palgrave Macmillan, 2014), 172–180.

24. On the ethnocultural approach to depicting the Chinese, see Zhang, *Migration and the Media*, 41–44.

25. Mark Goodall, *Sweet and Savage: The World through the Shockumentary Film Lens* (London: Headpress, 2006).

26. Mikita Brottman, "Mondo Horror: Carnivalizing the Taboo," in *The Horror Film*, ed. Stephen Prince (New Brunswick, NJ: Rutgers University Press, 2004), 168.

27. This insight builds upon Ibid., 168–169.

28. This association also resurfaced in certain comments by Italian politicians before the virus struck Italy on a large scale. On February 6, 2020, Gianfranco Librandi, a politician affiliated with the centrist and center-left political party Italia Viva, went on the television channel La 7 to recommend that in order for the Chinese to "stop eating wild animals, the solution is to

consume the Mediterranean diet." On February 27, 2020, Luca Zaia, then president of the Veneto region, who also served as the Minister of Agricultural, Food, and Forestry Policies between 2008 and 2010 in Silvio Berlusconi's government, said that the Chinese ate live mice. See La 7, "Coronavirus, Gianfranco Librandi: 'Basta mangiare animali selvaggi, soluzione è la dieta mediterranea,'" Feburary 6, 2020, https://www.la7.it/coffee-break/video/coronavirus-gianfranco-librandi-basta-mangiare-animali-selvaggi-soluzione-e-la-dieta-mediterranea-06-02-2020-306059, accessed May 14, 2022; and RaiNews, "Zaia: 'I cinesi mangiano topi vivi.' L'ambasciata di Pechino protesta, lui si scusa," February 29, 2020, https://www.rainews.it/archivio-rainews/articoli/zaia-cinesi-mangiano-topi-vivi-ambasciata-protesta-lui-si-scusa-6630af83-073d-49b3-8e60-0f47339f672d.html (accessed May 14, 2022).

29. Ku, *Dubious Gastronomy*, 134–135.

30. For extensive discussions about migrants' talking back to mainstream Italian society, see Graziella Parati, *Migration Italy: The Art of Talking Back in a Destination Culture* (Toronto: University of Toronto Press, 2005).

31. Harry Kashdan, "Eating to Become: Italian Counter-Narratives of Assimilation, Identity, and Migration," in *The Routledge Companion to Literature and Food*, ed. Lorna Piatti-Farnell and Donna Lee Brien (New York: Routledge, 2018), 175.

32. Graziella Parati, *Migrant Writers and Urban Space in Italy: Proximities and Affect in Literature and Film* (Cham, Switzerland: Palgrave Macmillan, 2017), 76.

33. Laura-Marzia Lenci, "Feeding the Body, Feeding the Language: Nourishment as Metaphor of Writing in Igiaba Scego's Literary Works," in *Food and Women in Italian Literature, Culture and Society: Eve's Sinful Bite*, ed. Claudia Bernardi, Francesca Calamita, and Daniele De Feo (London: Bloomsbury Academic, 2020), 128–137; Francesca Calamita, "*'Identica a loro?'* (In)digesting Food and Identity in Igiaba Scego's. 'Salsicce,'" in *(In)digestion in Literature and Film*, ed. Serena J. Rivera and Niki Kiviat (New York: Routledge, 2020), 186–200; and Federica Angelini, "Food and Identity in Laila Wadia and Igiaba Scego," *Anuario de Literatura Comparada* 3 (2013): 249–257.

34. Valentina Pedone, ed., *Il vicino cinese: la comunità cinese a Roma* (Rome: Nuove Edizioni Romane, 2008).

35. Christof Rapp, "The Nature and Goals of Rhetoric," in *A Companion to Aristotle*, ed. Georgios Anagnostopoulos (Chichester: Wiley-Blackwell, 2009), 581.

36. wei_alessandro, https://www.tiktok.com/@wei_alessandro/video/6844804678983765253?is_copy_url=1&is_from_webapp=v2&lang=en, July 2, 2020, accessed May 14, 2022.

37. dazibao, https://www.tiktok.com/@dazibao/video/6905033042880957697?is_copy_url=1&is_from_webapp=v1&lang=en&q=carne%20di%20cane%20cinesi%20italia&t=1652593264235%2C, December 11, 2020, accessed May 14, 2022.

38. For a survey of this literature written in Italian, see Gaoheng Zhang, "Contemporary Italian Novels on Chinese Immigration to Italy," *California Italian Studies* 4, no. 2 (2013): 1–38. For an analysis of Chinese-language literature authored by Chinese migrants living in Italy, see Valentina Pedone, "Self-narration as a 'Social Action' in the Works of the Sino-Italian Author Hu Lanbo," in *Exchanges and Parallels between Italy and East Asia*, ed. Gaoheng Zhang and Mario Mignone (Newcastle: Cambridge Scholars, 2020), 292–303.

39. Mimi Sheller and John Urry, "The New Mobilities Paradigm," *Environment and Planning* 38 (2006): 216.

4. FIGHTING "YELLOW MOZZARELLA": ITALIANS SAFEGUARD FOOD'S AUTHENTICITY

1. Emanuela Scarpellini, *Food and Foodways in Italy from 1861 to the Present* (New York: Palgrave Macmillan, 2016), 165.

2. Marco Fortis, *Il Made in Italy* (Bologna: Il Mulino, 1998).

3. Typing the keyword "Made in Italy" in a search engine at any major Italian news outlet will yield a significant quantity of coverage on the subject.

4. Gaoheng Zhang, *Migration and the Media: Debating Chinese Migration to Italy, 1992–2012* (Toronto: University of Toronto Press, 2019), 134–175.

5. For examples, see Carlo Andrea Finotto, "Made in Italy in Cina, questo sconosciuto (con poche eccezioni)," *Il Sole 24 Ore*, September 18, 2018; and Francesco Sisci, "In Cina inchiesta sui mobili Da Vinci, finto made in Italy," *Il Sole 24 Ore*, July 12, 2018.

6. Deborah Lupton, *Food, the Body, and the Self* (London: Sage, 1998), 152.

7. Valeria Siniscalchi, *Slow Food: The Economy and Politics of a Global Movement* (London: Bloomsbury, 2023), 166–167.

8. Giovanna De Luca, "*Into Paradiso* and *Mozzarella Stories*: Comedy, Mafia and immigration—an interview with Paola Randi and Edoardo De Angelis," *Journal of Italian Cinema and Media Studies* 3, no. 3 (2015): 383.

9. Áine O'Healy, *Migrant Anxieties: Italian Cinema in a Transnational Frame* (Bloomington: Indiana University Press, 2019), 187.

10. Helene A. Shugart, "Sumptuous Texts: Consuming 'Otherness' in the Food Film Genre," *Critical Studies in Media Communication* 25, no. 1 (2008): 72.

11. Vladimiro Polchi, "Se mozzarella e prosciutto li producono gli immigrati il made in Italy a tavola parla sempre più straniero," *La Repubblica*, April 28, 2015.

12. For an English-language example of this coverage, see Dany Mitzman, "The Sikhs who saved Parmesan," June 25, 2015, BBC Magazine, https://www.bbc.com/news/magazine-33149580, accessed May 22, 2020.

13. Emanuele Scarci, "Made in Italy terra di conquista. Ma siamo anche noi predatori," *Il Sole 24 Ore*, September 12, 2017.

14. Roberta Scagliarini, "Bright Food. 'Investiremo di più nella dieta mediterranea,'" *Corriere della Sera*, June 17, 2015.

15. For examples, see 时尚先生,"意大利知名橄榄油品牌翡丽百瑞（FILIPPO BERIO）中国上市," 风尚中国, August 12, 2015, http://m.fengsung.com/n-150812141920400.html, accessed November 16, 2023; and sohu.com, "法比奥：意大利百年橄榄油走上中国餐桌，背后是中意文化的交流与协同丨老外讲故事·海外员工看中国," September 23, 2022, https://www.sohu.com/a/587350420_121117454, accessed November 16, 2023.

16. Xinhua, "Chinese Olive Oil Wins Top Award in Int'l Competition in Greece," July 11, 2020, http://www.china.org.cn/business/2020-07/11/content_76261797.htm, accessed November 16, 2023; and Tommaso Cinquemani, "La Cina diventa produttrice di olio extravergine di oliva. E vince premi," AgroNotizie, January 8, 2021, https://agronotizie.imagelinenetwork.com/agricoltura-economia-politica/2021/01/08/la-cina-diventa-produttrice-di-olio-extravergine-di-oliva-e-vince-premi/68924, accessed November 16, 2023.

17. 闫姣, "东西问丨赵海云：从地中海'远嫁'而来的油橄榄, 如何适应'东方水土'?" 中国新闻网, May 10, 2023, http://www.chinaqw.com/yw/2023/05-10/357714.shtml, accessed November 16, 2023.

18. Zhang, *Migration and the Media*, 166–168.

19. Fabrizio Gatti, "Se il padrone è cinese. L'Italia dei padroni cinesi," *L'Espresso*, June 20, 2013.

20. Micol Sarfatti, "Sapessi come è strano lavorare per il signor Hu a Milano," *Corriere della Sera*, September 29, 2017.

21. For examples, see Andrea Galli, "Ogni giorno nasce un'impresa cinese," *Corriere della Sera*, September 22, 2009; and Laura Vincenti, "Bar e tabaccherie (sempre più) cinesi: 'Oggi sono uno su dieci,'" *Corriere della Sera*, November 18, 2019.

22. The website has since changed domain names. Alessandro M. Innocenti, "Alberghi e negozi in saldo sperando in un carico di yuan," *Corriere della Sera*, July 21, 2013.

23. For examples of such media coverage, see Vladimiro Polchi, "Capitali cinesi nelle nostre industrie. Pechino si compra l'Italia in crisi," *Le Inchieste* in

La Repubblica, October 4, 2013; Isidoro Trovato, "Le sette meraviglie italiane già comprate dai cinesi," *Corriere della Sera*, June 1, 2016; and Marco Ludovico, "Energia, reti, aziende strategiche: la mappa dei capitali cinesi in Italia," *Il Sole 24 Ore*, November 9, 2020.

24. Carlo Turchetti, "Italia. Il soccorso dei capitali del Dragone," *Corriere della Sera*, December 22, 2014.

25. Polchi, "Capitali cinesi nelle nostre industrie."

26. To view this commercial on YouTube, see https://www.youtube.com/watch?v=YKAuURrNNHc (accessed May 21, 2020). The "Paradise" advertisements inspired an episode of the Italian version of the sitcom *Camera Café*, titled "The Mysterious Chinese Man" (2017), in which the mythical Chinese businessman that purchases everything turns out to be a fraud. As another episode reveals, in reality he is a Vietnamese man who poses as the Chinese archetype to drink machine-made Italian coffee for free. See "Il cinese misterioso," Season 6, Episode 136, Rai Due, November 27, 2017, https://www.youtube.com/watch?v=Hf3JXCRx2Z4, accessed May 29, 2020; and "Lezione di cinesi/ Lesson by the Chinese," Season 6, Episode 8, Rai Due, September 6, 2017, https://www.youtube.com/watch?v=wokaVpbHUAQ, accessed May 29, 2020.

27. Such lampooning is missing from Lavazza's 1986 spot featuring several Italians dining in a Chinese restaurant. The focus there is still on the Italians' aversion to bizarre Chinese dishes, such as serpent-meat spring rolls, steamed jellyfish, and the so-called "ants climbing a tree" (glass noodles with ground pork). The presence of Lavazza coffee at the end of the meal provides much relief for the Italian diners. See https://www.youtube.com/watch?v=SKX5lCLbO70&t=4s, accessed May 21, 2020.

28. For a recent example, see Eric Sylvers, "Lavazza and Illy Say 'Basta' as Global Coffee Wars Come to Italy," *Wall Street Journal*, October 13, 2018.

29. https://www.youtube.com/watch?v=Jzs-kAyxnwc and https://www.youtube.com/watch?v=5QfZxjBxeJk, accessed May 21, 2020.

30. Filomena Greco, "Lavazza accelera sulla Cina e apre con il socio Yum mille caffetterie," *Il Sole 24 Ore*, September 23, 2021.

31. Daniela Polizzi, "Lavazza investe sull'Italia," *Corriere della Sera*, May 4, 2020.

32. Emanuele Scarci, "Lavazza fa shopping in Canada," *Il Sole 24 Ore*, May 25, 2017; and Scarci, "Made in Italy terra di conquista."

33. Sylvers, "Lavazza and Illy Say 'Basta' as Global Coffee Wars Come to Italy."

34. Sohu.com, "这家百年意大利咖啡品牌，将加大对云南咖啡豆采购量," October 15, 2023, https://www.sohu.com/a/728514693_121668715, accessed November 16, 2023.

35. 钟经文, "中国云南: 位处全球三大黄金咖啡产区," 江西网络广播电视台, https://cn.chinadaily.com.cn/a/202211/23/WS637d9e55a3109bd995a5199c.html, accessed November 16, 2023; and Yunnan Commercial Representative Office in Paris, France, "云南, 中国咖啡第一产区," http://oroyunnanfr.com/%E4%BA%91%E5%8D%97%E5%92%96%E5%95%A1/, accessed November 17, 2023.

36. 姚宇琛, "中国咖啡, 正在'被看到'," 农民日报, March 20, 2022, http://agri.china.com.cn/2022-03/29/content_41919463.htm, accessed November 17, 2022.

37. Direzione generale, Cinema e audiovisivo, "Accordi coproduzione cinematografica tra il Governo della Repubblica italiana e il Governo della Repubblica Popolare cinese," December 4, 2004, https://cinema.cultura.gov.it/normativa/normativa-internazionale/accordi-internazionali-di-coproduzione/accordo-di-coproduzione-cinematografica-tra-il-governo-della-repubblica-italiana-e-il-governo-della-repubblica-popolare-cinese/, accessed November 17, 2022. For Bortone's discussion of co-productions, see Laviosa, "*Caffè*—The First Sino-Italian co-production," 97.

38. Editorial, "Riso Gallo's rooster is back and updated with Armando Testa," July 10, 2017, https://newsroom.armandotesta.it/en/riso-gallos-rooster-is-back-and-updated-with-armando-testa/, accessed December 11, 2022.

39. Franco Tassi, "RISO GALLO—ETNICO VENERE—CINA," July 10, 2017, https://www.youtube.com/watch?v=DX002H6-bXM&ab_channel=ArmandoTestaSpA, accessed December 11, 2022.

40. Uncredited filmmaker for Armando Testa Agency, "Riso Gallo Venere—Soggetto Riso Nero e Rosso," May 11, 2020, https://www.youtube.com/watch?v=meXEBgCn2SY, accessed December 11, 2022.

41. The former description is archived at https://web.archive.org/web/20140726205411/http://www.risovenere.it/riso-venere/, accessed May 18, 2022.

42. https://www.risovenere.it/la-filiera-riso-venere/, accessed May 18, 2022.

43. Erika Camasso, "Ha ingolosito anche la Cina, il riso nero del dottor Wang," *Corriere della Sera*, September 9, 2005.

44. J. A. G. Roberts, *China to Chinatown: Chinese Food in the West* (London: Reaktion, 2002), 15.

45. Peter Naccarato, Zachary Nowak, and Elgin K. Eckert, "Afterword: Italy Represented," in *Representing Italy Through Food*, ed. Peter Naccarato, Zachary Nowak, and Elgin K. Eckert (London: Bloomsbury, 2017), 265.

46. Sandra Ponzanesi, "Beyond the Black Venus: Colonial Sexual Politics and Contemporary Visual Practices Revisited," in *ReSignification—European Blackamoors, Africana Readings*, ed. Awam Amkpa and Ellen Mary Toscano (Rome: Postcart, 2017), 137–147.

47. Carlos Augusto Monteiro, Geoffrey Cannon, Mark Lawrence, Maria Laura da Costa Louzada, and Priscila Pereira Machado, "Ultra-Processed Foods, Diet Quality, and Health Using the NOVA Classification System" (Rome: Food and Agriculture Organization of the United Nations, 2019), 11–12.

5. PIZZA HUT, FINE DINING, AND TRATTORIE: ITALIAN GASTRONOMY TOURISM IN CHINA

1. To view this post, see Sohu.com, "必胜客卖热干面了？中西合璧不只是跨界这么简单," July 19, 2020, https://www.sohu.com/a/408530834_120566500, accessed June 2, 2022.

2. This post is included on Sohu.com, "人民日报'简陋'的「热干面加油」海报，凭什么刷屏," February 27, 2020, https://www.sohu.com/a/376281946_416382, accessed June 2, 2022.

3. Frank Dikötter, *Things Modern: Material Culture and Everyday Life in China* (London: Hurst, 2007), 228–232.

4. For news about the Italian chef at the Forum, see coverage in *Yong Bao* 庸報, September 17–21, 23, 25 and October 8, 1934. On Chinese-language advertising about the Forum in the 1930s, see Gaoheng Zhang, "Mobility, Architecture, Chronotopes: Tianjin's Italian Concession, the 1930s," in *Cultural Mobilities Between China and Italy*, ed. Valentina Pedone and Gaoheng Zhang (Cham, Switzerland: Springer; Palgrave Macmillan, 2024), 113–135.

5. On Western food served in Tianjin's concessions, see Xin Jiang 姜新, "Wanqin minguo shiqi Tianjin zujie canyin wenhua de lishi jilu—Tianjin zujie yinshiye dang'an yanjiu" 晚清民国时期天津租界餐饮文化的历史记录—天津租界饮食业档案研究 [Historical Records of Food Cultures in the Tianjin Leased Territory during the Late Qing Dynasty and the Republican Period—Research on Archives of the Catering Industry of the Tianjin Leased Territory], *Chuxiong shifan xueyuan xuebao* 楚雄师范学院学报 2 (2017): 40–50.

6. For the newsreel, see "Roma. Gli spaghetti sono giunti in Cina," Settimanale Ciac/SC541, Istituto Luce, April 30, 1959.

7. Hongpei Zhang, "Beijing Maxim's: A Miniature of China's Reform and Opening-Up," *Global Times*, October 28, 2018, https://toula.it/toula-history/, accessed June 2, 2020.

8. Massimo Alberini, "Imporremo il risotto nel menù dei cinesi," *Corriere della Sera*, April 12, 1988.

9. Silvia Madiotto, "Coronavirus in Veneto: addio ad Arturo Filippini, maestro di stile e cucina," *Corriere del Veneto*, April 15, 2020.

10. On the inflation crisis, see Ezra F. Vogel 傅高义, *Deng Xiaoping shidai* 邓小平时代 [Deng Xiaoping and the Transformation of China], translated

from English by Feng Keli 冯克利 (Beijing: SDX Joint Publishing Company 三联书店, 2013), 455–459.

11. http://www.dianping.com/shanghai/ch10/g116, accessed June 2, 2020.

12. 巴贝拉意式休闲餐厅 (Ba Bei La Yishi Xiuxian Canting)/Babela's Kitchen, as it was operated during the mid-to-late 2000s, is an example of a Chinese-made Pizza Hut China imitation. Its owner, Chen Xingwei, intended to compete with Pizza Hut by offering both pizzas and Chinese dishes to satisfy customers' desire for both options during the same meal. See Joseph Constanty, "Chen Xingwei: Recipe for Success," *CNN*, November 17, 2009, http://travel.cnn.com/shanghai/none/chen-xingwei-recipe-success-681694/, accessed June 2, 2020.

13. Ann Swidler, *Talk of Love: How Culture Matters* (Chicago: University of Chicago Press, 2001), 24–40 and 71–88. For a discussion of what I call an Italian-Chinese migrant cultural repertoire, see Gaoheng Zhang, *Migration and the Media: Debating Chinese Migration to Italy, 1992–2012* (Toronto: University of Toronto Press, 2019), 10–12 and 37–44.

14. Lisa Rofel, *Desiring China: Experiments in Neoliberalism, Sexuality and Public Culture* (Durham, NC: Duke University Press, 2007), 118.

15. Claude Fischler, "Food, Self and Identity," *Social Science Information* 27, no. 2 (1988): 281–282.

16. Quoted in Sun Sun Lim and Cheryll Ruth R. Soriano, "A (Digital) Giant Awakens—Invigorating Media Studies with Asian Perspectives," in *Asian Perspectives on Digital Culture: Emerging Phenomena, Enduring Concepts*, ed. Daya Thussu, Sun Sun Lim, and Cheryll Soriano (New York: Routledge, 2016), 3.

17. Quoted in Wenhong Chen and Stephen D. Reese, "Introduction: A New Agenda: Digital Media and Civic Engagement in Networked China," in *Networked China: Global Dynamics of Digital Media and Civic Engagement*, ed. Wenhong Chen and Stephen D. Reese (New York: Routledge, 2015), 3.

18. Chen and Reese, "Introduction," 3.

19. Magda Antonioli Corigliano, "The Outbound Chinese Tourism to Italy: The New Graduates' Generation," *Journal of China Tourism Research* 7, no. 4 (2011): 402; and Han Shen, Ligang Peng, and Antonio Usai, "Perceiving the Tourism Image of Italy: A Study of the Destination Image Framework of Italy in the Chinese Market," *International Business Research* 11, no. 3 (2018): 33.

20. Isabelle de Solier, *Food and the Self: Consumption, Production, and Material Culture* (London: Bloomsbury Academic, 2013).

21. Deborah Lupton and Zeena Feldman, eds., *Digital Food Cultures* (New York: Routledge, 2020); and Tania Lewis, *Digital Food: From Paddock to Platform* (London: Bloomsbury Academic, 2020).

22. Alla Tovares and Cynthia Gordon, eds., *Identity and Ideology in Digital Food Discourse: Social Media Interactions Across Cultural Contexts* (London: Bloomsbury Academic, 2020), 2.

23. Marshall McLuhan, *Understanding Media: The Extension of Man* (New York: McGraw-Hill, 1964), 7.

24. Lim and Soriano, "A (Digital) Giant Awakens," 4.

25. Chen and Reese, "Introduction," 1.

26. For an overview of the restaurant sector in Beijing from the 1970s through the 1990s, see Yunxiang Yan, "Of Hamburger and Social Space: Consuming McDonald's in Beijing," in *Food and Culture: A Reader*, ed. Carole Counihan, Penny Van Esterik, and Carole M. Counihan (New York: Routledge, 2012), 454–456 and 464–466. This and the following paragraphs are based on Yan's account and are conceptually influenced by David Harvey, *A Brief History of Neoliberalism* (Oxford: Oxford University Press, 2005), 5–19.

27. Associated Press, "Pizza Hut Turns Over a Lot of Dough in Chinese Debut," *Los Angeles Times*, September 10, 1990.

28. Knight-Ridder News Service, "Festivities Mark Opening of China's first Pizza Hut," *Baltimore Sun*, September 11, 1990.

29. For the Associated Press news release, see AP News, "China's First Pizza Hut Opens in Beijing," *Associated Press*, September 10, 1990.

30. Pimo Hong 洪丕漠, "Bishengke bisabing" 必胜客比萨饼 [Pizza Hut Pizza], *Shipin yu shenghuo* 食品与生活 2 (1997): 32.

31. Lucy M. Long, *Culinary Tourism* (Lexington: University Press of Kentucky, 2013), 32–34.

32. Yum China Holdings, Inc., "Pizza Hut Celebrates 30th Anniversary in China," September 18, 2020, https://ir.yumchina.com/news-releases/news-release-details/pizza-hut-celebrates-30th-anniversary-china, accessed June 26, 2022.

33. For an analysis of Pizza Hut and community-oriented pizzeria in the United States, see Donna Gabaccia, *We Are What We Eat: Ethnic Food and the Making of Americans* (Cambridge, MA: Harvard University Press, 1998), 197–199.

34. 王圆磊, "必胜客中国三十年, 凭'新'而立," 国际品牌观察杂志/*Global Brand Insight*, October 19, 2020, http://www.c-gbi.com/v6/8893.html, accessed June 26, 2022.

35. Long, *Culinary Tourism*, 37–44.

36. For examples, see https://www.youtube.com/watch?v=7iVFAK74TGU and https://weibo.com/pizzahut, accessed June 10, 2022.

37. https://www.pizzahut.com.cn/About/PizzaHut_pizza, accessed June 2, 2020.

Notes to pages 141–146 231

38. The commercial can be viewed at https://www.youtube.com/watch?v
=HXPNTUt763U, accessed June 2, 2020. Starbucks may be viewed as another
case study of an American company adapting Italian culture for the Chinese.

39. 王圆磊, "必胜客中国三十年, 凭'新'而立."

40. Ilaria Boncori, *Expatriates in China: Experiences, Opportunities, and
Challenges* (London: Palgrave Macmillan, 2013), 35–37.

41. Examples of these events include https://ambpechino.esteri.it
/ambasciata_pechino/it/ambasciata/news/dall_ambasciata/2016/12/grande
-successo-per-il-programma.html, accessed June 6, 2020; https://
europeanartoftaste.com/zh-hant/ (accessed June 6, 2020); https://site.douban
.com/134032/, accessed June 7, 2020; http://www.lifeweek.com.cn/2011/1013
/35270.shtml, accessed June 7, 2020; Liu 刘新民, "进口贸易的有益尝试——记由上海
市食品进出口公司举办的"意大利食品推广周," 国际市场, June 15, 2002; Yang杨沐春,
"你看, 你看, 马可波罗的子孙——意大利食品和葡萄酒展示品尝会掠影," 中国酒,
April 15, 2003. For other events, see Angelo Camillo and Loredana Di Pietro,
"An Investigation on Cultural Cuisine of Mainland China: Management
Implications for Restaurant Operators," in *Handbook of Research on Global
Hospitality and Tourism Management*, ed. Angelo A. Camillo (Hershey, PA: IGI
Global, 2015), 25–26.

42. For examples of the cultural texts in the order in which they appear in this
paragraph, see the opening of Italy's Food Genius Academy in Shanghai in 2020;
https://class.hujiang.com/17378060/intro?uzhi=202,27984,110164,1283&singleId=
1e5bc2d2a41948c1b43aa19baaf417ff&ch_source=202; https://book.douban.com
/subject/30334422/;%20https://item.xhsd.com/items/1010000102525029; https://
www.bilibili.com/video/BV1rx41167w3/?from=search&seid=572102312433976 16
15; http://www.ifenglife.com/essay_show-18180-lh-36.html; http://wenzhang
.16fan.com/a/603740.html; https://dy.163.com/article/CHQK1SA80524BTE9
.html;NTESwebSI=4B19A1F4E092679101D4860BBDD991F3.hz-subscribe-web
-docker-cm-online-rpqqn-8gfzd-no6gz-957844999zp-8081; and https://www
.sohu.com/a/275144429_783336, accessed June 6, 2020.

43. https://www.bulgarihotels.com/en_US/beijing/bar-and-restaurants/il
-ristorante-niko-romito, accessed June 6, 2020.

44. Statistics from the Italian Trade Agency (ITA) show a gradual increase
in Italian food exports to China since the late 1990s. For statistics from the
late 1990s and early 2000s, see the tables in Romeo Orlandi, "La cucina
italiana in Cina: ideologia e commercio," *Mondo cinese* 112 (2002). For statistics
from the late 2010s, see https://www.ice.it/it/statistiche/tavolepaesi.aspx
?idPaese=720, accessed June 2, 2020.

45. Translations of this and subsequent quotes from *Shanghai solo andata* in
this section are mine.

46. https://www.simonettagarelli.com/simonetta/, accessed October 2, 2020.

47. Simone Cinotto, "Immigrant Tastemakers: Italian Cookbook Writers and the Transnational Formation of Taste in Postindustrial America (1973–2000)," in *New Italian Migrations to the United States: Vol. 1: Politics and History since 1945*, ed. Laura E. Ruberto and Joseph Sciorra (Urbana: University of Illinois Press, 2017), 139–166.

48. The biographical details are taken from http://www.operabombana.com/bombana/, accessed June 2, 2020.

49. On the reception of Fellini's films in South Korea, Japan, and China, see Hiju Kim, Hiromi Kaneda, and Gaoheng Zhang, "Federico Fellini's 2020 Centennial Screenings in South Korea, Japan, and China," *Italian Studies in Southern Africa/Studi d'Italianistica nell'Africa Australe* 35, no. 1 (2022): 165–203. For Chinese media's assessment of Fellini's cinema, see Gaoheng Zhang, "'Women with Big Breasts and Wide Hips': Federico Fellini's Cinema in Chinese Media Essays," in *Federico Fellini: Centennial Essays*, ed. Marco Malvestio, Jessica Whitehead, and Alberto Zambenedetti (Toronto: University of Toronto Press, 2025), 358–370.

50. http://www.dianping.com/shop/Ea6r7eSCe9h779JH, accessed June 2, 2020. Because of the nature of these restaurant reviews, I have not attempted to give the specific post addresses in this note.

51. Josée Johnston and Shyon Baumann, *Foodies: Democracy and Distinction in the Gourmet Foodscape* (New York: Routledge, 2014), 65–82.

52. Marisa Fumagalli, "Mozzarelle di bufala e vini toscani. Così il cibo tricolore diventa di moda," *Corriere della Sera*, December 10, 2004.

53. For example, from AGI, one of Italy's major news agencies, Elisabetta Tola, "Tutti i numeri sugli italiani all'estero," November 4, 2018, https://www.agi.it/data-journalism/italiani_estero_quanti_sono-4564494/news/2018-11-04/, accessed January 23, 2020; from *The Financial Times*, Renée Kaplan, "Italy counts the cost of its brain drain," November 7, 2019; from China's main news agency, Xinhua, Mu Xuequan, "Italy's brain drain continues amid persistent North-South gap in living standards: ISTAT," http://www.xinhuanet.com/english/2018-12/13/c_137672286.htm, accessed January 23, 2020.

54. I have included an anecdote regarding a Chinese migrant in Zhang, *Migration and the Media*, 208–209.

55. Noelle J. Molé, *Labor Disorders in Neoliberal Italy: Mobbing, Well-being, and the Workplace* (Bloomington: Indiana University Press, 2012), 26–27.

56. This and the following paragraphs draw from Esteri.it, "Anagrafe Italiani residenti all'estero," https://www.esteri.it/mae/it/servizi/italiani-all-estero/aire_0.html, accessed January 23, 2020; and Giovanna Di Vincenzo, "Italiani in Cina: dati sulle presenze e caratteristiche della collettività," in

Sulle orme di Marco Polo: Italiani in Cina, ed. Giovanna Di Vincenzo, Fabio Marcelli, and Maria Francesca Staiano (Todi: Tau Editrice, 2014), 57–64.

57. Di Vincenzo, "Italiani in Cina."

58. Giovanna Di Vincenzo and Maria Francesca Staiano, "Le problematiche e le necessità degli italiani in Cina," in *Sulle orme di Marco Polo: Italiani in Cina*, ed. Giovanna Di Vincenzo, Fabio Marcelli, and Maria Francesca Staiano (Todi: Tau Editrice, 2014), 85–107.

59. http://www.damarco.com.cn/index.php/en/about-us, accessed June 2, 2020.

60. Yao Minji, Ma Xuefeng, and Zhong Youyang, "Da Marco: Serving real Italian food in Shanghai since 1999," *SHINE*, September 24, 2019, https://www.shine.cn/news/metro/1909242625/, accessed June 13, 2022.

61. Lonelyplanet.com, https://www.lonelyplanet.com/china/shanghai/restaurants/da-marco/a/poi-eat/1096448/356068, accessed June 13, 2022.

62. For a comparable case concerning Italian ready-to-wear in China, see Gaoheng Zhang, *Fashion Communications Between Italy and China: Unfolding a Sartorial Relationship* (London: Bloomsbury, 2025).

63. http://www.thegoodfoodgroup.asia/mercanteeng#mercantewelcomeeng, accessed June 13, 2022. The English-language text is original.

64. On Maseroli and Yuan, see https://www.migrer.org/storie/omar-maseroli/, accessed December 14, 2022.

65. http://www.thegoodfoodgroup.asia/lievito-2#food-philosophy, accessed June 13, 2022.

66. Translations of quotes from this book are mine.

67. http://www.dianping.com/shop/G1lYK7GTQTLUH5Q5, accessed June 3, 2020.

68. Selena Schleh, "deCanto," *TimeOut Shanghai*, July 31, 2013, http://www.timeoutshanghai.com/venue/Restaurants__Cafes-European-Italian/13281/deCanto.html, accessed June 2, 2020.

69. http://www.dianping.com/shop/G1lYK7GTQTLUH5Q5, accessed June 3, 2020.

70. Lorenzo Ruggeri, "Italian Food, Five Asian Cities," *Gambero Rosso*, October 25, 2018, https://www.gamberorosso.it/en/news/restaurant-news/italian-food-five-asian-cities/, accessed June 6, 2020.

71. Accademiaitalianadellacucina.it, "Primo1," https://www.accademiaitalianadellacucina.it/it/ristoranti/ristorante/39864-primo1, accessed June 13, 2022. The translation is mine.

72. Sohu.com, "首位上榜《大红虾》的华人厨师—Jacky薛哲君," https://www.sohu.com/a/207345203_177903/, accessed June 6, 2020.

73. For an example of mentions of Italian truffles in relation to Garelli's practice analyzed above, see Brian Sun (bestfoodinchina.net), "Giovanni's (Sheraton Shanghai Hongqiao Hotel)," *China Daily*, July 28, 2010.

74. Editorial, "Apre in Cina la prima scuola di cucina italiana: ecco Food Genius Academy Shanghai," Reportergourmet.com, November 15, 2019, https://reportergourmet.com/150208/apre-in-cina-la-prima-scuola-di-cucina-italiana-ecco-food-genius-academy-shanghai.html, accessed June 6, 2020.

75. The details in this paragraph draw from the following list of mainstream Italian news coverage. Luca Zanini, "Uno chef italiano a Shanghai: così si tornerà al ristorante finita l'emergenza," *Corriere della Sera*, March 31, 2020, https://video.corriere.it/economia/per-te/chef-italiano-shanghai-cosi-si-tornera-ristorante-finita-l-emergenza/1131eb76-6d20-11ea-ba71-0c6303b9bf2d, accessed June 13, 2020; Massimiliano Tonelli, "Ecco come è stata la mia quarantena a Shanghai. Parla chef Riccardo La Perna," *Gambero Rosso*, March 31, 2020; and Livia Montagnoli, "La ripresa della ristorazione a Shanghai. Quali sono state le misure per ripartire?" *Gambero Rosso*, May 14, 2020.

76. Mark I. Choate, "Italian Emigration, Remittances and the Rise of Made-in-Italy," in *The Routledge History of Italian Americans*, ed. William J. Connell and Stanislao G. Pugliese (New York: Routledge, 2018), 337.

77. Boncori, *Expatriates in China*, 60–62.

6. Slow and Fast, Sweet and Sour: Chinese Foodie Travelers in Italy

1. 殳俏, "夏末秋初的无花果," *Sanlian Lifeweek*, October 29, 2012, http://www.lifeweek.com.cn/2012/1029/38982.shtml, accessed June 7, 2020.

2. 殳俏, "风流馄饨憨厚饺," *Sanlian Lifeweek*, September 13, 2011, http://www.lifeweek.com.cn/2011/0913/34875.shtml, accessed June 7, 2020.

3. 殳俏, "一碗面的乐趣和偏见," *Sanlian Lifeweek*, November 23, 2011, http://www.lifeweek.com.cn/2011/1123/35860.shtml, accessed June 7, 2020.

4. Josée Johnston and Shyon Baumann, *Foodies: Democracy and Distinction in the Gourmet Foodscape* (New York: Routledge, 2014), 2.

5. Ibid. For further explanations, Ibid., 48–60.

6. Wolfgang Arlt, *China's Outbound Tourism* (London: Routledge, 2006), 8–12.

7. Figures quoted in Magda Antonioli Corigliano, "The Outbound Chinese Tourism to Italy: The New Graduates' Generation," *Journal of China Tourism Research* 7, no. 4 (2011): 396–397.

8. https://www.unwto.org/tourism-data/country-profile-outbound-tourism, accessed June 25, 2022.

9. Corigliano, "Chinese Tourism to Italy," 397.
10. Silvia Gravili and Pierfelice Rosato, "Italy's Image as a Tourism Destination in the Chinese Leisure Traveler Market," *International Journal of Marketing Studies* 9, no. 5 (2017): 29.
11. Marina Palumbo, "L'Italia prima in Europa per i turisti cinesi," *La Stampa*, May 9, 2019.
12. Corigliano, "Chinese Tourism to Italy," 406.
13. Ibid., 405.
14. Gravili and Rosato, "Italy's Image as a Tourism Destination," 41–46.
15. Han Shen, Ligang Peng, and Antonio Usai, "Perceiving the Tourism Image of Italy: A Study of the Destination Image Framework of Italy in the Chinese Market," *International Business Research* 11, no. 3 (2018): 33.
16. 殳俏, "夏末秋初的无花果." Translations of Chinese quotes are mine in this section.
17. 殳俏, "风流馄饨憨厚饺."
18. 殳俏, "一碗面的乐趣和偏见."
19. 殳俏, "慢吞吞的柠檬," *Sanlian Lifeweek*, August 15, 2011, http://www.lifeweek.com.cn/2011/0815/34568.shtml, accessed June 7, 2020.
20. For a critical history of the Slow Food Movement, see Alison Leitch, "Slow Food and the Politics of 'Virtuous Globalization,'" in *Food and Culture: A Reader*, ed. Carole Counihan, Penny Van Esterik, and Carole M. Counihan (New York: Routledge, 2012), 409–425.
21. Carlnita Greene, "Competing Identities at the Table: Slow Food, Consumption, and the Performance of Social Style," in *Food as Communication: Communication as Food*, ed. Janet M. Cramer, Carlnita Greene, and Lynn Walters (New York: Peter Lang, 2011), 78–80.
22. 殳俏, "夏末秋初的无花果."
23. Ibid.
24. 殳俏, "夏天颤巍巍," *Sanlian Lifeweek*, July 20, 2012, http://www.lifeweek.com.cn/2012/0720/37950.shtml, accessed June 7, 2020.
25. 吴琪, "殳俏: 人和食物是平等的," *Sanlian Lifeweek*, January 22, 2006, http://old.lifeweek.com.cn//2006/0122/14462.shtml, accessed November 25, 2023.
26. Jennie Germann Molz, "Eating Difference: The Cosmopolitan Mobilities of Culinary Tourism," *Space and Culture* 10, no. 1 (2007): 77–93.
27. Editorial, "殳俏: 味道永远是食物的根本(组图)," Sina.com, March 4, 2009, style.sina.com.cn/taste/restau/2009-03-04/104735436.shtml, accessed November 25, 2023.
28. Nanxi Yan, "Slow Food in China: An Exploratory Study," Master of Arts Thesis, University of Waterloo, 2015, 13–14.

29. Ibid., 73–74 and 79–80.

30. For a chronology of important events of Slow Food Great China, see 慢食工作委员会, "何为慢食? 带你了解中国绿发会慢食工作委员会," Sohu.com, May 24, 2021, https://www.sohu.com/a/468356586_100001695, accessed November 25, 2023. For main events in the history of Slow Food International, see Slow Food International, "Our history," Slowfood.com, undated, https://www.slowfood.com/about-us/our-history/, accessed November 25, 2023.

31. Editorial, "纪录片《舌尖上的中国》研讨会发言摘登: 让世界感知中国味道," *Guang Ming Daily*, June 1, 2012.

32. Lanlan Kuang, "China's Emerging Food Media," *Gastronomica* 17, no. 3 (Fall 2017): 70–71 and 73–74.

33. Editorial, "舌尖体走红 你所不知道的《舌尖上的中国》," *Nanfang Dushi Bao*, https://web.archive.org/web/20140202180123/http://news.mtime.com/2012/05/29/1489377.html, accessed June 7, 2020.

34. Ibid. For the first season available from the official CCTV channel, see https://tv.cctv.com/2017/01/19/VIDAtIyRXSWBaJGZ1itGdZFE170119.shtml, accessed November 26, 2023. Carlo Petrini, *Buono, pulito e giusto. Principi di nuova gastronomia* (Torino: Einaudi, 2005).

35. Carlo Petrini, *Slow Food Nation: Why Our Food Should Be Good, Clean, and Fair* (New York: Rizzoli Ex Libris, 2007); and Carlo Petrini, 慢食运动: 为什么食品要讲究优良、清洁、公平? Translated by Yi Jie 尹捷 (Beijing: New Star Press 新星出版社, 2010).

36. Editorial, "舌尖体走红 你所不知道的《舌尖上的中国》." Ren is drawing from ideas presented in Petrini, *Slow Food Nation*, 55–88.

37. Editorial, "舌尖体走红 你所不知道的《舌尖上的中国》."

38. Zhang 张奕玮, "始于舌尖, 终于中国," 澎湃新闻, July 1, 2023, https://m.thepaper.cn/newsDetail_forward_23683325, accessed November 26, 2023.

39. Michaela DeSourcey, "Gastronationalism: Food Traditions and Authenticity Politics in the European Union," *American Sociological Review* 75, no. 3 (2010): 433.

40. Ibid., 449.

41. For an example, see Niu 牛梦笛 and Li 李蕾, "《舌尖上的中国》文化魅力的新开掘," 光明日报, June 6, 2012.

42. Kuang, "China's Emerging Food Media," 71.

43. For the series' official English website, see https://web.archive.org/web/20130801101616/http://english.cntv.cn/special/a_bite_of_china/homepage/index.shtml, accessed November 26, 2023. The French and Spanish versions can be accessed by navigating the tabs on the website.

44. For examples, see Niu 牛梦笛 and Li 李蕾, "《舌尖上的中国》文化魅力的新开掘" and Editorial, "纪录片《舌尖上的中国》研讨会发言摘登."

45. Janet Chrzan, "Slow Food: What, Why, and to Where?" *Food, Culture, and Society* 7 no. 2 (2004): 118.

46. For the initiative's Sina Weibo account, see https://weibo.com/yszg2012, accessed November 26, 2023.

47. 殳俏, "人與食物的美好關係," 一席/YiXi, September 23, 2017, https://www.youtube.com/watch?v=ctK97JNdiFQ, accessed November 26, 2023.

48. Chrzan, "Slow Food," 120.

49. Ibid., 127.

50. Ibid., 122.

51. Slow Food, "Slow Food Manifesto: International Movement for the Defense of and the Right to Pleasure," 1989.

52. Shen, Peng, and Usai, "Perceiving the Tourism Images of Italy," 33.

53. https://fs.ctrip.com/italypc, accessed June 25, 2022.

54. https://you.ctrip.com/restaurant/venice340.html, accessed June 25, 2022.

55. https://you.ctrip.com/travels/milan304.html, accessed June 25, 2022.

56. https://place.qyer.com/italy/, accessed June 16, 2020. Chinese tourism websites periodically change their home pages and navigation menus. Here and elsewhere in this section I capture the details available in June 2020.

57. https://place.qyer.com/italy/food/features247295/, accessed June 16, 2020.

58. https://guide.qyer.com/taste-of-italy/, accessed June 16, 2020.

59. https://guide.qyer.com/, accessed June 16, 2020.

60. https://place.qyer.com/poi/V2AJa1FuBzZTYVI6/, accessed June 16, 2020.

61. https://place.qyer.com/mguide/introduction/;https://place.qyer.com/italy/travel-notes/; and https://bbs.qyer.com/forum-13-1.html, accessed June 16, 2020.

62. Mike Gasher, "Media Convergence," *The Canadian Encyclopedia*, September 5, 2011, https://www.thecanadianencyclopedia.ca/en/article/media-convergence, accessed January 10, 2023.

63. https://www.iqiyi.com/a_19rrhxmrr5.html, accessed June 16, 2020. The third season of a popular show, titled 中餐厅/*Chinese Restaurant* (2019), features Taormina, Sicily. Celebrities cooked and managed a Chinese restaurant there. Some observations about Chinese eating western meals in the 2000s are provided in Romeo Orlandi, "La cucina italiana in Cina: ideologia e commercio," *Mondo cinese* 112 (2002).

64. Isabelle de Solier, *Food and the Self: Consumption, Production and Material Culture* (London: Bloomsbury Academic, 2013), 42–44.

65. Carlnita P. Greene and Janet M. Cramer, "Beyond Mere Sustenance: Food as Communication/Communication as Food," in *Food as Communication:*

Communication as Food, eds., Janet M. Cramer, Carlnita Greene, and Lynn Walters (New York: Peter Lang, 2011), xii.

66. This concern may be understood as a legacy of China's peasant and working-class nutritional needs, which is a constant theme in Chinese cultural beliefs about how people should relate to food. Memories of historical famines are constantly referenced in contemporary Chinese society through both news and entertainment media.

67. Pierre Bourdieu, "Distinction: A Social Critique of the Judgement of Taste," in *Food and Culture: A Reader*, ed. Carole Counihan and Penny Van Esterik (New York: Routledge, 2012), 38.

68. On neo-tribes and cosmopolitan attitudes among Chinese consumers, see LiAnne Yu, *Consumption in China: How China's New Consumer Ideology Is Shaping the Nation*, 2014), 102–118.

69. Eugenio Buzzetti, "'Caffè' arriva a Pechino, Bortone, 'non perdiamo il treno del cambiamento,'" AGI, November 23, 2016, https://www.agi.it/blog-italia/agi-china/_caffe_arriva_a_pechino_bortone_non_perdiamo_il_treno_del_cambiamento_-3229119/post/2016-11-24/, accessed November 22, 2023.

70. Francesco Gallo, "'La ricetta italiana,' un 'Vacanze romane' in salsa cinese," ANSA, April 21, 2022, https://www.ansa.it/sito/notizie/cultura/cinema/2022/04/21/la-ricetta-italiana-un-vacanze-romane-in-salsa-cinese_38956ccc-2652-43ac-af26-ad114b887eec.html, accessed November 22, 2023.

71. Stephen Teo, "The Chinese film market and the *Wolf Warrior* 2 phenomenon," *Screen*, 60, no. 2 (2019): 322.

72. Sky, "Antonino Chef Academy, chi è Federico Liu," Sky, November 12, 2019, https://tg24.sky.it/spettacolo/tv-show/2019/11/12/antonino-chef-academy-federico-liu, accessed November 24, 2023.

73. Lucy M. Long, *Culinary Tourism* (Lexington: University Press of Kentucky, 2013), 46.

CONCLUSION

1. For an analysis of different Italian regions' responses to the initial outbreak, see Gary P. Pisano, Raffaella Sadun, and Michele Zanini, "Lessons from Italy's Response to Coronavirus," *Harvard Business Review*, March 27, 2020.

2. Laura Mari, "Coronavirus, Sonia Zhou si arrende: chiude il ristorante e i cuochi tornano in Cina," *La Repubblica*, March 2, 2020.

BIBLIOGRAPHY

Abbas, Ackbar, and John Nguyet Erni. "General Introduction." In *Internationalizing Cultural Studies: An Anthology*, edited by Ackbar Abbas and John Nguyet Erni, 1–12. Malden, MA: Wiley-Blackwell, 2005.

Abu-Er-Rub, Laila, Christiane Brosius, Sebastian Meurer, Diamantis Panagiotopoulos, and Susan Richter. "Introduction: Engaging Transculturality." In *Engaging Transculturality: Concepts, Key Terms, Case Studies*, edited by Laila Abu-Er-Rub, Christiane Brosius, Sebastian Meurer, Diamiantis Panagiotopoulos, and Susan Richter, xxiii–xxxix. London: Routledge, 2019.

Adey, Peter, David Bissell, Kevin Hannam, Peter Merriman, and Mimi Sheller, eds. *The Routledge Handbook of Mobilities*. London: Routledge, 2013.

Alabiso, Duccio. *Shanghai Solo Andata: storie di giovani italiani in Cina*. Milano: Brioschi, 2011.

Anderson, E. N. *The Food of China*. New Haven, CT: Yale University Press, 1988.

Angelini, Federica. "Food and Identity in Laila Wadia and Igiaba Scego." *Anuario de Literatura Comparada* 3 (2013): 249–257.

Antonioli Corigliano, Magda. "The Outbound Chinese Tourism to Italy: The New Graduates' Generation." *Journal of China Tourism Research* 7, no. 4 (2011): 396–410.

Arlt, Wolfgang. *China's Outbound Tourism*. London: Routledge, 2006.

Ashley, Bob, Joanne Hollows, Steve Jones, and Ben Taylor. *Food and Cultural Studies*. New York: Routledge, 2004.

Barthes, Roland. "Toward a Psychosociology of Contemporary Food Consumption." In *Food and Culture: A Reader*, edited by Carole Counihan and Penny Van Esterik, 23–30. New York: Routledge, 2012.

Bender, Daniel E., and Simone Cinotto. "Introduction: Mobility and the Making of World Cuisines." In *Food Mobilities: Making World Cuisines*, edited by Daniel E. Bender and Simone Cinotto, 3–27. Toronto: University of Toronto Press, 2024.

Beriss, David. "Haute, Fast, and Historic: Restaurants and the Rise of Popular Culture." In *The Bloomsbury Handbook of Food and Popular Culture*, edited by Kathleen LeBesco and Peter Naccarato, 27–39. London: Bloomsbury Academic, 2018.

Berti, Fabio, and Valentina Pedone. "A Bridge between the Spiritual and the Worldly." In *Chinese Religions Going Global*, edited by Nanlai Cao, Giuseppe Giordan, and Fenggang Yang, 37–57. Leiden: Brill, 2020.

Bertozzi, Eddie. "The Possibility of Chineseness: Negotiating Chinese Identity in *Shun Li and the Poet* and *The Arrival of Wang*." *Journal of Italian Cinema and Media Studies* 2, no. 1 (2014): 59–73.

Biasin, Gian-Paolo. *The Flavors of Modernity: Food and the Novel*. Princeton, NJ: Princeton University Press, 1993.

Boncori, Ilaria. *Expatriates in China: Experiences, Opportunities and Challenges*. London: Palgrave Macmillan, 2013.

Bond, Emma. *Writing Migration through the Body*. Cham, Switzerland: Palgrave Macmillan, 2018.

Bondanella, Peter. *A History of Italian Cinema*. New York: Continuum, 2009.

Bower, Anne L., ed. *Reel Food: Essays on Food and Film*. New York: Routledge, 2004.

Brien, Donna Lee. "Food in the Singaporean Graphic Memoir." In *The Routledge Companion to Literature and Food*, edited by Lorna Piatti-Farnell and Donna Lee Brien, 219–231. New York: Routledge, 2018.

Bourdieu, Pierre. "Distinction: A Social Critique of the Judgement of Taste." In *Food and Culture: A Reader*, edited by Carole Counihan and Penny Van Esterik, 31–39. New York: Routledge, 2012.

Bressan, Nicoletta. "L'imprenditoria cinese in Italia: due casi studio. La ristorazione cinese a Milano e il distretto del porfido a Trento." Thesis, University of Trento, 2013.

Brottman, Mikita. "Mondo Horror: Carnivalizing the Taboo." In *The Horror Film*, edited by Stephen Prince, 167–188. New Brunswick, NJ: Rutgers University Press, 2004.

Burdett, Charles, Loredana Polezzi, and Barbara Spadaro, eds. *Transcultural Italies: Mobility, Memory and Translation*. Liverpool: Liverpool University Press, 2020.

Calamita, Francesca. "'*Identica a loro?*' (In)digesting Food and Identity in Igiaba Scego's. 'Salsicce.'" In *(In)digestion in Literature and Film*, edited by Serena J. Rivera and Niki Kiviat, 186–200. New York: Routledge, 2020.

Camillo, Angelo, and Loredana Di Pietro. "An Investigation on Cultural Cuisine of Mainland China: Management Implications for Restaurant Operators." In *Handbook of Research on Global Hospitality and Tourism*

Management, edited by Angelo A. Camillo, 23–36. Hershey, PA: IGI Global, 2015.
Capatti, Alberto, and Massimo Montanari. *Italian Cuisine: A Cultural History*. Translated by Áine O'Healy. New York: Columbia University Press, 2003.
Carolan, Mary Ann McDonald. *Orienting Italy: China through the Lens of Italian Filmmakers*. Buffalo: State University of New York, 2022.
Chan, Jachinson. *Chinese American Masculinities: From Fu Manchu to Bruce Lee*. New York: Routledge: 2001.
Chang, K. C., ed. *Food in Chinese Culture: Anthropological and Historical Perspectives*. New Haven, CT: Yale University Press, 1977.
Chen, Wenhong, and Stephen D. Reese. "Introduction: A New Agenda: Digital Media and Civic Engagement in Networked China." In *Networked China: Global Dynamics of Digital Media and Civic Engagement*, edited by Wenhong Chen and Stephen D. Reese, 1–16. New York: Routledge, 2015.
Chen, Yong. "Food, Race, and Ethnicity." In *The Oxford Handbook of Food History*, edited by Jefferey M. Pilcher, 429–441. Oxford: Oxford University Press, 2012.
———. *Chop Suey, USA: The Story of Chinese Food in America*. New York: Columbia University Press, 2014.
Cheng, Ann Anlin. "Digesting Asian America." In *The Cambridge Companion to Literature and Food*, edited by J. Michelle Coghlan, 215–227. Cambridge: Cambridge University Press, 2020.
Cheng, Vincent (Tzu-Wen). "'A Four-legged Duck?': Chinese Restaurant Culture in the United States from a Cross-Cultural/Inter-Cultural Communication Perspective." In *Food as Communication: Communication as Food*, edited by Janet M. Cramer, Carlnita Greene, and Lynn Walters, 195–216. New York: Peter Lang, 2011.
Choate, Mark I. "Italian Emigration, Remittances, and the Rise of Made-in-Italy." In *The Routledge History of Italian Americans*, edited by William J. Connell and Stanislao G. Pugliese, 337–348. New York: Routledge, 2018.
Chopra, Rohit. "Comic Books and the Culinary Logic of Late Capitalism." In *Food and Literature*, edited by Gitanjali G. Shahani, 237–249. Cambridge: Cambridge University Press, 2018.
Chow, Rey. *Ethics after Idealism: Theory, Culture, Ethnicity, Reading*. Bloomington: Indiana University Press, 1998.
Chrzan, Janet. "Slow Food: What, Why, and to Where?" *Food, Culture, and Society* 7, no. 2 (2004): 117–132.
Chung, Hillary, and Bernadette Luciano. "The Dis/locat/ing Migrant as an Agent of Transposition: Borensztein's *Un cuento chino* and Segre's *Io sono Li*." *Studies in European Cinema* 11, no. 3 (2014): 191–211.

Cinotto, Simone. *Gastrofascism and Empire: Food in Italian East Africa, 1935–1941*. London: Bloomsbury, 2024.

———. "Immigrant Tastemakers: Italian Cookbook Writers and the Transnational Formation of Taste in Postindustrial America (1973–2000)." In *New Italian Migrations to the United States: Vol. 1: Politics and History since 1945*, edited by Laura E. Ruberto and Joseph Sciorra, 139–166. Urbana: University of Illinois Press, 2017.

———. *The Italian American Table: Food, Family, and Community in New York City*. Urbana: University of Illinois Press, 2013.

Coghlan, J. Michelle, ed. *The Cambridge Companion to Literature and Food*. Cambridge: Cambridge University Press, 2020.

Cologna, Daniele Brigadoi. "Il quartiere cinese di Milano: territorio conteso o laboratorio di ridefinizione dell'identità sociale degli immigrati cinesi in Italia?" *Mondo cinese*, No. 134 (2008). https://www.tuttocina.it/Mondo_cinese/134/134_colo.htm. Accessed January 19, 2023, no pagination is given.

———. "L'importanza crescente degli studenti universitari cinesi per la società italiana." *Orizzonte Cina* 7, no. 6 (2016): 16–18.

———. "Intervista/Walter Sirtori e Hujian Zhou (Angiè)." *Mondo cinese*, no. 163 (2017): 103–119.

Couldry, Nick. "Sociology and Cultural Studies: An Interrupted Dialogue." In *Handbook of Cultural Sociology*, edited by John R. Hall, Laura Grindstaff and Minng-Cheng Lo, 77–86. London: Routledge, 2010.

Counihan, Carole, and Penny Van Esterik, eds. *Food and Culture: A Reader*. New York: Routledge, 2012.

Cramer, Janet M., Carlnita Greene, and Lynn Walters. "Beyond Mere Sustenance: Food as Communication/Communication as Food." In *Food as Communication: Communication as Food*, edited by Janet M. Cramer, Carlnita Greene, and Lynn Walters, ix–xviii. New York: Peter Lang, 2011.

Cresswell, Tim. *On the Move: Mobility in the Modern Western World*. New York: Routledge, 2006.

Curti, Roberto. *Italia odia: il cinema poliziesco italiano*. Torino: Lindau, 2007.

De Luca, Giovanna. "*Into Paradiso* and *Mozzarella Stories*: Comedy, Mafia and immigration—an interview with Paola Randi and Edoardo De Angelis." *Journal of Italian Cinema and Media Studies* 3, no. 3 (2015): 377–390.

de Solier, Isabelle. *Food and the Self: Consumption, Production and Material Culture*. London: Bloomsbury Academic, 2013.

Deleyto, Celestino. "Looking from the Border: A Cosmopolitan Approach to Contemporary Cinema." *Transnational Cinemas* 8, no. 2 (2017): 95–112.

Deng, Grazia Ting. *Chinese Espresso: Contested Race and Convivial Space in Contemporary Italy*. Princeton, NJ: Princeton University Press, 2024.

DeSourcey, Michaela. "Gastronationalism: Food Traditions and Authenticity Politics in the European Union." *American Sociological Review* 75, no. 3 (2010): 331–478.

Di Vincenzo, Giovanna. "Italiani in Cina: dati sulle presenze e caratteristiche della collettività." In *Sulle orme di Marco Polo: Italiani in Cina*, edited by Giovanna Di Vincenzo, Fabio Marcelli, and Maria Francesca Staiano, 57–64. Todi: Tau Editrice, 2014.

Di Vincenzo, Giovanna, and Maria Francesca Staiano. "Le problematiche e le necessità degli italiani in Cina." In *Sulle orme di Marco Polo: Italiani in Cina*, edited by Giovanna Di Vincenzo, Fabio Marcelli, and Maria Francesca Staiano, 85–107. Todi: Tau Editrice, 2014.

Dickinson, Roger. "Food and the Media: Production, Representation, and Consumption." In *The Handbook of Food Research*, edited by Anne Murcott, Warren Belasco, and Peter Jackson, 439–454. London: Bloomsbury Academic, 2013.

Dikötter, Frank. *Things Modern: Material Culture and Everyday Life in China*. London: Hurst, 2007.

Diner, Hasia R. *Hungering for America: Italian, Irish & Jewish Foodways in the Age of Migration*. Cambridge, MA: Harvard University Press, 2001.

Dolasinski, Lisa. "Mediating 'Sterile Masculinity': On Male Aging, Migration, and Biopolitics in a (Post)Berlusconi Italy." *Gender/Sexuality/Italy* 5 (2018): 80–106. https://www.gendersexualityitaly.com/5-media-ting-sterile-masculinity-on-male-aging-migration-and-biopolitics-in-a-postberlusconi-italy/. Accessed January 10, 2022.

Dott, Brian R. *The Chile Pepper in China: A Cultural Biography*. New York: Columbia University Press, 2020.

Douglas, Mary. *Purity and Danger: An Analysis of Concept of Pollution and Taboo*. London: Routledge, 2003.

Du Gay, Paul, Stuart Hall, Linda Janes, Anders Koed Madsen, Hugh Mackay, and Keith Negus. *Doing Cultural Studies: The Story of the Sony Walkman*. London: Sage, 1997.

During, Simon. *Cultural Studies: A Critical Introduction*. London: Routledge, 2005.

Eckert, Elgin K. "Inspector Montalbano *a tavola*: Food in Andrea Camilleri's Police Fiction." In *Representing Italy Through Food*, edited by Peter Naccarato, Zachary Nowak, and Elgin K. Eckert, 95–110. London: Bloomsbury, 2017.

Eckert, Elgin K., and Zachary Nowak. "*In cibo veritas*: Food Preparation and Consumption in Özpetek's "Queer" Flms." In *Representing Italy Through Food*, edited by Peter Naccarato, Zachary Nowak, and Elgin K. Eckert, 125–137. London: Bloomsbury, 2017.

Faucon, Térésa. "*Kung food*: chorégraphier les gestes culinaires." *Anthropology of Food*, no. 15 (2021). https://journals.openedition.org/aof/12825. Accessed December 2, 2023.

Feng, Jin. *Tasting Paradise on Earth: Jiangnan Foodways*. Seattle: University of Washington Press, 2019.

Ferry, Jane. *Food in Film: A Culinary Performance of Communication*. London: Routledge, 2015.

Fiore, Teresa. *Pre-Occupied Spaces: Remapping Italy's Transnational Migrations and Colonial Legacies*. New York: Fordham University Press, 2017.

Fischler, Claude. "Food, Self and Identity." *Social Science Information* 27, no. 2 (1988): 275–292.

Fortis, Marco. *Il Made in Italy*. Bologna: Il Mulino, 1998.

Gabaccia, Donna R. "Food, Mobility, and World History." In *The Oxford Handbook of Food History*, edited by Jefferey M. Pilcher, 305–320. Oxford: Oxford University Press, 2012.

———. *We Are What We Eat: Ethnic Food and the Making of Americans*. Cambridge, MA: Harvard University Press, 1998.

Gasher, Mike. "Media Convergence." *The Canadian Encyclopedia*. September 5, 2011. https://www.thecanadianencyclopedia.ca/en/article/media-convergence. Accessed January 10, 2023.

Gentilcore, David. *Italy and the Potato: A History, 1550–2000*. London: A & C Black, 2012.

———. *Pomodoro!: A History of the Tomato in Italy*. New York: Columbia University Press, 2010.

Germann Molz, Jennie. "Eating Difference: The Cosmopolitan Mobilities of Culinary Tourism." *Space and Culture* 10, no. 1 (2007): 77–93.

Gibson, Sarah. "Food Mobilities." *Space and Culture* 10, no. 1 (2007): 4–21.

Goodall, Mark. *Sweet and Savage: The World through the Shockumentary Film Lens*. London: Headpress, 2006.

Goody, Jack. *Food and Love: A Cultural History of East and West*. London: Verso, 2010.

Gravili, Silvia, and Pierfelice Rosato. "Italy's Image as a Tourism Destination in the Chinese Leisure Traveler Market." *International Journal of Marketing Studies* 9, no. 5 (2017): 28–55.

Greenblatt, Stephen, ed. *Cultural Mobility*. Cambridge: Cambridge University Press, 2010.

Greene, Carlnita. "Competing Identities at the Table: Slow Food, Consumption, and the Performance of Social Style." In *Food as Communication: Communication as Food*, edited by Janet M. Cramer, Carlnita Greene, and Lynn Walters, 75–93. New York: Peter Lang, 2011.

Greene, Carlnita P., and Janet M. Cramer. "Beyond Mere Sustenance: Food as Communication/Communication as Food." In *Food as Communication: Communication as Food*, edited by Janet M. Cramer, Carlnita Greene, and Lynn Walters, ix–xviii. New York: Peter Lang, 2011.
Griswold, Wendy. *Cultures and Societies in a Changing World.* Thousand Oaks, CA: Sage, 2013.
———. "A Methodological Framework for the Sociology of Culture." *Sociological Methodology* 17 (1987): 1–35.
Hannam, Kevin, Mimi Sheller, and John Urry. "Editorial: Mobilities, Immobilities and Moorings." *Mobilities* 1, no. 1 (2006): 1–22.
Harvey, David. *A Brief History of Neoliberalism.* Oxford: Oxford University Press, 2005.
Hayden, Tiana B., and Dhan Zunino Singh. "Food and mobility." *Journal of Transport History* 41, no. 2 (2020): 278–288.
Helstosky, Carol. *Garlic and Oil: Politics and Food in Italy.* Oxford: Berg, 2004.
Hirst, Bamboo. *Il riso non cresce sugli alberi.* Milano: La Tartaruga Edizioni, 1988.
Hom, Stephanie Malia. *Empire's Mobius Strip: Historical Echoes in Italy's Crisis of Migration and Detention.* Ithaca, NY: Cornell University Press, 2019.
Hong, Pimo 洪丕漠, "Bishengke bisabing" 必胜客比萨饼. [Pizzahut Pizza]. *Shipin yu shenghuo* 食品与生活 2 (1997): 32.
Hu, Lala. *Semi di tè.* Busto Arsizio: People, 2020.
Hu, Lanbo, ed. *Noi restiamo qui: come la comunità cinese ha vissuto l'epidemia.* Roma: Cina in Italia, 2020.
Humble, Nicola. *The Literature of Food: An Introduction from 1830 to Present.* London: Bloomsbury Academic, 2020.
Illouz, Eva. *Oprah Winfrey and the Glamour of Misery: An Essay on Popular Culture.* New York: Columbia University Press, 2003.
Inglis, David, Andrew Blaikie, and Robin Wagner-Pacifici. "Editorial: Sociology, Culture and the Twenty-First Century," *Cultural Sociology* 1, no. 1 (2007): 5–22.
Jiang, Xin 姜新. "Wanqin minguo shiqi Tianjin zujie canyin wenhua de lishi jilu—Tianjin zujie yinshiye dang'an yanjiu" 晚清民国时期天津租界餐饮文化的历史记录— 天津租界饮食业档案研究. [Historical Records of Food Cultures in the Tianjin Leased Territory during the Late Qing Dynasty and the Republican Period——Research on Archives of the Catering Industry of the Tianjin Leased Territory]. *Chuxiong shifan xueyuan xuebao* 楚雄师范学院学报 2 (2017): 40–50.
Johnston, Josée, and Shyon Baumann. *Foodies: Democracy and Distinction in the Gourmet Foodscape.* 2nd edition. New York: Routledge, 2014.

Kashdan, Harry. "Eating to Become: Italian Counter-Narratives of Assimilation, Identity, and Migration." In *The Routledge Companion to Literature and Food*, edited by Lorna Piatti-Farnell and Donna Lee Brien, 175–183. New York: Routledge, 2018.

Kim, Hiju, Hiromi Kaneda, and Gaoheng Zhang. "Federico Fellini's 2020 Centennial Screenings in South Korea, Japan, and China." *Italian Studies in Southern Africa/Studi d'Italianistica nell'Africa Australe* 35, no. 1 (2022): 165–203.

Ku, Robert Ji-Song. *Dubious Gastronomy: The Cultural Politics of Eating Asian in the USA*. Honolulu: University of Hawai'i Press, 2014.

Kuang, Lanlan. "China's Emerging Food Media." *Gastronomica* 17, no. 3 (Fall 2017): 68–81.

Kubati, Ron. "Comunità chiuse: *Io sono Li, La giusta distanza* e *Cose dell'altro mondo*." *NEMLA Italian Studies, Special Issue: New Perspectives on Veneto Literary and Cultural Itineraries* xxxv (2013): 221–244.

Laviosa, Flavia. "*Caffè*—The First Sino-Italian co-production: An interview with Cristiano Bortone." *Journal of Italian Cinema and Media Studies* 5, no. 1 (2017): 93–98.

LeBesco, Kathleen, and Peter Naccarato, eds. *The Bloomsbury Handbook of Food and Popular Culture*. London: Bloomsbury Academic, 2018.

Leckie, Jacqueline, Angela McCarthy, and Angela Wanhalla. "Introduction: Migrant Cross-cultural Encounters in Asia and the Pacific." In *Migrant Cross-cultural Encounters in Asia and the Pacific*, edited by Jacqueline Leckie, Angela McCarthy, and Angela Wanhalla, 1–16. London: Routledge, 2016.

Leer, Jonatan, and Karen Klitgaard Povlsen, eds. *Food and Media: Practices, Distinctions and Heterotopias*. New York: Routledge, 2016.

Leighton, Stephen. "Passions and Persuasion." In *A Companion to Aristotle*, edited by Georgios Anagnostopoulos, 597–611. Malden, MA: Wiley-Blackwell, 2009.

Leitch, Alison. "Slow Food and the Politics of 'Virtuous Globalization.'" In *Food and Culture: A Reader*, edited by Carole Counihan, Penny Van Esterik, and Carole M. Counihan, 409–425. New York: Routledge, 2012.

Lenci, Laura-Marzia. "Feeding the Body, Feeding the Language: Nourishment as Metaphor of Writing in Igiaba Scego's Literary Works." In *Food and Women in Italian Literature, Culture and Society: Eve's Sinful Bite*, edited by Claudia Bernardi, Francesca Calamita, and Daniele De Feo, 128–137. London: Bloomsbury Academic, 2020.

Lewis, Tania. *Digital Food: From Paddock to Platform*. London: Bloomsbury Academic, 2020.

Lim, Sun Sun, and Cheryll Ruth R. Soriano, "A (Digital) Giant Awakens—Invigorating Media Studies with Asian Perspectives." In *Asian Perspectives* on *Digital Culture: Emerging Phenomena, Enduring Concepts*, edited by Daya Thussu, Sun Sun Lim, and Cheryll Soriano, 3–14. New York: Routledge, 2016.

Lindenfeld, Laura, and Fabio Parasecoli. "Food and Cinema: An Evolving Relationship." In *The Bloomsbury Handbook of Food and Popular Culture*, edited by Kathleen LeBesco and Peter Naccarato, 27–39. London: Bloomsbury Academic, 2018.

Liu, Haiming. *From Canton Restaurant to Panda Express: A History of Chinese Food in the United States*. New Brunswick, NJ: Rutgers University Press, 2015.

Lizie, Arthur. "Food and Communication." In *Routledge International Handbook of Food Studies*, edited by Ken Albala, 27–38. London: Routledge, 2012.

Long, Lucy M. *Culinary Tourism*. Lexington: University Press of Kentucky, 2013.

Louie, Kam. *Theorising Chinese Masculinity: Society and Gender in China*. Cambridge: Cambridge University Press, 2002.

Lu, Shun, and Gary Alan Fine. "The Presentation of Ethnic Authenticity: Chinese Food as a Social Accomplishment." *Sociological Quarterly* 36, no. 3 (1995): 535–553.

Lupton, Deborah. *Food, the Body, and the Self*. London: Sage, 1998.

Lupton, Deborah, and Zeena Feldman, eds. *Digital Food Cultures*. New York: Routledge, 2020.

Marchetti, Gina. *Romance and the "Yellow Peril": Race, Sex, and Discursive Strategies in Hollywood Fiction*. Berkeley: University of California Press, 1993.

McKenzie, Rory. "Italy's *ragioniere*? The National and International Relevance of Ugo Fantozzi." *Journal of Italian Cinema and Media Studies* 9, no. 2 (2021): 245–260.

McLuhan, Marshall. *Understanding Media: The Extension of Man*. New York: McGraw-Hill, 1964.

McMenamin, Amanda Eaton. "Eating to Live, Living to Tell: Foundational Food in the Latina Testimonial Text." In *The Routledge Companion to Literature and Food*, edited by Lorna Piatti-Farnell and Donna Lee Brien, 450–459. New York: Routledge, 2018.

Mendelson, Anne. *Chow Chop Suey: Food and the Chinese American Journey*. New York: Columbia University Press, 2016.

Ministero del Lavoro e delle Politiche Sociali. "La comunità cinese in Italia: Rapporto annuale sulla presenza dei migranti." Rome: Ministero del Lavoro e delle Politiche Sociali, 2021.

Mintz, Sidney W. "Foreword: Food for Thought." In *The Globalization of Chinese Food*, edited by David Y. H. Wu and Sidney C. H. Cheung, xii–xx. Honolulu: University of Hawai'i Press, 2002.

Molé, Noelle J. *Labor Disorders in Neoliberal Italy: Mobbing, Well-being, and the Workplace*. Bloomington: Indiana University Press, 2012.

Moliterno, Gino J. "*Mondo Cane* and the Invention of the Shockumentary." In *The Italian Cinema Book*, edited by Peter Bondanella, 172–180. Cham, Switzerland: Palgrave Macmillan, 2014.

Monteiro, Carlos Augusto, Geoffrey Cannon, Mark Lawrence, Maria Laura da Costa Louzada, and Priscila Pereira Machado. "Ultra-Processed Foods, Diet Quality, and Health Using the NOVA Classification System." Rome: Food and Agriculture Organization of the United Nations, 2019.

Moon, Krystyn R. *Yellowface: Creating the Chinese in American Popular Music and Performance, 1850s–1920s*. New Brunswick, NJ: Rutgers University Press, 2004.

Mountfort, Paul. "*Tintin* and the Secrets of Food: The Body Fantastic, Cultural Others, and Limits of Language." In *The Routledge Companion to Literature and Food*, edited by Lorna Piatti-Farnell and Donna Lee Brien, 101–110. New York: Routledge, 2018.

Mudu, Pierpaolo. "The People's Food: The Ingredients of 'Ethnic' Hierarchies and the Development of Chinese Restaurants in Rome." *GeoJournal* 68, no. 2/3 (2007): 195–210.

Naccarato, Peter. "There's a Mobster in the Kitchen: Cooking, Eating, and Complications of Gender in *The Godfather* and *Goodfellas*." In *Representing Italy Through Food*, edited by Peter Naccarato, Zachary Nowak, and Elgin K. Eckert, 111–124. London: Bloomsbury, 2017.

Naccarato, Peter, Zachary Nowak, and Elgin K. Eckert. "Afterword: Italy Represented." In *Representing Italy Through Food*, edited by Peter Naccarato, Zachary Nowak, and Elgin K. Eckert, 263–265. London: Bloomsbury, 2017.

———. eds. *Representing Italy Through Food*. London: Bloomsbury, 2017.

Nathan, Vetri. *Marvelous Bodies: Italy's New Migrant Cinema*. West Lafayette, Indiana: Purdue University Press, 2017.

Nelson, Cary, Paula A. Treichler, and Lawrence Grossberg. "Cultural Studies: An Introduction." In *Cultural Studies*, edited by Lawrence Grossberg, Cary Nelson, and Paula A. Treichler, 1–19. New York: Routledge, 1992.

Nguyen, Viet Thanh. *Race and Resistance: Literature and Politics in Asian America*. Oxford: Oxford University Press, 2002.

O'Healy, Áine. *Migrant Anxieties: Italian Cinema in a Transnational Frame*. Bloomington: Indiana University Press, 2019.

Orlandi, Romeo. "La cucina italiana in Cina: ideologia e commercio." *Mondo cinese* 112 (2002): https://www.tuttocina.it/Mondo_cinese/112/112_orla.htm. Accessed January 15, 2022.

Parasecoli, Fabio. *Bite Me: Food in Popular Culture*. Oxford: Berg, 2008.
———. "Chinese Food Ways in Italy." *Chinese Food in Europe* 12, no. 2 (2005): 5, 8, and 16.
———. *Food*. Cambridge, MA: MIT Press, 2019.
———. "Food, Cultural Studies, and Popular Culture." In *Routledge International Handbook of Food Studies*, edited by Ken Albala, 274–281. London: Routledge, 2013.
———. "Gluttonous Crimes: *Chew*, Comic Books, and the Ingestion of Masculinity." *Women's Studies International Forum* 44 (May–June 2014): 236–246.
———. "The Invention of Authentic Italian Food: Narratives, Rhetoric, and Media." In *Italians and Food*, edited by Roberta Sassatelli, 17–42. Cham, Switzerland: Palgrave Macmillan, 2019.
Parati, Graziella. *Migration Italy: The Art of Talking Back in a Destination Culture*. Toronto: University of Toronto Press, 2005.
———. *Migrant Writers and Urban Space in Italy: Proximities and Affect in Literature and Film*. Cham, Switzerland: Palgrave Macmillan, 2017.
Pedone, Valentina, ed. *Il vicino cinese: la comunità cinese a Roma*. Rome: Nuove Edizioni Romane, 2008.
———. "Self-Narration as a 'Social Action' in the Works of the Sino-Italian Author Hu Lanbo." In *Exchanges and Parallels between Italy and East Asia*, edited by Gaoheng Zhang and Mario Mignone, 292–303. Newcastle: Cambridge Scholars, 2020.
Pedone, Valentina, and Gaoheng Zhang. "Introduction." In *Cultural Mobilities Between China and Italy*, edited by Valentina Pedone and Gaoheng Zhang, 1–36. Cham, Switzerland: Springer; Palgrave Macmillan, 2024.
Petrini, Carlo. *Buono, pulito e giusto. Principi di nuova gastronomia*. Torino: Einaudi, 2005.
———. *Slow Food: The Case for Taste*. Translated by William McCuaig. New York: Columbia University Press, 2003.
———. *Slow Food Nation: Why Our Food Should Be Good, Clean, and Fair*. Translated by Clara Furlan and Jonathan Hunt. New York: Rizzoli Ex Libris, 2007.
———. 慢食运动: 为什么食品要讲究优良、清洁、公平? Translated by Yi Jie 尹捷. Beijing: New Star Press 新星出版社, 2010.
Piatti-Farnell, Lorna, and Donna Lee Brien. *The Routledge Companion to Literature and Food*. New York: Routledge, 2018.
Pieke, Frank N., and Tabitha Speelman. "Chinese Investment Strategies and Migration—Does Diaspora Matter?" In *Chinese Migration and Economic Relations with Europe*, edited by Marco Sanfilippo and Agnieszka Weinar, 12–32. New York: Routledge, 2016.

Pilcher, Jeffrey M. *Food in World History*. New York: Routledge, 2006.
Ponzanesi, Sandra. "Beyond the Black Venus: Colonial Sexual Politics and Contemporary Visual Practices Revisited." In *ReSignification—European Blackamoors, Africana Readings*, edited by Awam Amkpa and Ellen Mary Toscano, 137–147. Rome: Postcart, 2017.
Poole, Gaye. *Reel Meals, Set Meals: Food in Film and Theatre*. Sydney: Currency Press, 1999.
Precup, Mihaela. "Food, Memory, and Ethics in Graphic Narratives." In *The Routledge Companion to Literature and Food*, edited by Lorna Piatti-Farnell and Donna Lee Brien, 470–480. New York: Routledge, 2018.
Probyn, Elspeth. *Carnal Appetites: FoodSexIdentities*. London: Routledge, 2000.
Rabbiosi, Chiara. "Locating Italianicity Through Food and Tourism: Playing with Geographical Associations." In *Italians and Food*, edited by Roberta Sassatelli, 71–100. Cham, Switzerland: Palgrave Macmillan, 2019.
Rapp, Christof. "The Nature and Goals of Rhetoric." In *A Companion to Aristotle*, edited by Georgios Anagnostopoulos, 577–596. Malden, MA: Wiley-Blackwell, 2009.
Ray, Krishnendu. *The Ethnic Restaurateur*. London: Bloomsbury, 2016.
Redi, Federica. "Bacchette e forchette: la diffusione della cucina cinese in Italia." *Mondo cinese* 95 (1997): 41–67.
Ricatti, Francesco. "Humiliation and Love: Villaggio, Benigni, and the Cultural Politics of Emotions." *Incontri: Rivista europea di studi italiani* 29, no. 2 (2014): 8–18.
Roberts, J. A. G. *China to Chinatown: Chinese Food in the West*. London: Reaktion, 2002.
Rofel, Lisa. *Desiring China: Experiments in Neoliberalism, Sexuality, and Public Culture*. Durham, NC: Duke University Press, 2007.
Sassatelli, Roberta, ed. *Italians and Food*. Cham, Switzerland: Palgrave Macmillan, 2019.
Scarpellini, Emanuela. *Food and Foodways in Italy from 1861 to the Present*. Translated by Noor Giovanni Mazhar. New York: Palgrave Macmillan, 2016.
Schuster, Paulette K. "Interconnectivities: Mobility, Food and Place." In *Handbook of Culture and Migration*, edited by Jeffrey H. Cohen and Ibrahim Sirkeci, 386–395. Cheltenham, UK: Edward Elgar, 2021.
Scibetta, Andrea. "Chinese Migration(s) to Italy Beyond Stereotypes and Simplistic Views: The Case of the Graphic Novels *Primavere e Autunni* and *Chinamen*." In *Tracing Pathways: Interdisciplinary Studies on Modern and Contemporary East Asia*, edited by Diego Cucinelli and Andrea Scibetta, 91–108. Firenze: Firenze University Press, 2020.

Shahani, Gitanjali G. "Introduction." In *Food and Literature*, edited by Gitanjali G. Shahani, 1–35. Cambridge: Cambridge University Press, 2018.
———. ed. *Food and Literature*. Cambridge: Cambridge University Press, 2018.
Sheller, Mimi, and John Urry. "The New Mobilities Paradigm." *Environment and Planning* 38 (2006): 207–226.
Shen, Han, Ligang Peng, and Antonio Usai. "Perceiving the Tourism Image of Italy: A Study of the Destination Image Framework of Italy in the Chinese Market." *International Business Research* 11, no. 3 (2018): 30–47.
Shi, Yang Shi. *Cuore di seta*. Milano: Mondadori, 2017.
Shugart, Helene A. "Sumptuous Texts: Consuming 'Otherness' in the Food Film Genre." *Critical Studies in Media Communication* 25, no. 1 (2008): 68–90.
Simoons, Frederick J. *Food in China: A Cultural and Historical Inquiry*. Boca Raton: CRC Press, 1990.
Siniscalchi, Valeria. *Slow Food: The Economy and Politics of a Global Movement*. London: Bloomsbury, 2023.
Slow Food. "Slow Food Manifesto: International Movement for the Defense of and the Right to Pleasure." 1989. https://slowfood.com/filemanager/Convivium%20Leader%20Area/Manifesto_ENG.pdf. Accessed November 26, 2023.
Spadaro, Barbara. "Transnational Italian Comics: Graphic Journalism across Memories and Cultures." In *Transcultural Italies: Mobility, Memory and Translation*, edited by Charles Burdett, Loredana Polezzi, and Barbara Spadaro, 287–308. Liverpool: Liverpool University Press, 2020.
Storey, John. *From Popular Culture to Everyday Life*. New York: Routledge, 2014.
Swidler, Ann. *Talk of Love: How Culture Matters*. Chicago: University of Chicago Press, 2001.
Tajima-Peña, Renee. "Lotus Blossoms Don't Bleed: Images of Asian Women." In *Making Waves: An Anthology of Writings by and about Asian American Women*, edited by Asian Women United, 308–317. Boston: Beacon Press, 1989.
Teo, Stephen. "The Chinese Film Market and the *Wolf Warrior* 2 Phenomenon." *Screen* 60, no. 2 (2019): 322–331.
Tigner, Amy L., and Allison Carruth. *Literature and Food Studies*. New York: Routledge, 2018.
Tovares, Alla, and Cynthia Gordon, eds. *Identity and Ideology in Digital Food Discourse: Social Media Interactions Across Cultural Contexts*. London: Bloomsbury Academic, 2020.

Urry, John. *Mobilities*. Cambridge: Polity, 2007.
Urry, John, and Jonas Larsen. *The Tourist Gaze 3.0*. London: Sage, 2011.
Vogel, Ezra F. 傅高义. *Deng Xiaoping shidai* 邓小平时代 [Deng Xiaoping and the Transformation of China]. Translated from English by Feng Keli 冯克利. Beijing: SDX Joint Publishing Company 三联书店, 2013.
Volgger, Michael, and Harald Pechlaner. "Responses to Chinese Tourists' Interest in Wine and Food: An Italian Perspective." In *Food, Wine and China: A Tourism Perspective*, edited by Christof Pforr and Ian Phau, 219–237. New York: Routledge, 2018.
Wong, Aliza S. "Authenticity *all'italiana*: Food Discourses, Diasporas, and the Limits of Cuisine in Contemporary Italy." In *Representing Italy Through Food*, edited by Peter Naccarato, Zachary Nowak, and Elgin K. Eckert, 33–54. London: Bloomsbury, 2017.
Wu, David Y. H., and Sidney C. H. Cheung, eds. *The Globalization of Chinese Food*. Honolulu: University of Hawai'i Press, 2002.
Xu, Wenying. *Eating Identities: Reading Food in Asian American Literature*. Honolulu: University of Hawai'i Press, 2008.
Yan, Nanxi. "Slow Food in China: An Exploratory Study." Master of Arts Thesis. University of Waterloo, 2015.
Yan, Yunxiang. "Of Hamburger and Social Space: Consuming McDonald's in Beijing." In *Food and Culture: A Reader*, edited by Carole Counihan, Penny Van Esterik, and Carole M. Counihan, 449–471. New York: Routledge, 2012.
Yu, LiAnne. *Consumption in China: How China's New Consumer Ideology Is Shaping the Nation*. Cambridge: Polity, 2014.
Zanini, Livio. "Non solo involtini primavera: Dinamiche dell'imprenditoria cinese nel settore della ristorazione in Veneto." In *Cinesi tra le maglie del lavoro*, edited by Maurizio Rasera and Devi Sacchetto, 145–178. Milano: Franco Angeli, 2018.
Zanoni, Elizabeth. *Migrant Marketplaces: Food and Italians in North and South America*. Urbana: University of Illinois Press, 2018.
Zhang, Gaoheng. "The *Chinaman* and the *Cinesina*: Gendering Chinese Migrants in Italian Novels." *Journal of Romance Studies* 19, no. 1 (2019): 69–97.
———. "Chinese Migrants and the 'Chinese Mafia' in Contemporary Italian Culture." In *Transcending Borders: Selected Papers in East Asian Studies*, edited by Valentina Pedone and Sagiyama Ikuko, 67–86. Firenze: Firenze University Press, 2016.
———. "Chinese Migrants, Morality, and Film Ethics in Italian Cinema." *Journal of Modern Italian Studies* 22, no. 3 (2017): 385–405.

———. "Contemporary Italian Novels on Chinese Immigration to Italy." *California Italian Studies* 4, no. 2 (2013): 1–38.
———. *Fashion Communications Between Italy and China: Unfolding a Sartorial Relationship*. London: Bloomsbury, 2025.
———. "Frames and Agendas in Italian Films about Chinese Migrants." *LEA—Lingue e letterature d'Oriente e d'Occidente* 8 (2019): 123–137.
———. *Migration and the Media: Debating Chinese Migration to Italy, 1992–2012*. Toronto: University of Toronto Press, 2019.
———. "Mobility, Architecture, Chronotopes: Tianjin's Italian Concession, the 1930s." In *Cultural Mobilities Between China and Italy*, edited by Valentina Pedone and Gaoheng Zhang, 113–135. Cham, Switzerland: Springer; Palgrave Macmillan, 2024.
———. "The Three Riddles in Puccini's *Turandot*: Masculinity, Empire, and Orientalism." In *Der musikalisch modellierte Mann: Interkulturelle und interdisziplinäre Männlichkeitsstudien zur Oper und Literatur des 19. und frühen 20. Jahrhunderts*, edited by Ester Saletta and Barbara Hindinger, 397–416. Vienna: Praesens, 2012.
———. "'Women with Big Breasts and Wide Hips': Federico Fellini's Cinema in Chinese Media Essays." In *Federico Fellini: Centennial Essays*, edited by Marco Malvestio, Jessica Whitehead, and Alberto Zambenedetti, 358–370. Toronto: University of Toronto Press, 2025.

INDEX

2018XFun Foodie Club (iQIYI), 177–180

Accademia Italiana della Cucina, 156, 157
Africa, 183
al dente, 130, 149
Albania, 115
Alberini, Massimo, 34, 48, 130
Amalfi coast, 166
ambivalence, food and, 8, 11, 70, 162, 173–174, 180
American Chinese food, 16, 28, 39, 40, 46–51
American fast food, 7–8, 28, 43–46, 135–136
Amsterdam, 46
Anagrafe degli Italiani Residenti all'Estero (AIRE), 150–152
animal rights, 91, 97–98
Antonino Chef Academy, 187
Antwerp, 121, 122
Aperol spritz, 184
assimilation narratives, 69–70
Australian food, 144–145
authenticity, food's, 14, 34, 35, 47, 49, 105–126, 137, 143, 145–146, 149–150, 153–158, 171–172

Baghdad, 121
Barcelona, 177
Bay, Allan, 26, 50

Beijing, 46, 48, 120, 122, 129, 136, 144, 148, 151, 153–155, 169, 183
Beijing Maxim's, 129
Belgium, 120
Belt and Road Initiative, 31–32
Berio, Filippo, 114
bistecca alla fiorentina, 177
A Bite of China (Xiaoqing Chen), 169–172
Black Venus, 125
Bombana, Umberto, 148–150, 187
Bonilli, Stefano, 25
Bra, 169
brain drain, 150
Bright Food, 114
British Broadcasting Corporation (BBC), 170
Buddhist temples, 30
Bulgari-Marriott, 144
bullyism, 72–73
business culture, 16, 159, 135–142, 175
Buzzati, Dino, 25, 44–46

cactus, 167
Canadian food, 144–145
Caffè (Cristiano Bortone), 120–123, 180
California, 92, 94
Camorra, 67–68, 112
Campania, 71, 105, 110
Cannavacciuolo, Antonino, 187
capital, migrants', 33, 107, 111–112, 114–119

255

capitals, food, 8, 26, 28, 47, 77–78
Capri, 178
casual dining, 138
Cenci in Cina (Marco Limberti), 108–110, 185
Charlie Chan, 76, 79–80
chauvinism, food, 71, 124
ChemChina, 116
Chengdu, 169
Chicago, 46
Chinaman, 55–56, 78–80, 117, 118, 123, 125
Chinamen: Un secolo di cinesi a Milano (Ciaj Rocchi and Matteo Demonte), 78–80, 140
Chinatown, 30, 46, 74, 77, 86
Chinese Americans, 66–80, 92
Chinese Exclusion Act, 96
Chinese Italians, 30, 37, 101, 155–157. *See also* second-generation Chinese migrants
chop suey, 50, 205n36
chopsticks, 2, 25, 44, 71, 78, 98
cinesina, 45, 55–56, 72–73, 110
Cio-Cio San, 68
coffee, 116–120, 125, 143, 179
coffee bars, 29, 36, 38, 70–71, 115
Cold War, 44, 45
colonialism, 34
comfort food, 185–186
communications, food, 17–20, 39, 72–73, 133, 178, 209–210n63
consumer culture, 5, 42, 91
cooking, 109, 185–187
cookbooks, 49, 143–144, 147
Cosa nostra, 58, 65, 90
cosmopolitanism, 8, 23, 45–46, 74, 77–78, 89, 101, 128, 132, 162, 165, 168, 189, 193
COVID-19 pandemic, 1–3, 20, 26, 41, 42, 73, 78, 83, 101, 118, 127–128, 130, 148, 157, 163, 180
crime journalism, 55, 65, 69, 98
crime narrative, 57–66, 98–99
Ctrip.com, 175–177

Cultural Revolution, 41, 129, 135, 146–147
cultural sociology, 210n64, 211n69
cultural studies, 203–204n26, 211n69

Da Marco, 152–153
deCanto Restaurant, 156
delivery, food, 42, 48, 157
Delitto al ristorante cinese (Bruno Corbucci), 59–61, 74
Deng, Xiaoping, 129, 130
Denominazione d'Origine Protetta (DOP), 111
Deoleo, 119
Dianping.com, 130–131, 148–149, 156
didacticism, 101, 165, 179
digital culture, food and, 133–135, 189, 192
documentary cinema, food and, 60, 95, 129, 144, 169–172
dogmeat eating, 9, 21–22, 83–103, 118, 137, 192, 194
Domino's Pizza, 137
dumplings, 5–6, 78, 166, 171

Eat Pray Love (Ryan Murphy), 183
eating, 12, 15, 25, 27, 34, 58, 75–76, 77, 84, 93–94, 135–136, 167, 168, 179–180, 186
Emilia-Romagna, 154
entrepreneurship, food: and the Chinese case in Italy, 32–42, 115–116; and the Italian case in China, 150–158
ethics, representational, 57–64, 94–95, 111–112
ethnic cuisine, 15, 35, 54, 85, 90, 194
European Union, 31, 111, 143, 151
expatriates, 31, 143, 151–152, 158

fake foods, 107–114
family, food and, 186, 188
Fantozzi (Luciano Salce), 88–96, 97–98, 194
fashion, 108, 153, 184

Fellini, Federico, 4, 148
femininities, 66–73, 80, 110, 112, 147, 182–183, 187–188. *See also* masculinities
fine dining, 8, 129–130, 135, 142–150
First Opium War, 129, 194
Florence, 32, 39, 164, 165
Fondazione Migrantes, 151
foodie culture, 149, 161–162, 162–163, 177–180, 192
foodscape, 8, 28, 34, 39, 50–51, 55, 128, 133, 152
foodways, 9, 13, 15, 23, 27, 85, 91, 96, 101, 140, 161
Franchi, Elisabetta, 83–84
French food, 26, 129, 130, 132, 155, 158, 167, 180, 194–195
Fu Manchu, 56, 62–63, 64, 75, 76, 117
fundamentalism, food, 162, 174

Gambero Rosso, 3, 25, 153, 156–157
Gansu, 115
gastronationalism, 162, 171
gelati, 184
gender, food and, 13–14, 21, 38–39, 45. *See also* femininities; masculinities; sexuality, food and
globalization, food and, 15, 44, 106, 118, 167, 172
The Good Earth (Sidney Franklin), 64
Gorbaciof (Stefano Incerti), 67–68, 74
Grand Kempinski Hotel, 145
Grand Tour, 164, 183, 184
graphic novels, food and, 73–80
Guangdong, 50, 151

Hang Zhou, 2, 3, 66
haute cuisine, 26, 39–41, 47, 149. *See also* working-class food
Hirst, Bamboo, 49
Hollywood cinema, 62, 67–68, 69, 183
Hong Kong, 32, 46, 48, 59, 77, 79, 93, 94, 147, 148, 151, 169
human rights, 97–98

humor, 101, 118
Hunan, 41
hybridized food, 39, 47, 50, 77, 124, 132, 139, 142, 146, 155–157, 159, 168

identity-making, 5, 27, 56, 79, 126, 132, 133, 135, 147, 161–162, 178, 189, 193
industrialized food, 35, 44
ingredients, 107, 119–125, 137, 144–145, 149, 153, 154, 165, 179
interracial romance, 66–73, 154
Io sono Li (Andrea Segre), 70–72, 75
Istituto Luce, 129
Italian Americans, 33, 142, 147
Italian Communist Party, 172
Italian National Tourist Board, 175
Italian-style food, 106–107, 131, 135–142

Japanese food, 26, 36, 89–90, 91, 144, 167, 194–195
jellies, fruit, 167
Jolie Plus, 117–118
journalism, food, 164–174
The Joy Luck Club (Wayne Wang), 63

Kentucky Fried Chicken (KFC), 136, 141, 142
kitchens, representations of, 33, 39, 63, 67, 75, 108–109
Korean food, 36, 92
kung fu (martial arts), 62, 72–73, 74, 75–76
Kung Fu (various directors), 64

labor, migrants', 107–114
Laika, 2–4, 195
Lamborghini hotels, Tonino, 145
Lanzhou, 166
Latin Americans, 36
Lavazza, 116–119, 123, 226n27
Lee, Bruce, 56, 75, 79–80
lemon, 149, 161, 166–167, 178
Lombardy, 39, 195
London, 16, 26, 32, 46, 145

Long Wei (Diego Cajelli), 74–77
Los Angeles, 49
Lucca, 54, 114

Macau, 147, 148, 169
Madama Butterfly (Luigi Illica, Giuseppe Giacosa, and Giacomo Puccini), 68
Made in Italy: cachet, 114–115, 126, 118–119, 144, 145–146, 147, 157, 158, 193; cultural exports, 148; expertise, 107–126, 145, 181; industries, 8, 107–108, 153; products, 184–185
Mafia, Chinese, 59, 60–62, 64, 65, 69, 70, 90, 92
Malaysia, 94
Mao, Zedong, 41
Maoism, 7, 41–42
Margherita pizza, 176
The Mask of Fu Manchu (Charles Brabin), 63
masculinities, 73–80, 110, 112, 182–183. *See also* femininities
Mattarella, Sergio, 2
McDonald's, 43–44, 136, 141, 142
meal sequence, 35, 47, 149, 165, 179
media convergence, 178
menus, 39–42, 47–48, 139, 140, 144, 153
Mercante, 153–155
Michelin, 148
migration, labor, 7, 28–31
migrations, Chinese: and expatriates, 31; and labor migrants, 28–31; and students, 31, 39, 177
migrations, Italian: in China, 150–152, 158; and food, 34
Milan, 2, 16, 20, 25, 28, 30, 32, 33, 36, 39, 42, 45, 46, 50, 73–80, 86, 129, 164, 192, 195
Il mio nome è Shangai Joe (Mario Caiano), 64
mobilities: body and, 103; cultural, 6–7, 168; food, 4–5, 12–13, 120–123, 141–142; global, 122–123; historical, 4–5, 12; intersecting, 11–17; physical, 4, 6–7
model minority, 76, 80
Mondo Cane (Gualtiero Jacopetti, Franco Prosperi, and Paolo Cavara), 93–96
mozzarella, 22, 71, 105–106, 110–114, 125, 145

Naples, 97, 142, 176, 178
National Geographic, 170
neoliberalism, 34, 42, 55, 101, 142, 145, 150, 159
Nestlé, 118, 120
New Guinea, 94
New York City, 16, 26, 28, 46–47, 50, 192
noodles, 127, 149
NOVA system, 125
Novara, 124

olive oil, 114–115, 125, 154
Open Door Policy, 8, 29, 129, 135, 192–193
organized crime, 55, 66, 67–68, 70, 74, 79
Orientalization, 34, 45, 68, 70, 89–90, 98, 111, 137, 147
osteria, 34, 70–71, 152, 178

panini, 178
panna cotta, 167
Papa John's, 137
"Paradise" (Lavazza), 117–119, 192
pairing of food, 165, 166, 167
Paris, 32, 46
pasta, 127, 131, 140, 144, 149, 166
Petrini, Carlo, 168, 170
Philippines, 124
Piazza Vittorio, 2, 30, 96–97, 100
Piedmont, 124, 156, 169
pilgrimage, food, 178
Pirelli, 116
pizzas, 5–6, 97, 131, 136, 140, 141, 149

Pizza Hut China, 8, 23, 127–128, 131, 132, 135–142, 155, 158–159, 162, 168, 175, 188, 189, 193
pleasure, food and, 168, 173–174
Po River, 124
poliziesco (crime film), food and, 57–58
Polo, Marco, 6
popular culture, food and, 9, 54, 181
populism, 100–101, 126
Positano, 166, 168, 178
postmodern, 42, 63, 89–90
Prato, 30, 40, 108, 115
Primo1, 156–157
processed food, 107, 125
Pu'er, 120, 122

Questa notte è ancora nostra (Paolo Genovese and Luca Miniero), 68–70, 77
Qing dynasty, 117, 129
Qyer.com, 176–177

racialization, food and, 13–14, 21, 85–103, 105–106, 110
racism, 3, 36–37, 63, 71, 72–73, 76
Raggi, Virginia, 2
ravioli, 144, 161, 166
reality television, 177–180, 181
repertoire, culinary, 22–23, 128–135, 158–159
Republic of China, 129, 194
restaurant reviews, 25–26, 39–51, 130, 148–149, 156, 177
restaurants, representations of, 53–81
rhetoric, 72, 79, 87, 92, 99–101, 106, 113, 119, 219n31
Ricci, Matteo, 6
rice, 123–125, 149. See also risotto; staple foods
La ricetta italiana (Zuxin Hou), 180–189
Riso Gallo, 123–124
riso Venere, 123–124
risotto, 130, 149, 166. See also rice; staple foods

Ritz-Carlton, 145
Roman Holiday (William Wyler), 181–189
romantic comedy, food and, 68–70, 180–189
Rome, 2, 16, 26, 28, 30, 31, 32, 34, 36, 39, 45, 49, 50, 59, 121, 164, 179, 180–189, 192
Romito, Niko, 144–145, 152, 154

safety, food, 3, 152
Sala, Giuseppe, 2
Salov, 114, 116
salvation narratives, 67–68
San Francisco, 26, 46
Saudi Arabia, 147
Scontro di civiltà per un ascensore a Piazza Vittorio (Amara Lakhous), 96–102
second-generation Chinese migrants, 30, 33, 69–70, 79. See also Chinese Italians
Second World War, 158
semiotics, food and, 209n61
Settimana della Cucina Italiana nel Mondo, 143
Severe Acute Respiratory Syndrome (SARS), 20, 35–36, 37, 42, 43, 88, 89, 117, 195
sexuality, food and, 76–77. See also gender, food and
Shang-Chi, 75
Shanghai, 118, 130, 136, 144, 146, 148, 150, 151, 152–153, 156, 157, 169
Shanghai solo andata (Duccio Alabiso), 146–147
Sheraton Shanghai Hongqiao Hotel, 146
Shu, Qiao, 161–162, 164–174, 193
Sichuan, 41
Silk Road, 147
Singapore, 94
Sinophobia, 66, 96
Slow Food, 23, 43–44, 111, 131, 161, 162, 166–174, 188, 189, 193
Slow Food International, 169

social media, food and, 38, 42, 175, 176, 182
Sorrento, 178
Sotto il ristorante cinese (Bruno Bozzetto), 57–59, 61–66
spaghetti, 127, 129, 137, 141, 149, 176, 186–187
Spanish food, 130
staple foods, 170. *See also* rice; risotto
Starbucks, 118, 119, 120
star chefs, 130, 131, 148–150, 187
Starwood Hotels, 147
La stella che non c'è (Gianni Amelio), 122
stereotypes, food: negative, 35–36, 41, 45, 60, 61, 117, 123–124, 222–223n28; positive, 73–80, 155
Storia di un ristorante italiano in Cina (Giovanni Messina), 155–156
street food, 178
supplì, 178
Switzerland, 97, 98, 101

taboos, food, 86–88
Taiwan, 32, 45, 59, 60–61, 94
takeaway food, 41, 49
terroir, 110, 124, 154, 165
Tianjin, 7, 129
tiramisu, 149, 166
tortellini, 144, 166
Toulà, 129–130
tourism: culinary, 15, 27, 43, 58, 78, 127–159, 161–162, 175–180; leisure, 7, 15, 36, 39, 163–164; outbound Chinese, 163–164, 175; websites, 174–177
traceability, 124
tradition, culinary, 40–41, 48, 91, 106, 130, 154, 166
transculturality, 5–6, 16–17, 142, 163, 171–172, 186
transnationalism, 6, 37, 106, 116, 117, 118–119, 142–150, 153
trattoria, 34, 150–158

Treviso, 129
Trieste, 121, 122
Tripadvisor.com, 39–42, 154
truffle, 149, 157, 178, 179
Turandot, 68
Turandot (Giuseppe Adami, Renato Simoni, and Giacomo Puccini), 68
Turin, 116

Udine, 180
Under the Tuscan Sun (Audrey Wells), 183
United Nations (UN), 125, 163

Veneto, 36, 129, 130
Venice, 32, 36, 70, 144, 164, 176
Vercelli, 124
Vespa, 184, 188
Via Paolo Sarpi, 2, 30, 74, 75, 86
Via Pistoiese, 30
Vicenza, 37
Vietnam, 119
viscerality, food and, 102–103

Wenzhou, 29, 156
Wolf Warrior 2 (Wu Jing), 183
wontons, 166
working-class food, 41–42, 47–48, 172. *See also* haute cuisine
World Tourism Organization (UNWTO), 163
World Trade Organization (WTO), 143
Wuhan, 127, 139

Yellow Peril, 58, 62–63, 66
Yellowface, 58, 59, 63–64, 118, 125
Yueshi China (Changzhen Ren), 173
Yugoslavia, 70
Yulin, 83
Yum China Holdings, Inc., 118, 138, 139
Yunnan, 119–120, 121, 122, 157, 169

Zhejiang, 29, 40, 50, 151
Zhou, Sonia, 3–4, 195

GAOHENG ZHANG is Associate Professor of Italian Studies at the University of British Columbia. His recent books include two monographs, *Fashion Communications Between Italy and China: Unfolding a Sartorial Relationship* (Bloomsbury, 2025) and *Migration and the Media: Debating Chinese Migration to Italy, 1992–2012* (Toronto, 2019), and a co-edited volume, *Cultural Mobilities Between China and Italy* (Palgrave Macmillan, 2024).

Critical Studies in Italian Migrations

Nancy C. Carnevale and Laura E. Ruberto, *series editors*

Heather Renee Sottong, *Transnational Dante: Inventing Argentine Cultural Identity*
Giulia Riccò, *The Italian Colony of São Paulo: Race, Class, and Cultural Capital in Brazil*
Gaoheng Zhang, *Italian Dumplings and Chinese Pizzas: Transcultural Food Mobilities*

www.ingramcontent.com/pod-product-compliance
Lightning Source LLC
Chambersburg PA
CBHW031145020426
42333CB00013B/518